THE SULLIVAN EXPEDITION of 1779

The Regimental Rosters of Men

Albert Hazen Wright

HERITAGE BOOKS
2008

HERITAGE BOOKS
AN IMPRINT OF HERITAGE BOOKS, INC.

Books, CDs, and more—Worldwide

For our listing of thousands of titles see our website
at
www.HeritageBooks.com

A Facsimile Reprint
Published 2008 by
HERITAGE BOOKS, INC.
Publishing Division
100 Railroad Ave. #104
Westminster, Maryland 21157

Originally published 1943

With aid and encouragement from
Boldman, George	Kerns, M. R.
Clinton, Gordon A.	Rollo, Donald N.
Corson, Dale R.	Seeley, Ralph
Heidt, William	Stickler, Merril

Cornell University
Corning-Painted Post Historical Society
DeWitt Historical Society, Tompkins County
Niagara County Historical Society
Tioga County Historical Society

— Publisher's Notice —
In reprints such as this, it is often not possible to remove blemishes from the original. Also, pages 162a and 162b are missing from the index. We feel the contents of this book warrant its reissue despite these blemishes and hope you will agree and read it with pleasure.

International Standard Book Number: 978-1-58549-826-0

THE REGIMENTAL ROSTERS OF THE SULLIVAN EXPEDITION, 1779

Preface

As one of the avocational byproducts we have pursued for 30 years, we present the study of The Sullivan Expedition of 1779. It began with a severe winter meeting of AAAS in New York when it was difficult to go from place to place and then miss the speaker sought. We inferred the newspapers of 1779 had Sullivan material and we began with the old holdings of the Astor and Lenox library with parts of the New York Public Library, and struck "gold" at once. That success prompted us to try several other avenues and approaches. At the Semicentenial (1929) someone remarked "Wouldn't it be fine if we knew how many soldiers of that expedition settled or came to live in western New York and northeastern Pennsylvania. I suppose it is too late to know who were on the expedition?" In an enthusiastic moment I said it could be done. That incident continued to be a "red rag" to me. Years later at Concord, N.H. when we saw the 72 volumed set (N.H. Hist. Soc.) of the pension records of N. H. Revolutionary soldiers, we began the roster of the 3 N. H. Regiments on this Expedition of 1779. The trail led from Concord to Boston, Providence, Hartford, New York, Albany, Trenton, Philadelphia, Harrisburg and Washington. The roster is finished, but the Pennsylvania Brigade is somewhat problematic because there are no 1779 musters, payrolls or other contemporary lists of the 4th, 11th, and the independent companies of Gen. Hand's forces.

This roster record came from several state archives, libraries and state historical societies. The greatest sources of material were N. H. State Historical Society, Massachusetts State Archives, N. Y. Historical Society, Penn Historical Society, the wonderful Pennsylvania State Archives set, and foremost the Adjutant General's Division of National Archives. All were helpful with their treasures: muster rolls, payrolls, adjutant's accounts, etc., and as a consequence we make the roster to be 5865+ men. It is herein presented in the hope that future generations may honor these forbears who helped to forge our country's outlook and may resolve not to let anyone pervert or corrupt our hard won liberties.

THESE STUDIES OF 1942-1949 WERE EMBODIED IN AN IMMENSE 1142-PAGED MANUSCRIPT, THEREFORE THIS SHORT PAPER IS A MERE LIST OF THE PEOPLE ON THE TRIP.

THE REGIMENTAL ROSTERS OF THE SULLIVAN EXPEDITION, 1779

Introduction

In our paper on the Contemporary Newspaper Comment (Studies in History Nos. 5-8, 1943) of the Sullivan Expedition 1779, we began our General Introduction thus

"Forty or more journals, narratives, memoirs and orderly books extant or previously known have given you the daily doings of the army. In the centennial days of 1879 the master hands of Rev. David Craft, General John S. Clark, Hon. George S. Conover and other equally gifted contemporaries of these or other professions gave you the localities, personae and major outlines of the general narrative of this well-known expedition. Since then some twenty-five or thirty spirited and scholarly persons such as E. Cruikshank, William S. Stryker, A. Tiffany Norton, Simon S. Adler, Wm. Elliot Griffis, Louise Welles Murray, Mary Elwood Cheney, Oscar Rising, to the present (written in 1929) state historian, Dr. A. Flick have filled in the story point by point. What remains? No one has made a complete roster of Sullivans army. All routes not covered by Lieut. Lodge's (Erskine-DeWitt) maps should be studied, all detachments and their route of assembling, the names of the privates lost and wounded never has been assembled (now being tried by the author). Newspaper and magazine accounts after 1779, obituaries of participants, pension applications of participants, numbers of descendants of Sullivan soldiers in Western New York, and countless other worthwhile studies are at our door if with patience we work diligently and intelligently like the great three C's of Sullivan bibliography, Craft, Clark, and Conover."

Someone remarked how fine it would be if we knew how many of these campaigners settled in Western and Central New York and Northeastern Pennsylvania but held the roster could not be completed at this date. This is an attempt to accomplish that very task thought impossible. Many more source journals, orderly books have appeared since the publication of the journals in 1887. Today the number would reach sixty instead of forty as quoted above.

Roster of Sullivan Expedition of 1779

General Commanding and his Staff

Major General John Sullivan	Commander in Chief
Major Wm. Pierce	Aide-de-Camp
Capt. Lieut. Jonathan Dayton (3rd N.J.)	Aide-de-Camp
Major Adam Hoops	Aide-de-Camp, Asst. Quartermaster
Major Nicholas VanCortlandt	Aide-de-Camp
Lieut. Col. Francis Barber	Adjutant General, Sub inspector
Major Nicholas Fish (2nd N.Y.)	Adjutant General Oct. 16, 1779

Lieut. John Stagg (Spencers or 5 N.J.)	Asst. to Adjutant General
Col. Bryan Bruen (Probably the "Mr Brenion", Commissary to Adjutant Gen., Commander, and Col. Proctor's Artillery (see journals, also Brewer Hubley 166)	Private Secretary
Lieut. Robert Pemberton	Judge Advocate
Lieut. Col. Pierre Regnier (Transferred to N.Y. Brigade)	Subinspector
Dr. Francis Hagan	Surgeon in Chief
Dr. Andrew Laidley	Hospital at Easton
Rev. Samuel Kirkland	Chaplain
Rev. Samuel Kirkland	Interpreter
James Deane	Interpreter
Capt. Benjamin Lodge	Surveyor
Capt. John Franklin	Guide
Lieut. John Jenkins	Guide
Rev. Samuel Kirkland	Guide
Capt. Jehoiakim (Stockbridge Indian)	Guide
Hanyost (Oneida Indian)	Guide
Col. John Harper	Guide
Capt. (Gerrit?) Putnam	Guide
Col. Cornelius Sheriff	Deputy Quartermaster General
Maj. Douw	Deputy Quartermaster General
Col. Cook	Depy. QM G. at Sunbury
George Ross	Depy. QM G. at Lancaster
Col. Cornelius Cox	Depy. QM G. at Estherton
Major Adams Hoops	Assistant Quartermaster
Armstrong	Assistant Quartermaster
Capt. Wm. Sproat	Deputy Quartermaster
Lieut. David Kirkpatrick (Malcolm's)	Asst. Depy. QM General
Capt. Alexander Patterson	Asst. Depy. QM General
Ludwig	Baker in Chief
Stewart	Bullock Guard
Col. Daniel Topham	Commissary, Clothier, Conductor of Military Stores
Sergt. Patrick Sullivan (Hubleys)	Asst. to Commiss. Military Stores
Col. John Steele	Deputy Commiss. Issues
Lieut. Col. Persifer Frazier	Deputy Commissary General
Lieut. John Woodman (Weidman, German)	Deputy Commissary
Lieut. Robert Pemberton	Deputy Commissary
Col. B. Brenion (see Bruen)	Commissary to Adj. Gen.
	Commander, 4th Pa. Artill.
W. McGlaughlin (3rd N.Y.)	Asst. Commiss. Issues
	Conductor of Stores
Neilson	Asst. Commiss. Issues
Gibbons	Asst. Commiss. Issues
John Pratt	Asst. Commiss. Issues at Ft. Sullivan, Oct. 1, 1779
Col. Robert Hopper	Commissary of Transportation
Col. Henry Antis	Conductor of Boats
Maj. Morrison	Commander of Fleet
Col. Wm. Bond	Collector of horses and drivers
	Lt. Conductor of Boats

John Hubley	Conductor of Stores
Capt. Gifford	In Charge of Cattle
James Cooke	Express Rider
James Funston	Issuer of Clothing

First Brigade

William Maxwell	Brigadier-General
Aaron Ogden (Captain 1st N.J.)	Aide-de-Camp
John Ross (Major 2nd N.J.)	Brigade Major and Inspector
Nathan Wilkinson (2nd Lieut. 3rd N.J.)	Brigade Quartermaster
Andrew Hunter	Chaplain
Matthias Ogden	Colonel 1st N.J. Regiment
Israel Shreve	Colonel 2nd N.J. Regiment
Elias Dayton	Colonel 3rd N.J. Regiment
Oliver Spencer	Colonel Spencer's (5th) N.J. Regiment

Was Sheldon's Cavalry along?

Second Brigade

Enoch Poor	Brigade General
Jeremiah Fogg	Aide-de-Camp, July 2, 1779
Elihu Marshall (From 2nd N.Y. but his regiment in Poor's Brig. in 1779 to Aug. 1779)	Brigade Major
Jeremy Pritchard	Brigade Major Aug. 16, 1779
Wm. Scott	Major, Brigade Major Nov. 5, 1779
Dudley L. Chase	Lieut. Brigade Quartermaster
Joseph Ciley	Colonel 1st N.H. Regiment
George Reid	Lieut. Col. 2nd N.H. Regiment
Henry Dearborn	Lieut. Col. 3rd N.H. Regiment
Daniel Whiting	Major 6th Mass. Regiment after Aug. 1779

Third Brigade

Edward Hand	Brigade General
Jonathan Snowden	Aide-de-Camp (Lieut. 1st N.J.)
William Sprout	Captain, Aide-de-Camp
William Sproat	Captain, Brigade Major and Inspect.
William Rogers D.D.	Chaplain
William Kinnerly	Brigade Surgeon
John Van Anglen (From 1st N.J. Reg.)	Commissary
Wm. Butler	Lieut. Colonel 4th Pa. Regiment
Adam Hubley	Lieut. Colonel 11th Pa. Regiment
Daniel Burchardt	Major, Pa. German Battalion
Thomas Proctor	Colonel Penn. 4th Artillery
James Parr	Major Morgan's Rifle Corps

John Paul Schotts	Captain Schott's Rifle Corps
Anthony Selin	Captain Schott's Rifle Corps
Simon Spaulding	Captain Independent Wyoming Co.
John Franklin	Captain

Fourth Brigade

James Clinton	Brigadier-General
	Aide-de-Camp
Leonard Bleecker	Brigade Major
Nicholas Fish	Brigade Major and Inspector
John Pratt	Asst. Commissary Gen. (of Issues)
Henry Glenn	Asst. Commissary Gen. (of Issues)
John Gano	Chaplain
Stephen McCrea	Brigade Surgeon
Philip VanCortlandt	Lieut. Colonel 2nd N.Y. Regiment
Peter Gansevoort	Col. 3rd N.Y. Regiment
Frederick Weissenfels	Lieut. Col. 4th N.Y. Regiment
Lewis Dubois	Col. 5th N.Y. Regiment
John Lamb	Col. Artill. Detachment

Number

A. Count made in 1949.

Approximate Number on Expedition (6000)

First Brigade - Gen. Wm. Maxwell

1st N.J. Regt.	351
2nd N.J. Regt.	375
3rd N.J. Regt.	347
5th N.J. Regt. (Spencers)	338
	1411

Second Brigade - Gen. Enoch Poor

1st N.H. Regt.	463
2nd N.H. Regt.	414
3rd N.H. Regt.	346
6th Mass. Regt.	313
	1536

Third Brigade - Gen. Edward Hand

4th Pa. Regt.	199
German Regt.	400
Wyo. Cos. (2)	125
Schotts and Selins	50
4th Pa. Artillery	174
Morgans Riflemen, about	100
11th Pa. Regt., about	350
	1398

Fourth Brigade - Gen. James Clinton

2nd N.Y. Regt.	281
3rd N.Y. Regt.	458
4th N.Y. Regt.	367
5th N.Y. Regt.	383
Lamb's Artillery	31
	1520

First Total	1411
Second Total	1536
Third Total	1398
Fourth Total	1520
Total	5865
General Staff	30
Final Total	5895

Above 6000 (i.e., counting boatmen, drivers of cattle and horses, hospital and medical help, commissary and quartermaster help.)

B. Count made in 1965. Total 5992 or 6150 if Armand's Legion be counted general staff, 53; 1st brigade, 1443; 2nd brigade, 1536; 3rd brigade 1455; 4th brigade, 1505.

If it be objected that 6000 be too high an estimate of Sullivan's forces, consider these statements:

1. Many a time it has been said one-third of Washington's army of regular soldiers, not militia, was on the Sullivan Expedition.

2. Lieut. Colonel Dearborn's journal more or less bears it out.

   a. On Aug. 25, 1779 he said "Our whole force that will march from here is about 5000 men Officers included nine pieces of Artillery".

   b. On Aug. 26, 1779 he stated "A garison of 300 men is left at this place (Tioga Point) under the Command of Col. Shreeve".

   c. On July 31 he wrote that they moved from Wyoming at 2 o'clock with 120 boats, about 1200 pack horses and 700 beef cattle.

   d. On Aug. 15, 1000 men chosen to march eastward to join Gen. Clinton. The arms at Tioga was big enough to withstand attack even if 1000 men were thus deputied.

   e. On Aug. 19, "Gen. Clinton joined us at 10 o'clock with 2000 men including Officers, boatmen, etc. He had 208 batteaux with provisions..."

Let's analyze this statement with our numbers. From Otsego, Clinton has his N. Y. brigade plus the 6th Massachusetts plus 4th Pa. Artillery plus Morgans riflemen. Our figures are

New York Brigade	1520
6th Massachusetts	313
4th Pa. Artillery	174
Morgan's Riflemen	100
Total	2107

All in all 6000 is not an impossible determination of the actual number of General Sullivan's army, if this 2107 be added to Sullivan's 3500 men fit for action at Ft. Sullivan.

Transportation Corps

Colonel William Bond
Colonel Henry Antis
Major   Morrison
Capt. William Gifford
   and others

In the fleet, collectors of horses and drivers (horses and cattle), and guards of such, and similar workers, were a large force whose number can never be determined. Surely all the boatmen, pack horse drivers, cattle drivers, bullock guards, etc. were not all soldiers thus assigned.

If one canvass only five of the journals he will see what a task, supplies must have been. For example:

Gookin (104) gives 300 horses from Wyoming for Poor, 300 for Maxwell, 200 for Hand, and 100 for Proctor. In addition he gives 120 boats and 800 head of cattle.

Norris (227) has 1200 pack horses and 500 head of cattle.

Webb (286) gives 300 boats, 800 head of cattle, 500 horses, 500 wagons.

Clinton (V, 861, 122) in two different places has 200 or 208 batteaux.

Dearborn (65, 71) has on July 24, 70 boats from Sunbury and on July 28, 80 waggons from Easton and on Aug. 25 records a great difficulty of lack of horses for moving supplies and provisions.

The number of boatmen, drivers, etc. is at this date impossible of determination. The following letter shows one of the difficulties. In Pa. Archives o.s. VII: 568, 569) appears an "Extract of a Letter from Major General Sullivan to Congress, 1779. Dated Headquarters, Wyoming, July 21, 1779. General Washington in consequence of my letters wrote the executive council of Pennsylvania for Rangers and Riflemen. They engaged seven hundred and twenty, and the President frequently wrote me that they would be ready in season, not a man of them has joined us, nor are any about to do it, the reason assigned by them, is that the quartermaster gave such extravagant prices to boatmen that they all enlisted into the boat service --but this is evidently a mistake for we have not a hundred boatmen engaged for the army, and but forty-two pack horsemen, so that I must drought for boatmen and pack horsemen."

Volunteers (Pioneers)

Colonel John Harper

This group has always puzzled us. Craft in his address (p. 365) remarked "Among the companies which were thus sent out, was a party of volunteers under Colonel John Harper..." He is speaking of Lieut. John Jenkin's September 9 note (p. 174), "Yesterday, Col. Harper, with a number of volunteers, destroyed a small town called Scauwaga, about ten miles from Canadaseago (Geneva)."

Bleecker in two instances at the beginning of the New York troops' march wrote as follows: "The Volunteers in Camp, commanded by Captain Harper and Putnam will go with the fatigue Party as Guides" (p. 70). "No Provision to be issued to the Volunteers unless the Returns are signed by Captain Harper" (p. 76).

We can find no musters, payrolls, adjutant journals, indicating a corps under Col. Harper. We have sought the evidence at Albany, New York City, and Washington. There is partial evidence for such an organization in 1780 but not in 1779. We will therefore have to treat Col. Harper and Putnam (Is it Gerrit?) as Guides and the word volunteers in quotes as small letters, i.e. volunteers from the main army. A small corps may have existed in 1779 but the evidence is not at hand. For example, from an Orderly Book July 27 - Sept. 28, 1779 for Aug. 24 we observe the note "Pioneers to be commanded by a Captain and sub draught from the line". Or on Aug. 27 we have "One man more from each Regiment to be added to Capt. Cieling's Corps of Pioneers". On Sept. 2 and Sept. 10 are much more re the role of the Pioneers from each Brigade. Therefore we treat Colonel Harper as such a commander.

Colonel E. Sheldon

According to the journals of the Sullivan Expedition 1779 (Albany 1887, p. 216) a "detachment of cavalry from Col. E. Sheldon's Regiment" was attached to General Maxwell's Brigade for the Expedition. In the same publication Craft in his address (p. 341) said the center or main division of the army "was to be made up of three Brigades--the New Jersey, commanded by Brigadier Wm. Maxwell--; also Davis Forman's Regiment and Colonel Elisha Sheldon's Connecticut Riflemen, both subsequently merged into Spencer's Regiment..."

In his N. J. Official Register ... Revolutionary War 1872, Stryker (p. 58, 59) writes "Sheldon's Regiment sometimes called the Second Regiment, Light Dragoons, was commanded by Colonel Elisha Sheldon of Connecticut. Although the State had an officer in this organization, most of the soldiers joined the companies commanded by officers of other States."

According to Connecticut in the Revolution 45 N. J. residents were in Sheldon's regiment, 42 being in Capt. David Edgar troop. We have been unable as Hartford, Trenton and Washington to show that Capt. David Edgar was on the trip. Neither have we connected the other 4 troops of Sheldon's Regiment (such as Strithers, Hoagland) with the expedition. It is true that 24 privates of this regiment were at one time in the 5th N. J. Regiment but not in any of the nine 1779 companies of Spencer's outfit.

1st BRIGADE (General Maxwell)

Adjutant General William S. Stryker (1884) gave a fine historical sketch of Maxwell's Brigade. It was entitled General Maxwell's Brigade of the New Jersey Continental Line in the expedition against the Indians in the year 1779. It was read before the New Jersey Historical Society, of their meeting at Trenton, January 17th, 1881. Our list of the makeup of each company of the four regiments differs but slightly from him. Our lists are based on muster rolls of the U. S. Adjutant General deposit in National Archives. Later (1941) the New Jersey Historical Records Survey Program sponsored by the New Jersey State Planning Board made an index to Stryker's List of Revolutionary soldiers, not solely those of the 1779 trip. New Jersey, considering its historical losses such as the Federal Census reports of 1790, 1800, 1810, and 1820 and other items, has reasons to thank Stryker for a welcome contribution

1st New Jersey Regiment

We have attempted to determine solely the troops on the expedition in 1779. These accounts can in no way be interpreted as approaching a complete history of each regiment. All pertinent data of 1779 has been sought. For example, in Stryker we found 738 privates ascribed to the 1st Regiment--7 fifers, 14 drummers, 31 corporals, and 54 sergeants or a total of 834 in all. Of these 232 were on this trip. Ogden's Regiment had about 330 men or about one hundred who were not in those 834 listed. Doubtless most of them will appear in the more recent file of 40,000 revolutionary names (line and militia) which the Adjutant General's Office in Trenton, New Jersey now has. In June, 1942 we read the Orderly Book Nov. 20, 1777 to Feb. 27, 1778 of Jacob Piatt, Adjutant of the 1st New Jersey Battalion. On the last ten pages are the weekly returns of Feb. 6, Feb. 13, Feb. 20, and Feb. 28, 1778. The last total, Capt. Longstreet, 12, Capt. Baldwin, 43, Capt. Morrison, 31, Capt. Flavhanan, 25, Capt. V. Angel, 38, Capt. Mead, 29, and Capt. V. Vorhies, 31, or a total of 252. Inasmuch as we once made a list of these privates of 840 or 850 men we will not attempt to analyze all the men preceding and after the expedition who were absent from the expedition. What a fine problem for some scholar.

First New Jersey Regiment

Matthias Ogden Colonel
David Brearly Lieut. Colonel
Daniel Piatt Major
Peter Van Vorhies Paymaster
Cyrus D'Hart Paymaster
Peter Lott Quartermaster
Jacob Piatt Adjutant
Ephraim Whitlock Adjutant
Wm. Barnett (Bennett) Surgeon
Jacob Harres Surgeon Mate
Jonathan Forman Captain
Giles Mead Captain
Alexander Mitchell Captain
Peter Van Voorhies Captain
John Holmes Captain
Aaron Ogden Captain
Jacob Piatt Capt. Lieut.
John Van Angeln 1st Lieut.
   (Commissary Gen. Hand)

Wm. Piatt 1st Lieut.
Cyrus D'Hart 1st Lieut.
John Howell 1st Lieut.
Wm. Barton 1st Lieut.
Absalom Martin 1st Lieut.
Peter Lott 1st Lieut.
Ephraim Whitlock 1st Lieut.
Eben Burrows 1st Lieut.
Jonathan Snowden 2nd Lieut.
   (Aide de Camp Gen. Hand)
Absalom Bonham 2nd Lieut.
Samuel Seeley 2nd Lieut.
Silas Parrott Ensign
Aaron Rhea Ensign
Asher Levy (Lewis) Ensign
John Bishop Ensign
John Geary Ensign
Thomas Knapp Sergeant Major
Wm. Hamilton Quartermaster

Corrections or additions to Greenough's Roster:

1. "Cyrus D'Hart, 1st Lieut. and Paymaster Apr. 22, 1778-1781" Hedman and Greenough
2. (Yet) Peter Van Vorhies, Paymaster Muster Roll April, May, 1779
3. Substitute Wm. Barrett for David Ewing, Surgeon
4. Substitute Jacob Harris for Stephen Ball, Surgeon's Mate
5. Peter Lott, 1st Lieut, not 2nd Lieut.
6. Jona Snowden, 2nd Lieut, not 1st Lieut. which finally came Oct. 26, 1779
7. Asher Levi or Levy or Lewis, Ensign, might be omitted. He resigned June 14, 1779
8. John Geary (Garey), Ensign
9. Add: Thomas Knapp, Sergeant Major
       William Hamilton, Q.M. Sergt.
       David Bertron, Fife Major
       Richard Tobbs (Jobs), Drum Major

First Company

(Colonel's Company)

Matthias Ogden Colonel
Jacob Piatt Capt. Lieut.
Jonathan Snowden 2nd Lieut.
Joseph Fulkerson Sergeant
Joshua Townley Sergeant

Charles Burdeau (Badeau) Sergt.
John Woodruff Corporal
Thos. Skilman Corporal
Wm. Walker Fifer

Privates

- Geo. Augustine
- James Brook
- Hyram Casterlin
- Daniel Crowell
- Nathaniel Danheim (Dunham)
- Jonas Dones
- Wm. Ervin (Erwin)
- Jonathan Force
- Judiah (Jedediah) Freeman
- Jno Fulligan (Trilligan)
- William Harris
- John Hopkins
- John Lisk
- David Loyd
- John Loyd
- Patrick Lyon
- Cornelius Miller
- Wm. Moore
- John Strobridge (Strawbridge)
- John Snow
- Job Stites (Stiles)
- Abram Storm
- Meseck Walker
- Ebenezer Ward (Armourer at Wyoming)
- Elihu Webster (Wagoner for Gen. Maxwell)
- Thomas White
- James Willcox
- John Willson

Comparison with Stryker's (1885:40) list

1. Stryker has Bertram, David Private but a David Bertow Fifer in his Major's Co. and we have David Bertron Fife Major in the Major's Co. Normally the Fife Major might be in the Colonel's Company.

Second Company

Lieut. Colonel's Co.

- Eden Burrows   1st Lieut.
- Samuel Seeley   2nd Lieut.
- Zabez Abbey   Sergeant
- John Minthorn (Minton)   Sergeant
- George Hall   Sergeant
- John Hasbrooks   Sergeant
- Powell Allison   Corporal
- William Bird   Corporal
- Rufus Randolph   Corporal
- David Dunbar   Drum & Fife
- William Darby   Drum & Fife
- John Nicholls   Drum & Fife

Privates

- Daniel Boosey
- John Boston
- Samuel Clarke
- Wm. Clarke
- Nicholas Cline
- Benjamin Cornton (Coddington)
- Aaron Crane
- Daniel Cranie
- Edmund Crane
- Elijah Crane
- Ezekiel Crane
- John Flynn
- Samuel Freeman
- Nathan Hall
- Michael Higgins
- Joseph Howard
- Mich. Jones
- Benjamin Lush (Lisk)
- Andrew May
- Henry McCann
- James Meads
- Thos. Morgan
- Abram Mulatt
- Thomas Pendergrass
- Daniel Tuttle
- Moses Willson
- George Wood

Comparison with Stryker's (1885:41) list

1. Stryker has a Robert Blower and Thomas Meeker in this company but each was sick at Elizabethtown. Francis Cain is not in our list.

Third Company

(Major's Company)

William Piatt 1st Lieut.	John Hubble Corporal
Silas Parr (Parrot) Ensign	Benjamin Osburn Corporal
James Holmes Sergeant	Joseph Stout Corporal
Wm. Holbrook Sergeant	James Perdon Drum
Philip McCray (McCrea) Sergeant	David Bertron Fife Major

Privates

Daniel Braty	Coonrad Midjeo
Solomon Cagan	Nathaniel Osmun
Edward Carnine	John Piatt Volunteer
Thomas Cartwright	Moses Quick
Joseph Crane	John Rush
John Cunningham	Ahyah (Abijah) Sander (Scudder)
James Farmer	Peter Taylor
Edward Gage	Joseph Town
Wm. Jones	Garret Williamson
William Lay	Isaac Wood
Enoch Leonard	Isaac Woolley
John Linwood	David Wright
Charles McGlocken	Joseph Wright
Wm. McMullin	Samuel Wright

Comparison with Stryker's (1885:41) list

1. He has 8 not in our list. They are omitted from our list for these reasons:

Farrow, Abraham	Sick at Springfield
Prickett, Azariah	Stryker also gives him in the 4th where we place him
McManis, Wm.)	
Quimby, John)	
Smith, John)	Sick absent
Templeton, James)	
Ryan, Thomas	Taken by prior enlistment 13 May

Fourth Company

Jonathan Forman   Captain
Cyrus D'Hart   1st Lieut.
Absalom Bonham   2nd Lieut.
Charles Gambertson   Sergeant
Abraham Van dn Hale (Vanderhall)   Sergt.
John Chasey   Sergeant

Andrew Wilson   Corporal   ) Reduced
William Ribbetts   Corporal) Sept. 1
David Amy   Corporal
John Roberts   Drum
Robert Codington   Fife

Privates

Jacob Adams
Rheuben Ayres
Moses Beadle
Jno Carry
Ephraim Eilach
William Farr
Henry Grey
John Hance
Patrick Henderson
Joseph Hillsey
George Hobble
Ebenezer Jones
John Jones
Anthony King
Joseph Lacey
John Moony

John Newton
Arthus O'Neal
Luke Osborne
Matthias Roll
John Saulsbry
Lorrence Smith
Wm. Stuart
Sol Thorp
( )ariah (Azh) Tuckett
John Tuttle
Francis Walkers
Jacob Whitchal
Thomas Williams
Isaac Woolsey
Wm. Wood

Comparison with Stryker's List (1885:42)

1. Stryker has Jacob Lacey and Stephen Eslick. We have an Ephm. Eilach.

Fifth Company

Giles (Yellis) Mead   Captain
William Barton   1st Lieut.
Aaron Rhea   Ensign
Joseph Long   Sergeant
Peter Weaverlin   Sergeant

William Bradshaw   Sergeant
William Bradshaw   Corporal
William Erwin   Corporal
David Lee   Corporal
Richard Shires (Shiras)   Drum

Privates

Matthew Bevins
Timy Breaze
Benjamin Bunnel
John Burnet
Richard Carton (Carter)
Richard Clark
John Comfort

Ebenezer Cutter
John Dennison
Israel Earl
Wm. Erwin
David Fowler
George Frazier
Wm. Gibbs

Samuel Grey
Robert Hampstead
Michael Hayes
Joseph Hornblower
Henry Lennington
Benjamin Lewis
Lurring Loyns
John Rarity

Jacob Ricker
Michael Smith
Joseph Sooper
John Thomas
Benjamin Thurston
David White
Jno Yattie (Yates)

Sixth Company

Alexander Mitchell   Captain
Absalom Martin   1st Lieut.
Asher Levi   Ensign   Resigned
Robert Logan   Sergeant
Abram Hudson   Sergeant

John Hardcastle   Sergeant
Philip Minthorn   Corporal
David Carter   Corporal
Joseph King   Drum & Fife
Isaac Seers (Sears)   Drum & Fife

Privates

Charles Bloomfield
John Browne
William Browne
George Clifton
John Collins
Jona Crane
John Davis
Jere Day
Isaac Dickinson
Benjamin Eaton
Wm. Finley
John Fordice
Gab Hutchings
Stephen Leonard
Abraham Losey

John McLaughlin
William Minthorn
David Mott
David Mumford
Nicholas Pearson
Thomas Perry
John Potter
Thad Rice
Thomas Royal
Levi Shaddick
Adam Showers
Ben Tharp
Price Thompson
Daniel Tuttle
John Williams

Comparison with Stryker's (1885:43) list.

Stryker has: 1.   John Frost, Corporal, but he was sick at Elizabethtown
              2.   Richard Pearson

Seventh Company

Peter Van Voorhies   Captain
Peter Lott   1st Lieut.
John Gary   Ensign
Jacob Williamson   Sergeant
Simon V. Horn   Sergeant
Tunis Voorhies   Sergeant

John Tilton   Sergeant
Christ. McManus   Sergeant
John Rose   Corporal
Richard Jackson   Corporal
Wm. Dear   Fifer

Privates

Joshua Bell	John Johnson
John Boyd	Israel Miels
John Dean	Thos. Newton
Henry Dunfield	William Stillwell
Peter Erwin	George V. Northand (Van Ostrand)
John Fulmon (Fulmore)	John Venett
Daniel Gregg	John Wilson
William Hatchett (Matchett)	Thomas Wilson
Samuel Hill	Amos Witmore

Comparison with Stryker's (1885:44) list

Stryker adds: John Bowers, Drummer, and privates John Simpson and Wm. Vredenburgh. But we have Wm. Vredenburgh = Wm. Fradenburgh "taken by the Marylanders ye 15th of May 1779"

Eighth Company

John Holmes Captain	Andrew McClure Sergeant
Ephraim Whillock 1st Lieut.	James Rice Corporal
John Bishop Ensign	Michel Lane Corporal
George Gray Sergeant	William Creamer Fifer
James Billard Sergeant	

Privates

Samuel Anderson	Moses Horan
William Anderson	Frederick Kizer (Kyson)
Moses Applegate	Thomas Lyal
(Caspar Behall)	Daniel Martin
Daniel Blew	John Moore
John Bryant	William T. Murdock
John Coryell	John Pierce
Tunis Covert	Isaac Price
John Embly	Caspar Russell
Alex Eslick	Wm. Shuffley
John Giddeman	Amos Stackhouse
Thomas Halfpenny	William Thomas
Andrew Hamilton	Wm. Yates
Powles Hopsiker	

Comparison with Stryker's (1885:p. 44) list

1. Stryker has: Wright has:

Peter Dougherty   Drummer
Joseph Craven   Private   Left sick Westfield
Wm. Donaldson   Private   Left sick Turkey Hill
Phenix Jewett   Private

Thos. Jewett with Col. Biddle
omitted Apr.-June 1779 payroll

Ninth Company

Aaron Ogden   Captain
John Howell   1st Lieut.
Joseph Jones   Sergeant

Benjamin Bedell   Sergeant
Ezekiel Howard   Corporal
Jacob Woolley   Drum

Privates

Morris Akers (Ader)
Jacob Bedell
James Cammell (Campbell)
George Carter
Job Coleman
John George
Matthew Gracey
Dennis Hays
Jonas Kent
Joseph King
John Le Grange
Benjamin Legur
Robert Little
Joseph Osborne

Stephen Osborne
Stephen Plum
George Reade
Levy Ross
Samuel Sears
David Sergeant
James Sherwood
John Todd
William Wallace
Wm. Watson
Robert Wherry
James Whitehead
Aaron Willis

Comparison with Stryker's (1885:45) list

1. Stryker has Benjamin Bryant Private

2nd New Jersey Regiment

We have compared these muster rolls of 1779 with a list of the privates of the 2nd Regiment as designated by Stryker. In another compilation someone made 669 privates in the 2nd Regiment. We counted 547 in Stryker's list and at least 214 of these men were on the trip in 1779. There are 84 new names to the Stryker list as there are 17 new sergeants, 6 new corporals, and 7 new men of the drum corps. An actual count of our final sheets shows on the trip for this regiment, 289 enlisted men, 25 corporals, 16 drum and fife, 31 sergeants, 4 2nd lieutenants, 5 1st lieutenants, 1 surgeon, 1 surgeon's mate, 1 capt. lieut., 6 captains, 1 major, 1 lt. colonel and one colonel. We have then 21 above sergeants, 72 sergeants, corporals, drum corps, 289 enlisted men or a total of 382 men. It is manifest that 289 privates out of a total (in its whole history of the regiment) of 547 or 669 men, many were enlisted for the war and it further shows how many of the New Jersey men stuck by their job.

There are at least 4 journals or narratives from members of this regiment, namely, Dr. Ebenezer Elmer, 1st Lieut. John Shreve and 2nd Lieut. Samuel Shute. Gee's account of Fort Sullivan where Colonel Shreve commanded also helps in the history of this regiment.

2nd New Jersey Regiment

Isaac Shreve   Colonel
Wm. D'Hart   Lieut. Colonel
John Ross   Major
Luther Halsey   Adjutant
Derrick Lane   Quarter Master
John Peck   Paymaster

Ebenezer Elmer   Surgeon
Moses G. Elmer   Surgeon's Mate
Wm. Barr   Sergeant Major
Barnet Mooney   Sergeant Major
Geo. McDonald   Quartermaster Sergt.
Wm. Burtless   Drum Major

Additions or corrections to Greenough's Roster:

1. Derrick Lane, Capt. Lieutenant
2. John Shreve, 1st Lieutenant
3. George Walker, 2nd Lieutenant
4. Joseph Buck, 2nd Lieutenant
5. John Hollinshead, Captain until July 5, Aug. 2 or Aug. 23, 1779
6. Jesse Paul

First Company

(Colonel Company)

Isaac Shreve   Colonel
Samuel Hendry   Capt. Lieut.
John Shreve   2nd Lieut.
George Peelor   Sergeant
Wm. Turner   Sergeant

John Seeley   Sergeant
John Patterson   Corporal
James Penton   Corporal
James Gibson   Corporal
Thos. Stillinger   Fifer

Privates

Joseph Babcock (Badcock)	Wm. Clark
Thos. Brown	Andrew Cox
John Campbell	John Duffy
Joseph Charters	John Ferral
James Fletcher	Dennis Lynch
Wm. Fletchers	Randle McDuffy
Daniel Fogg	George Megonigal (MeGonigal)
Wm. Francis	Reuben Mills
Joshua Giffens	Harmon Persons (Pierson)
Eli Gladhill	John Reed
Jno Gurrell	Levi Springer
Thomas Hamilton	Thos. Stephles (Steeples)
James Hill (Hall)	Cornelius Stevenson
Henry Hillabrant	Absalom Tims (Tinis)
John Lloid	Wm. Williams

Second Company

(Lt. Colonel's Co.)

Wm. D'Hart Lt. Colonel	Kendrick Bowen (Borhan) Sergeant
Samuel Naglee 1st Lieut.	Chas. Kennedy Corporal
Jonathan Rhea 2nd Lieut.	Noah Ogden Drum
John Johnston Sergeant	Barny Hortwick Fife
Jordon Hopson Sergeant	

Privates

Elijah Anderson	Matthias Hortwick
Pompey Black	Peter Lowing
John Blackston	Wm. Lynch
Henry Burke	Stephen Masters
Richard Caseby	Edward Maze
John Chester	James McBurney
Michael Clarke	James McCullough
Matthew Conner	Zachariah Peterson
John Derry	Thomas Pollard
Isaac Doty	Henry Sigler
Philip Dunfield	John Smith
Henry Fagan	James Thomson
John Gasright	Shadrick Titus
Levi Griffiths (Griffey)	John Ward

Comparison with Stryker's (1885:47) list shows:

1. Henry Dunfield which we have as Philip Dunfield. He Stryker, has many Dunfields in 1st New Jersey Regiment.

Third Company

(Major's Co.)

John Ross Major	Thomas Patter (Patton) Sergeant
Abel Wayman 1st Lieut.	Richard Abbott Corporal
Joseph Buck Ensign	John Thomas Corporal
John Johnston Sergeant	Jesse Edwards Corporal
Samuel Elwell Sergeant	Jacob Wallinger Drummer

Privates

Stephen Bayley	James Emmerton
James Boites	Wm. Gaskell
Samuel Bowen	John Gerald
James Christy	Wm. Griffeth
Jacob Cook	John Guy
Josiah Cramer	Joshua Hacket
Hugh Crely	Dennis Hinds
Dolph Ebenhardt	Patrick Kelly
Wm. Kerrell	Joseph Polk
James Kinsey	Wm. Prince
Shedrick Kinsey	Robert Proctor
Patrick McAnally	Leo Sandall
Wm. McDade	John Slaughter
Frederick Miller	Chas. Stephens
Jos. Miller	George Tainey (Farney)
Neal O'Neal	Wm. Taylor
John Osman	Robert Woodsides

Comparison with Stryker's (1885:48) List adds the name of James Dalton private.

Fourth Company

John Hollinghead Capt.	Andrew Mason Corporal
Luther Halsey Lieut.	John Smith Corporal
John Peck Lieut.	Thos. Furgason Corporal
John Goldy Sergeant	Frederick Yority Corporal
Martin Johnson Sergeant	Wm. Blair Drum & Fife
Andrew Lykins Sergeant	Able Corson Drum & Fife
Andrew Mason Sergeant	

Privates

James Batling	Obadiah Clutch
John Bennett	James Condon
John Berkins	John Crump
Daniel Britton	Patrick Early
John Clemons	John Edwards

Remington Ewing
David Fisher
Jacob Force
John Golden
Robert Grigg
Philip Kaith (Kaits)
Joseph Land
Richard Long
Thos. Neal
Philip Nolt

Henry O'Neal
Philip Peters
John Robinson
John Shelock (Shearlock)
John Smith
Wm. Strong
Patrick Sullivan
Adam Vincent
Bowen Watts
James Welch
Frederick Yority

Comparison with Stryker's List (1885:49) shows he had:

1. Joseph Berktaler and Daniel Harris but we did not put them in the list because each was "sick at Burlington".

Fifth Company

John Noble Cummings   Captain
Samuel M. Shute   2nd Lieut.
Abram Loper   Sergeant
Chas. McMillan   Sergeant
Benajah Hewett   Sergeant

Isaac Johnston   Corporal
George Waggoner   Corporal
Wm. Rose   Corporal
Michl Faginer   Drum & Fife
Jno Seythin (Sithin)   Fife

Privates

Consider Adition
Thomas Bennet
Thomas Burrell
Robt. Campbell
Daniel Carty
John Carty
Richard Chew
Timothy Conner
Andrew Cramer
Jonathan Daniels
Adm Demaris
Wm. Dixon
John Du Croy
John Edwards
James Fanning
Lawr Ferrin
Robt. Findley
Joseph Floyd

Jacob Gray
Thomas Green
Thomas Harwood
John Insell
John Ireland
David James
Lanet Lambert
John Moore
Isaac Nixon
Peter Ryggar (Bijggar)
Daniel Scull
Anias Strattin
John Taylor
Jona Terry
Robert Thompson
John Williams
Henry Wolf
Ebenzr Woodruff

Comparison with Stryker's List (1885:50) shows:

1. John Sanders but by July-Sept. 1779 musters "John Sanders joined July 1". Did he join at Wyoming or Peekskill or New Jersey?

Sixth Company

Samuel Reading   Captain
George Walker   Ensign
David Gilmore   Sergeant
John Disney   Sergeant
Silas Newton   Sergeant
John Williams   Corporal
John Van Dike   Corporal
Peter Brown   Drum

Privates

- John Civery (Curry)
- Geo. Dotmouth (Dotworth)
- Robt. Fricklen
- Benj. Gartenhous (Garlinghouse)
- Wm. Griggs
- Benj. Horn
- John Huntley
- Jacob Keen
- Philip Lock
- Vincent Luwry
- Wm. Lye
- Alexander McCawly
- Const. McCowen
- James McDonald
- Alex McGregor
- Jeremy McMahon
- Phillip March
- Emans Medaugh (Medock)
- David Peck
- George St. Clare
- Samuel Stanley
- Wm. Watson
- Thos. Welch
- Peter White

Seventh Company

Nathaniel Bowman   Captain
Samuel Conn   1st Lieut.
John Curtis   Sergeant
Almarin Brooks   Sergeant
Isaac Carty   Corporal
George Guinnop   Corporal
Joseph Bennett   Corporal
Henry Graham   Drummer
Samuel Sickels   Fifer

Privates

- Jonathan Baxter
- Josiah Bell
- Zebulon Brown
- Enas Campbell
- Henry Carrigan
- Henry Climhorn
- Joseph Cornick
- Abraham Cox
- Oliver Cromwell
- Wm. Curley
- Ashbrook Dixon
- Francis Dorton
- Andrew Downing
- Wm. Everingham
- John Finch
- Thomas Finn
- John Flake
- John Foster
- Daniel Guffy
- Benjamin Guinnop
- Henry Haldron
- Jacob Hall
- James Irwin
- William Irwin
- Jacob Little
- Walker Lounsbury
- John McQuay
- Joseph Merriam
- Thos. Middleton
- Richard Mills
- Isaiah Nichols
- Neal Nimnough
- Joshua Psandler
- David Quigley
- John Seely
- Nathaniel Shepard
- Wm. Shoemaker
- Alexander Stewart
- Joseph Swan
- Thos. Watkins
- Thos. White
- Wm. Wright
- Thos. Young

Comparison with Stryker's (1885:51) List shows a Joshua Finley not in our list. The nearest we have to this name is "Joseph Finnerty, war prisoner with enemy". We also have a Thomas Young who deserted June 17.

Eighth Company

Jonathan Phillips   Captain
Abraham Appleton   1st Lieut.
Martin Hill   Sergeant
John Gavin   Sergeant
William Gibson   Sergeant

Ezekiel Jobs   Corporal
John Curley   Corporal
John Tater   Corporal
Wm. Burtless   Drum
Robert Fowler   Fife

Privates

Amos Akers
John Ames
Wm. Barret
Arhab Beth
David Brown
Able Bunton
John Coalman
John O. Flaugherty
Shepard Grimes
Thomas Hoolden
John Jobs
Samuel Jobs
Lot Lovelott
John Lyons

Hugh McClean
Wm. McGee
Patrick O'Briant
John Phennimore
Francis Phillips
Peter Powell
Wm. Price
Wm. Pully
Amos Reed
Thos. Reed
John Say
Matthew Thomas
Patrick Toole
Benjamin Voglum

Ninth Company

Wm. Helms   Captain
Derrick Lane   Lieutenant
Benajah Osman   2nd Lieut.
Asay Jones   Sergeant
Thos. Evans   Sergeant
John Poten   Sergeant

Samuel Landon   Sergeant
Robert Watts   Corporal
John Strimple   Corporal
Isaac Williss   Corporal
Abram Rogers (Razer)   Drummer

Privates

Daniel Burns	Wm. Morgan
James Burns	John O'Neal
George Campbell	John Perry
John Chubb	John Poole
Thomas Davis	James Rankins
Jonathan Dunham	George Rockley
David Fanney	Jesse Saxton
John Fleming	Jacob Shaver
Joseph Fox	Joseph Shaver
James Galliher	John Smith
James Glann	John Space
Edward Hawkings	Wm. Sutton
Jonathan Hickman	Hindk V. Wye
John Hoovy	Sam Whitehead
John McCollum	

Third New Jersey Regiment

From a muster roll (Adjutant General's Office, Washington, D. C. Jacket 35-1 Item 103) taken July 7, 1779 at Wyoming we find this staff:

Elias Dayton Colonel	Samuel Sheppard Lieut.
Francis Barber Lieut. Colonel	Ephraim Derby Lieut.
John Conway Major	Edmund D. Thomas Lieut.
Lewis F. Dunham Surgeon	John Reed Lieut.
Ephraim Lorce Surgeon's Mate	Benjamin Horn Lieut.
Joseph I. Anderson Paymaster	Jno Runcastle Lieut.
Samuel Sheppard Adjutant	Wm. Kirsey . Ensign 2nd Lieut.
Ephraim Derby Quartermaster	Nathaniel Wilkinson Ensign
Wm. Gifford Captain	2nd Lieut. Brigade Q.M.
Richard Cox Captain	Wessel F. Stout Ensign 2nd Lieut.
Jeremiah Ballard Captain	Comm. with Boats
Joseph I. Anderson Captain	Jervais Bloomfield 2nd Lieut.
Bateman Loyd Captain	James D. Camp Ensign
Seth Johnson Captain	James Rogers Ensign
Jonathan Dayton Captain Lieut.	George Grant Sergt. Major
John Blair Lieut.	Moses Sproule Q.M. Sergt.
Nathaniel Leonard Lieut.	Morris Wooton Dr. Major

The muster rolls of 1779 reveal of the 315 men Stryker assigned to this regiment in its history that 194 or almost 2/3 of them were on this trip. In the interpretation of names, care has to be exercised. For example, Caesar may be Casar, Seasor; or O'Mack be O'Mock, Mack or Aumacher; or Manning be Harring, Hayning, Manning; or Mustis be Mericus. Never will it be entirely accurate until someone checks all the Washington Adjutant General Office muster rolls along with the 40,000 cards which the New Jersey Adjutant General Office has. Had we not these certain musters of 1779 the above task is what we would have to undertake to arrive at the New Jersey men of this trip for the 3rd, 2nd and 1st New Jersey regiments. Even then the New Jersey evidence (much copies) never would have solved the problem. The Adjutant General's Office (7th and Pennsylvania Ave.) made for the solution.

From Stryker we secured a list of 50 sergeants, corporals, drummers and fifers as of the 3rd regiment not of 1779 solely. 45 of these are found in the musters of 1779 and the total of sergeants, corporals, drummers and fifers for 1779 was 67 or 22 more than the 45 or 17 more than the 50 of Stryker. It shows many stuck very loyally by their jobs.

Corrections or additions to Greenough's Roster:

1. Lewis F. Dunham resigned March 1778 sick at Norris Town.
2. Benj. Horne, 2nd Lieut. Nov. 22, 1777.
3. John Blair, 2nd Lieut May 1, 1777; 1st Lieut. Nov. 1, 1779.
4. John Kersey, Ensign Nov. 1, 1777; 2nd Lieut (sometimes on trip).
5. Francis Barber, Lieut. Colonel at first.
6. John Conway, Major then Lieut. Col. either Apr. 7, 1779 or July 5, 1779 or Aug. 23, 1779 (see Bleecker).
7. Wessel F. Stout also Quartermaster.
8. Ephraim Loring or Lorce, Surgeon Mate.
9. Jonathan Dayton, Capt. Lieut.
10. Add: George Grant, Sergeant Major
    Moses Sproule, Quartermaster Sergeant
    Morris Wooton, Dr Major

Third New Jersey Regiment

First Company

(Colonel Company)

Elias Dayton Colonel	Morris Wooton Drum Major
Jonathan Dayton Captain Lieut.	Ephraim Howard Drummer
William Kersey Ensign	Moses Sproule Quartermaster Sergt.
George Grant Sergeant Major	Samuel Johnson Corporal
Thomas Dixon Sergeant	William Andrews Corporal
William Gibson Sergeant	Edward Howell Corporal
James Shay (Sharp) Sergeant	

Privates

Abel Adams	John Howard
Peter Bereau (Bercaw)	Joseph Johnson
Edward Brady	George Leedbetter
Paul Brewer	Jacob Likens
Francis Carbury	William Lyons
Aaron Deacon	John McCully
Thomas Dixon	James Morris
Daniel Donelly	Thomas Morris
Daniel Ellis	Benjamin Norcross
John Emmons	Abram Peterson
Joseph Gale	Jaspar Potts
John Higgins	Patrick Ryan
Thomas Holland	Jonas Sherwood
	John Snider

Comparison with Stryker's List (1885:53):

1. Stryker gives John Guy, James D. Harmad and Jonathan Shoars. The last may be our Jonas Sherwood of the Aug. - Sept. 1779 payroll.

Second Company

Francis Barber Lieut. Colonel
John Conway Lieut. Colonel
John Blair Lieutenant
Moses Sproule Sergeant (Promoted to Quartermaster June 1, 1779)
Joseph Benham Sergeant
Edward McHughes (McCugo, McHuge) Sergt.

Zebulon Parks Sergeant
Zebulon Parks Corporal
John Truax Corporal
John Van Marter Corporal
Johiab Hull Drummer
James Kilpatrick Fifer

Privates

James Begert
Ephraim Bonham
Conklin Budd
Jediah Burrell
Thomas Carhart
Charles Connel
Charles Cosgrove
Joseph Cox
Joseph Dean
Josiah Halstead
John Hooper
John Howell
Joseph Howerd
Benjamin McDonald
Joseph McIntire
Joseph Moore
Jacob Moorehouse

Eliakim Ogden
John Oakley
John Orr
Gerstrom Parker
Giles Reed
John Ricker
Swain Russell
John Sanders
Timothy Sullivan
Richard Sweeten (Sweating)
Henry Timy (Tummey)
James Van ormond
William Vaughan
Jacob Valentine
James Wilson
Francis Wood

Comparison with Stryker's (1885:54) List:

1. Stryker has Richard Handley and David Welch, privates, on the trip.

Third Company

(Major's Company)

John Conway Major
John Hollinshead Major
Nathl. Leonard Lieutenant

Nathan Wilkinson Ensign
John Miller Sergeant
Jonathan Nicklas Sergeant

Job Brown   Sergeant
Daniel Davis   Corporal
Phillips Goggin   Corporal

Martin Chandler   Drummer
James Barrow   Fifer

Privates

Peter Barney
Thomas Bleckman
Michel Boney
Daniel Brewster
John Burross
Samuel Dowdney
Patrick Dunlevi
Joseph Garretson
Bennet Garrison
John Haines
John Harding

Abram Hazelton
Alexander Jones
Nathan Kimble
Ellithan Langley
Micah Mall (Maule)
Levi Peters
Samuel Potter
James Ray
Edward Russell
Theophilus Shapher
Daniel Sullivan

Fourth Company

William Gifford   Captain
Samuel Sheppard   Lieut.
James De Camp   Ensign
Isaac Jones   Sergeant

Thomas Ireland   Sergeant
Jacob Longhouse   Sergeant
James Bowers   Drummer
David Rogers   Fifer

Privates

Hugh Agar (Augur)
Justis Ball
James Blain
Robert Campbell
Lawrence Carney
Moses Day
Ichabod Forster
Jacob Fox
John Green
Thomas Hilliard
James Horne
John Hutch
John Ketchum
Anthony King

John Lipes
David Martin
Henry McCabe
Chas. Morgan
Thomas Omack
David Reese
Stephen Roberts
David Royal
John Royal
John Shearman
Richard Sennet
James V. Varrick
Garrat Voorhes
Henry Wade

Comparison with Stryker's (1885:55) List:

1. He has John Carr, private, on the trip, but "John Carr (was) sick Cumd. Co...."

Fifth Company

Richard Cox   Captain
Ephraim Darby   1st Lieut.
Wessel T. Stout   2nd Lieut.
Thomas Cobb   Sergeant
Samuel Wigton   Sergeant
James Raymond   Sergeant

John Crill   Corporal
Jedidiah Lyon   Corporal
William Broderick   Corporal
John Jobes   Fifer
Chas. Aman (Oman, Osmun)
  Drummer until July 1, 1779,
  then reduced

Privates

Andrew (William) Anderson
Barney Bangheart
Jemmerson Banks
Samuel Bonnell
Luke Country
James D'Wight
John D'Wight
Elihu Howard
George Johnston
William Lambert
William Mapes
John Martin
John McGinta
Josh Middleton

David Morris
Chas. Osman (Oman) Reduced
Henry Perry
Robert Pickett
William Pinkney
John Price
Isaac Robbins
John Roe
Peter Smith
Christ Snyder
Wm. Stives
Peter Tharp
Samuel Worden

Sixth Company

Jeremiah Ballard   Captain
Edmund B. Thomas   Lieutenant
James Rodgers   Ensign
John Howe   Sergeant
John Hill   Sergeant

Jacob Kent   Sergeant
Peter Smith   Corporal
Thomas Manning   Corporal
Cornelius Drake   Corporal
James Loyd   Fifer

Privates

William Bishop
Joseph Boltor
Samuel Brown
Wooldrick Bulbury
Zachariah Burrell
Henry Casey
Jonathan Conkling
George Corwine
Luke Devore
John English
Joseph Fowler
Davis (David) Gordon
Daniel Guard
Theo Hathaway
Armstrong Jones
James Joy
Henry Kitchen

William Logan
Abram Ludlow
Thomas Martin
James Matthews
William Meade
Solomon Monson
Adamiram Parrott
John Price
Stephen Price
Adamiram Prudden
Joseph Rowe (Rose)
Coonrad Runyon
James Swift
William Tuttle
John Tway
Isaac Ward
Aaron Young

Seventh Company

Joseph I. Anderson Captain	Jacob Sickle Corporal
John Reed 1st Lieutenant	James Riley Corporal
Wm. Hood Sergeant	Alexander Love Corporal
James Beach Sergeant	William Gibson Drummer
William Ross Sergeant	William Radley Fifer

Privates

Daries Anderson	William Johnston
Abraham Borden	Zephaniah Leonard
Jacob Briant	Daniel Mahone
John Bruer	Timothy McKinney
Abraham Casterlin	Alexander Montgomery
Samuel Chandler	John Murphy
John Colston	Stephen Murtis
Amos Crossman	Isaiah Reed
William Dugan	John Rounsavell
John Dunavan	Isaac Stephens
George Garvin	Nathan Tarbill
John Grace	Morgan Thomas
William Griffin	Valentine Thomas
Jeremiah Hackett	William Van Horn
George Hottman	John Whitaker

Comparison with Stryker's (1885:55) List: He has the following with my comments.

1. John Burton "Wounded at New Brunswick"
2. John Hepner "Wounded in Salem Co."
3. John Walters "Wounded in Salem Co."
4. John Redman "Govnr Leavingston's"
5. John Grace "Absent on leave"
6. Joseph Fowler

Eighth Company

(Bateman Loyd Captain Prisoner absent)	Joseph Goulder Sergeant
Benjamin Horn 1st Lieutenant	Daniel Woodruff Corporal
John Reucastle 1st Lieutenant	Elias Lyons Corporal
Timothy Sexton Sergeant	Samuel Clark Corporal
John Cavanaugh Sergeant	Stephen Hatfield Drum & Fife

Privates

Robert Burk
Henry Clayton
Noathan Davy
John Dogherty
George Fidis
John Finley
Eliphalet Herbert
Elisha Hobbs
James Martin
Daniel McDonald
John Nosler
Joseph Osburn

Benjamin Price
Isaac Robertson
Cornelius Robsen
John Rose
John Roseborough
Laurence Seary
John Seasor
Caspar Sweden
Samuel Tendcal
James Wells
Michel Welts (Walsh)

Comparison with Stryker's (1885:58) List: He has

1. Peter Norris and John Foster, privates, but the muster roll for June has "John Foster deserted" and "Peter Norris" sick Norristown. The August payroll has John Foster's and Daniel Season's names erased. My list has a John Season "On Command Lieut. Horn Easton Oct. 17, 1779"

Ninth Company

Seth Johnson   Captain
Jarvis Bloomfield   2nd Lieutenant
Nathan Welch   Sergeant
William Russell   Sergeant
Ebenezer Carlile   Sergeant

Godph. Blekner   Corporal
Matthias Shirts   Corporal
John Smith   Corporal
Aaron Thompson   Fifer

Privates

John Bandal
Samuel Bohanon
Andrew Campbell
William Canoday (Hanaday)
            (Kennedy)
Samuel Chambers
Josiah Cogswell
Robert Delimore
William Flowars
Pat Hartt
George Hayning
Hugh Healey
Peter Hinds
Andrew Horneforth
Joseph Humphries

Samuel Johnson
Ambar Jonas
Bartn Keley
Ephrain Kibbe
Lot Lambert
Hugh McCoaklin
John McMillin
Luis Noel
John O'Brian
George Powars
John Smith
Thomas Soper
John Spicer
Timothy Tway
John Woodruff

29

Comparison with Stryker's (1885:59) List: Stryker has a James Chambers; we have a Samuel Chambers; Wm. Kennedy (we, Wm. Canoday, Hanaday); he has a Hugh McLaughlin (we, Hugh McCoaklin). Our list has a Peter Hynds who was "reduced May 28, 1779".

Spencer's (Fifth New Jersey) Regiment

At Trenton and Washington the author had the most difficulty in assembling and classifying the makeup of Spencer's Regiment than any other group because of its numerous elements. It was a Continental regiment, not state, variously called Independent, Spencer's and 5th New Jersey Regiment. Then it had the remains of the 5 other independent groups. Had we not the muster or payrolls of 1779 it would be an impossible task. Then confusion sometimes arises even in journals of the expedition. For example, the Sergeant Major George Grant of the 3rd New Jersey Regiment who knew there were the 1st, 2nd and 3rd New Jersey regiments on the trip meant to say there was a 4th New Jersey Regiment instead of "the 4th Regiment!

The numbering would have been impossible without the actual muster rolls and Thulman's orderly book consolidation order of July 27. Stryker did well with the evidence then at his hand. Even yet it is difficult to understand the regiment. Did Huntley's and Kearsley's companies stay with Spencer's Regiment?

We are not positive we have the clear picture of the shakedown of this composite regiment after its consolidation of many elements like Forman's, Malcolm's and others. Yet we doubtless have seen to date more material than any previous author.

If we combine the muster roll for March, April, May and June, 1779 (A.G.O. 161-22) with the July, August and September, 1776 (161-26) roll, we have a staff as follows:

Oliver Spencer   Colonel
William S. Smith   Lt. Colonel
Peter Thulman   Adjutant
John Santford   Pay Master
John (or Wm.) Beach   Quartermaster
John McEwen   Quartermaster
Jahas Campfield   Surgeon
John Darcy   Surgeon Mate
Benjamin Weatherby   Captain
John Burrowes   Captain
John Santford   Captain
James Broderick   Captain
Nathaniel Tom   Captain
Abraham Nealy   Captain

Jno Combs   Captain
James Bonnel   Captain
William Beach   Captain Lieut. and Captain
David Kirkpatrick   Lieut.
Finch Gildersleeve   Lieut.
Anthony Maxwell   Lieut.
Peter Thulman   Lieut.
Robert Thulman   Lieut.
Wm. Bull   Lieut.
Jno Stagg   Lieut.
John Orr   Lieut.
Jno McEwen   Ensign
Jno Reid   Ensign

Spencer's (Fifth New Jersey) Regiment

First Company

John Burrowes   Captain
Robert Pemberton   1st Lieutenant
David Kirkpatrick   1st Lieutenant
Thomas Roberts   Sergeant, later Sergt. Major
Benj. Paul   Sergeant Reduced
Michael Erickson   Sergeant
Frederick Mapes   Sergeant
John Brown   Sergeant
John O Neill   Corporal
Jacob Allen   Corporal
Henry Reed   Corporal
Joshua Sullivan   Fifer

Privates

Samuel Bennett
John Berry
John Bolton
Wm. Britton
Thos. Clevenger
John Fisher
Alexander Gale
Wm. Gordon
Edward Griffey (Gussee)
Joseph Griffey
Humphrey Jeffrey
Henry Johnson
Stephen McCormick
Richard Mitchell
George Mount
Peter Peterson
Wm. Robins (Robinson)
Edmund Robinson
James Smith
Matthew Smith
Samuel Samith
Elisha Stout
Benj. Tharp
Wm. Thompson
Holmes Throckmorton
Elijah Tice
Peter Van Cleaf
Eseck Van Dorn
Hendrick Voorhees
Jededeah Woolley

This agrees with Stryker's list except we add Roberts, Paul and Clevenger and eliminate Martin Myers, Nicholas Stephens, Abel Thorp, the last three who were sick and absent.

Second Company

(James Broderick's Co.)

James Broderick (Braddock)   Captain
Finch Gildersleeve   Lieutenant
Benjamin Edsall   Sergeant Deserted June 11
Jacob Wandle   Sergeant
Wm. Casey   Sergeant
Wm. Lewis   Corporal
Anthony Parcall   Fifer

Privates

- Henry Blaricum
- Isaac Breasted
- Abraham Cole
- John Conkling
- Thos. Decker
- Leonard Devons (Divins)
- Samuel Decker
- Anthony Dougherty
- Henry Dow
- Peter Edsell
- Stephen Gregory (Gouger)
- Thomas Gregory
- John Lane
- Isaac Lopus
- Wm. Morrell
- Philip Morse (Moss)
- John Quick
- Lewis Reed
- Thomas Reynolds
- Ephraim Rose
- Aaron Stiles
- Ephraim Sutton
- Luke Thomas
- James Walling
- David Wandle
- Ephraim Woodruff

Our list of privates agrees with Stryker's list except for two, Joseph Hedger and Robert Waller, who were absent.

Third Company

Weatherby's Co.

- Benjamin Weatherby   Captain
- David Kirkpatrick   Lieutenant
- John McEwen   Ensign
- Hector McNeal   Sergeant
- Thomas Garrons   Sergeant
- John Britton   Sergeant
- Hubart Burke   Sergeant
- John Johnson   Corporal
- Jeremiah Gathright   Drummer
- Benj. Applegate   Drummer
- Henry Gathright   Fifer

Privates

- Benjamin Allen
- Benjamin Applegate
- Daniel Bates
- Daniel Britton
- Henry Cherry
- Norris Clark
- Cornelius Conklin
- John Davis
- James Donaldson
- John Donaldson
- George Feathers
- Andrew Johnson
- Lewis Johnson
- James Lewis
- Philip McCracken
- Joseph McPherson
- Michael Meeker
- James Millson
- Samuel Morgan
- Ludlow Ogden
- Thomas Price
- David Scudder
- Wm. Smith
- Daniel Woodruff
- Philip Young

Our list is the same as Stryker except for Michael Hagerty who was sick at Yellow Springs from March - October, 1779 at Yellow Springs.

Fourth Company

(Capt. Santford's Co.)
(Tomm's and Santford's Cos. combined)

John Santford   Captain
Anthony Maxwell   Lieutenant
Finch Gildersleeve   Lieutenant
Wm. Rogers   Sergeant
Reese Williams   Sergeant
Wieder Kidder   Sergeant

Wm. Davidson   Sergeant
Samuel Clark   Corporal
Isaac Monhart   Corporal
Jacob Ezeler   Fifer
John Bogart   Fifer
Joseph Hicks   Drummer

Privates

John Alexander
John Allen
Benj. Allison
Jas. Allison
Albert Begun
George Bowls
David Brush
Alexander Campbell
John Cook
William Cox
Stephen Crane
Joseph Goold
John Gondee
Robert Hadlock
Wm. Hawthorn
Wm. Hillings (Holly)
James Jenkins

David Kelly
Jacob Kinch
Wm. Lane
Samuel Manning
Phineas Mapes
Edward McHenry
Thos. McKey
John McLellan (McCallen)
John McMasters
John Mosure (Mosier)
John Ray
John Steward
Joseph Sheldon
Peter Sullivan
Benj. Tharp
James Tinkham

Fifth Company

(M. T. Forman's and John Combs Co. Forman's Regt.)

John Combs   Captain
Robert Pemberton   Lieutenant
Peter Thulman   Lieutenant
Philip Chaplin   Sergeant

Samuel Reading   Sergeant
Alexander Duncan   Corporal
Richard Mann   Corporal

Privates

James Austin	John Kelly
Daniel Birmingham	Daniel Lewis
Joseph Edmondson	Andrew Patterson
David Ford	Wm. Rogers
John Goldsworthy	Wm. Taylor
Isaac Henderson	Wm. White
Edward Kelly	Isaac Williams

Sixth Company

(Neely's Co.)

Abraham Neely Captain	Wm. Miles Corporal
Peter Thulman Lieutenant	John Riley Corporal
Uzal Meeker Lieutenant	Thos. Donaldson Corporal
Allen McLean Sergeant	Thos. Dawson Drummer
Garret Sickles Sergeant	Joseph Jacobs Drummer
James Robinson Corporal	John Unbehand Fifer

Privates

John Brown	Ezekiel Mott
Wm. Carr	Samuel Neucy
George Colton	Elijah Riphey
Thos. Donaldson	Daniel Robinson
James Dorry	Martin Rutt
Michael Grow	John Ryan
Matthew Hill	Peter Sheridan
Wm. Howell	Peter Shoemaker
Richard Hutchinson	Joseph Smith
Matthew Johnson	Peter Stephens
John Lyby	Daniel Sweeney
John McDonell	John Thomas
Malcolm McKinsey	Martin Van Every
Patrick McLane	James Wetherhawk
	James Wyer

From Stryker's List we have eliminated Corp. Wm. Peck Mason at West Point. Maybe his Peter Sheridan is our Peter Shoemaker. We have added Wm. Carr, John Davis, Matthew Johnson, John Lybey, John McDonell, Samuel Neuey, Martin Rutt (died June 1), Joseph Smith, Daniel Sweeney, Martin Van Every and James Wetherhawk. Most of these additions came from the Major's Co. of March - June 1779.

Seventh Company

(Capt. David Lyons' Co.)

James Bonnel   Captain
(John Stagg   with Adj. Genl.)
John Reed   Ensign
John Reed   Sergeant
Thomas Hoyt   Sergeant
Thomas Jackes   Sergeant

Wm. Crookshank   Sergeant
James Delaney   Corporal
Barney Mooney   Corporal
Albert Vores (Voorhis   Corporal
Barney Bailey   Drummer
Wm. Vallence   Drummer

Privates

Joseph Allison
Robert Bochanon
John Conkling
Daniel Davis
John Davis
Daniel Frazy
Zebedee Frazy
Wm. Gannon
Chas. Gordon
Pierson Green
Gilbert Grotoclas (Gillis)
Wm. Hennis
Aaron Hoofman
Gato Johnson
John Ketcher (Kecher, T. Lecher, Thecher)

Jack Lawrence
John Leighton (Lightning)
Robert Little
Michael Magrew
Hugh McConnell
John Mulvany
Thomas Parks
John Rich (Thich)
Henry Snyder
James Southerland
John Sullivan
Matthias Vallentine
Abraham Van Vleet
Thos. Vane (Vance)
Wm. Yeardon (Yadin, Yeomans)

Eighth Company

Colonel's Company

William Beach   Capt. Lieut.
   Resigned July 5, 1779
William Bull   Capt. Lieut
   July 5, 1779
Moses Ogden   Sergeant
Wm. McGill   Sergeant
Robert Dugan   Sergeant
After (Arthur) Paul   Sergeant

Jonas Tompkins   Sergeant
John Organ   Corporal
Josiah Hunt   Corporal
Seth Jewell   Corporal
James Marshall   Corporal
Joseph Squire   Corporal
Elias Newman   Corporal
   (Numan)

Privates

- James Anson
- Cornelius Ball
- John Bell
- Aaron Brink
- Henry Brink
- Lackey Brown (Malarkey)
- James Burgess
- Joseph Crofat (Crofort, Crawford)
- Amos Day
- George Graham (Grame)
- James Halliday
- David Haycock
- Christopher Hite
- Abraham Jones
- Joseph Jones
- John McKinsey
- Patrick Mulholland
- Matthew Organ
- Matthew Pierson
- Samuel Pierson
- Wm. Reed
- Richard Rosecrans (Rosengrants)
- George Secheveral
- Daniel Smith
- Hugh Steward
- John Syron
- John White
- Henry Williams

Spencer's Ninth Company

Lt. Colonel's Co.

- Wm. Smith   Lieut. Colonel
- Wm. Bull   Lieutenant until July 5, 1779
- John Orr   Lieutenant
- Samuel Sly Sergeant
- John Horton Sergeant
- Thomas Watson Sergeant
- Wm. Bray   Corporal
- Wm. Peck   Drummer

Privates

- Abraham Brannon
- Michael Brannon
- Reuben Brannon
- Thomas Cannon
- Martin Crook
- Silas Daily
- Elias Davis
- Jacob Decker
- James Downs
- Thomas Dunlap
- George Gardner
- James Graham
- Alexander Harrington
- John Harrington
- Jacob Harrison
- David Jacobs
- Edward Keeler
- Moses Mengas
- Christopher Millspaugh
- Daniel Reed
- James Rogers
- Samuel Rogers
- John Scott
- James Stroughan
- Peter Swan
- Michael Teets
- Wm. Teets
- John Winn
- David Young

Second Brigade
(General Poor)

Sixth Massachusetts Regiment

(Late Ichabod Alden's, later Jno Brooks' Seventh Regiment)

This memorable regiment probably made greater sacrifices than any other regiment of the North. When we chanced on a settlement (MSA XXVIII, 86) of the rank of 12 regiments and 89 captains the names: (4th Capt. Thomas Nixon, Aug. 6, 1776; 4th Capt. Wm. Stacey, Jan. 1, 1777; 11th Capt. David Whiting, Sept. 29, 1776; 33rd Capt. Luke Day, Jan. 1, 1777; 44th Capt. John Reed, Jan. 1, 1777; 51st Capt. Daniel Lane, Jan. 1, 1777; Capt. Wm. H. Ballard, July 1, 1775; Capt. Asa Coburn, Jan. 1, 1777) we thrilled with pride at the accomplishments of these men and their cohorts. Once the old regiment was affectionately called Nixon's, then after Col. Ichabod Alden who was killed in battle Nov. 11, 1778. Lieut. Colonel William Stacy had little opportunity to command being taken prisoner Nov. 11, 1778. Its upper command had so suffered in Nov. 1778 that Major David Whiting commanded through the Sullivan Expedition. On its return to the Hudson River in late fall or early winter, 1779, Lieut. Colonel John Brooks became its leader and it became known as the 7th Regiment. The staff did not suffer so badly as the high command. They lost Francis Suza DeBeer, Surgeon Mate, as prisoner Nov. 11, 1778, and did not replace him at once. William Hickling, the paymaster, was replaced Oct. 1, 1778 by Joseph Tucker but Adjutant William White and Surgeon Ezekiel Brown carried on as formerly. The Massachusetts State Archives helped us immeasurably in determining the Sullivan participants of these companies of the famous Cherry Valley outfit.

Sixth Massachusetts Regiment

(Nixon's, late Ichabod Alden's, later Jno Brooks' 7th Regiment)

Date	Name	Rank
Nov. 6, 1776	Daniel Whiting	Major
Sept. 29, 1778	"	Lieutenant Colonel
Jan. 1, 1777	Wm. White	Adjutant
Oct. 1, 1778	"	Lieutenant
June 5, 1779	"	Captain Lieutenant
Jan. 1, 1777	Wm. McKendry	Quartermaster
Oct. 1, 1778	"	Ensign
Jan. 1, 1777	Joseph Tucker	Ensign
Oct. 1, 1778	"	Paymaster
Jan. 1, 1777	Ezekiel Brown	Surgeon
Jan. 1, 1777	Wm. Hudson Ballard	Captain
("	Asa Coburn	")
"	Luke Day	"
"	Benj. Warren	"
"	John Reed	"
"	Daniel Lane	"

June 5, 1779	Jonas Parker	Captain
Oct. 1, 1778	"	Captain Lieutenant
June 5, 1779	Wm. White	Captain Lieutenant
Oct. 1, 1778	"	Lieutenant
Jan. 1, 1777	Jas. Lunt	Lieutenant
"	Samuel Buffington	"
"	Wm. Curtis	"
"	Eliphalet Thorp	"
Jan. 1, 1777	Eben Peabody	"
"	Robert Givens	"
"	Stephen Carter	"
Nov. 19, 1777	Elijah Day	"
July 5, 1779	Luther Trowbridge	"
Jan. 1, 1777	Levi Parker	Ensign
"	Richard Bagnall	"
"	Joseph Tucker	"
Oct. 1, 1778	Wm. McKendry	"

Corrections and Comments on Greenough's Roster (Sullivan Journals 1887, pp. 322, 323).

1. Daniel Whiting. Add Lieutenant Colonel Sept. 29, 1778.
2. Wm. White. Add Captain Lieutenant June 5, 1779.
3. James Lunt. Find no evidence of Adjutant.
4. Wm. McKendry. Ensign instead of Lieutenant.
5. Francis (Ira P.) De Bar. Surgeon's Mate. Not on trip. (Francis S. Z. De Bur) Taken prisoner Nov. 11, 1778.
6. Wm. Hudson Ballard. Add to list as 1st Captain.
7. Jonas Parker. Add Captain June 5, 1779.
8. James Lunt. Neither Adjutant nor Quartermaster.
9. Lieutenants' ranks uncertain, but different from Greenough's.

First Company

William Ballard   Captain
James Lunt   Lieutenant
Levi Parker   Ensign
Henry Stiles   Sergeant Major
Parker Emmons   Sergeant
Peter Wright   Sergeant
Amos Lunt   Sergeant

John Ashley (Ackley)   Drum Major
Jacob Robbins   Drummer
Gad Smith   QM Sergeant
Francis Smith   Corporal
Ephraim Warren   Corporal
Henry Eviced (Evierd)   Fife Major
Zachh Longley   Fife

Privates

Jedediah Adams	Joshua Moody
Joseph Allen	John Patch
Elnan Clarke	Isaac Proctor
Ebenezer Cory	Abijah Read
Oliver Cory	Elear Read
Samuel Craft	? Elnathan Read
Wm. Davis	? Jeremiah Robbins
? Ephraim Dutton	Amos Russell
Wm. Dutton	Boston Ting
Joseph Falmth	Cornwell Ting
Joshua Fassett	Joseph Underwood
Smith Foster	Jacob Wendall
Oliver Heald	Joseph Young
Jonathan Hildreth	

Second Company

(Light Infantry Company)

(Asa Coburn Captain Absent on trip)	James Butterfield Sergeant
Samuel Buffington Lieutenant	Toss Page Corporal
Robert Givens Lieutenant	Samuel Stebbins Corporal
John Brown Sergeant	David Collins Corporal
_____ Sergeant	Wm. McCondry Drummer
	Zebulon Herrick Fifer

Privates

John Allen	Samuel
Joseph Brown	Wm. Hannum
Thomas Burges	Jonas Kump
Jesse Ceaser	Nathan Lewis
Abijah Chadwick	Wm. Lord
Enoch Cleveland	Wm. Mills
Samuel Cole	John Mitchell
Nathl. Cotton	Jacob Mynear
Jesse N. Court (McCourt)	Andw. Ostrander
Enock Dill	Charles Otto
Mias Dolph	Joseph Pike
Daniel Driskill	Samuel Queen
John Fadden	Henry Rednat
Josiah Farrington	Wm. Soliom
George Gambel	Stephen Staples
Isaac Glenney	Samuel Stenson
Daniel Gould	David Teanning (Scanning, Seanning)
Joshua Gray	Stephen Tempel

Isaac Tibbits
Thomas Tilley (Silley)
Enock Toad
Joseph Walker
Fred Whentworth

Simeon Whitton
Thomas Willis
Alex Wilson
John Wooster
Stephen Wyatt

Third Company

Luke Day   Captain
Wm. White   Lieutenant
Elijah Day   Lieutenant
William Tryon   Sergeant
Elihu Warner   Sergeant

James Fadden   Sergeant
Elijah Bliss   Corporal
David French   Corporal
Stephen Shepard   Corporal
Joseph Burk   Drummer

Privates

Cato Abbott
Frank Aine (Rine or Pirce)
(Fradrack Airs (Aires))
Edward Bates
Tomas Belknap
Felley (Tilley) Burk
Ebenezer Cole
Wm. Culberson
Samuel Fall
Joseph Fothergill
Thomas Goldthwait
Amos Hardy
Daniel Hithcock

John Lebirt (Lebort)
Daniel Mc Daniel
Michael Mead
Ashell Mighells
George Mills
Martin Nash
Jesse Read
Thomas Saffin
Andrew Shankling
Thomas Torrance
Jacob Valentine
Zaccheus Walking
John Wheeler

Fourth Company

Benjamin Warren   Captain
Richard Bagnall   Ensign
Robert Donham   Sergeant
Ebenezer Howard   Sergeant
Joseph Bartlett   Sergeant

Benj. Glasier (Glanir)   Corporal
Bennet Simmons   Corporal
Samuel Drew   Corporal
Joziah Roberts   Drummer
Josiah Gorham   Fifer

Privates

Oliver Barnes
Reuben Chase
Jeremiah (John) Cobb
Wm. Duggin
Wm. Glasier

John (Josiah) Gorhom
Richard Harper
Thomas June
Loring Kingman
Benjamin Le Mine

Abisha Packard
Michel Pies (Pier)
Jonathan Polden
Wm. Polden
Prince Redwood

Thomas Turner
William Wallis
Hugh Warwick
Patrick Whalen
Asa Woodworth

Fifth Company

John Reed   Captain
Joseph Tucker   Ensign
Robert Jack   Sergeant
Adam Hunter   Sergeant
John Barton   Corporal

Joseph Holden (Hunter)   Corporal
John Randel   Corporal
Nathan Millwood   Drummer
Adam Williams   Fifer

Privates

Daniel Blazdell
Jonathan Blazdell
Daniel Cornish
Daniel Danforth
Martin Grant
Patrick Heffner (Hefferon
Enos Hudson
Elisha Lake
Nephm Leavit (Liffit)

John McManero (McMannos)
Abraham Melson
Luke Nicholson
Daniel Redlon (Ridley)
David Sparks
Thos. Stanley
Samuel Tilley
Wm. Tucker
John Wheeler (Whalin)
Benj. Willson

Sixth Company

Daniel Lane   Captain
Ebenezer Peabody   Lieutenant
Wm. McKendry   Ensign
Stephen Morrill (Merrill or tt)
   Sergeant
John Dain (Dean or Dian)   Sergt.
Thomas Paine   Sergeant

Enos Runnells   Corporal
Jonathan Gillman   Corporal
Nathan Woodman   Corporal
Thomas Brimigion (Brimigent)
   Drummer
Isaac Lane   Fifer

Privates

Joshua Bangs
John Cox
Jothom Doyle
John Edgerley (Edsley)
Benj. Elwell
John Elwell
Wm. Hancock
John Harris
Peter Jordan
David Kimball
Daniel Merritt

Wm. Merritt
Abraham Millet
James Mosely
Nathan Partig (Partridge)
Clements Pennell (Pencell)
John Piene (Pine)
Daniel Ridloe (Ridlon)
Benj. Tileston (Silston)
Samuel Webber
Nathan Woodman Jr.

Seventh Company

William Curtis   Lieutenant
Stephen Carter   Lieutenant
Hezekiah Cutting Sergeant
Theodore Smith   Sergeant
Samuel Lancaster Sergeant

Samuel Wheeler   Corporal
John Banker   Corporal
Simeon Page   Corporal
Jesse Parker   Drummer
Wm. Vame   Fifer

Privates

Ephraim Ames
Boston Ballard
Moses Bedunah
Wm. Brittain
John Brown
Paul Brown
Jack Canada
Ezekiel Chace
Joseph Chandler
John Cile
Joseph Crumell
Moses George
Jehial Hurd

Ira Jonson
Wm. Jordan
John Kidder
Wm. Knight
Wm. Love
John May
Jesse Parker (Barker)
Ebenezer Pease
Jonas Richardson
Ezra Root (Rood)
Thomas Secomb
John Snelton
Solomon Steel

Eighth Company

(Formerly Wm. Patrick's Company)

Daniel Whiting   Major
Eliphalet Thorp   Lieutenant
Elkanah Hixson   Sergeant
Elijah Dickerman Sergeant
Jonathan Clark   Sergeant

Elkanah Petingall Corporal
Rufus Hayward (Woodward) Corporal
Wm. Handley   Corporal
Wm. Hewins   Corporal
Robert Billings   Drummer
Zebrina Lyon   Fifer

Privates

Eben Capen
Jacob French
John Ganson
Cato Hails
Jonathan Hawes (Haw)
Silvanus Hill (Hall)

Moses Hayward
Cato Johnston
Jos. Jones
Davis Kinney
Charliton Lines
John Lucius

John Madden
Amos Mendall
John Peirce
Jonas Rich
Sam Temple

Thomas Tennant
John Tolman
Saml. Tolman
Eben Wentworth
Enoch Wentworth

Ninth Company

Jonas Parker   Captain Lieutenant
Luther Trowbridge   Lieutenant
Joseph How   Sergeant
John Barker   Sergeant
David Mitting   Sergeant

Ephraim Barker   Corporal
James   Corporal
John Shaffer   Corporal
David Mitchell   Drummer
John Didrich   Fifer

Privates

John Ditman
Christian Entret
Henry Entret
Thomas Gosling
Joseph Grant
Christian Hon
Jacob Johnson
Ralph Metcalf
Adam Mier
John Mier

John Mitchell
Wm. Moake
John Morrison
James Nathan
John Otto
James Pierce
Anton Shoppo
John Stacy
Jona Stratton

First New Hampshire Regiment

I. Officers Present:

    (John Stark, Colonel) Resigned.
    Joseph Cilley, Colonel.
    George Reid, Lt. Colonel (see 2nd N.H. Regiment.)
    Jeremiah Gilman, Lt. Colonel.
    William Scott, Major.
    Benjamin Kimball, Capt. & Paymaster. Killed Aug. 23, 1779.
    Thomas Blake, Lieut. & Paymaster. Aug. 24, 1779.
    (Caleb Stark) & Adjutant) Brig. Maj. with Gen. Stark.
    Jeremiah Pritchard, Lieut. & Adjutant.
    Joseph Mills,   not until May 1, 1780.
    Josiah Munroe, Lieut. & Quartermaster, Aug. 23, Munro.
    Jonathan Willard, Quartermaster, not until July 5, 1780.
    John Hale, Surgeon.
    William Hale, Hospital Steward.
    Jonathan Pool, Surgeon's mate.
    Amos Morrill, Captain.
    Jason Wait, Captain.
    (John House, Captain, Resigned Mar. 4, 1778).
    Amos Emerson, Captain.
    Ebenezer Frye, Captain.
    Isaac Farwell, Captain.
    Nathaniel Hutchins, Captain.
    Simon Sartwell, Capt. Lieut. (with rank of Capt. Sept. 20, 1777).
    Moody Dustin, 1st. Lieut. (with rank of Capt. Mar. 5, 1778).
    Nathaniel McCauley, 1st. Lieut.
    Josiah Munroe, 1st Lieut.
    Daniel Clapp, 1st Lieut.
    William Hutchins, 1st Lieut. Resigned June 23, 1779.
    Asa Senter, 1st Lieut.
    Jeremiah Pritchard, 1st Lieut.
    Bezaleel Howe, 1st Lieut. June 23, 1779.
    "   " , 2nd Lieut. Nov. 8, 1776 to June 23, 1779.
    Simon Morrill, 2nd Lieut.
    Jonathan Willard, 2nd Lieut., 1st Lieut. Aug. 23, 1779.
    Joshua Thompson, 2nd Lieut.
    Thomas Blake, 2nd Lieut.
    Jonathan Perkins, Ensign.
    Joseph Mills, Ensign, engaged March 19, 1779.
    Hubbard Carter, Ensign.
    Samuel Thompson, Ensign.

Those in parentheses () were absent (see next list).

We have no muster rolls for 1779 except for Capt. Hutchins' Company, so cannot assign the 1st and 2nd Lieutenants and Ensigns to their respective companies with certainty. The Captains of the Companies of course can be determined and some probable alignment of Lieutenants and Ensigns. We cannot positively assign Messrs. Sartwell, Dustin, Munroe, Hutchins (Wm.), Senter, Pritchard, Howe, Blake, Thompson--nine in all. If any one ever finds any 1779 muster rolls of this regiment they should be published.

II. Officers Absent.

Promoted to another position or group.

Resigned:
  John Stark, Colonel, March 23, 1777.
  John House, Captain, March 4, 1778.
  James Taggart, 1st Lieut. Aug. 23, 1778.
  William Lee, 2nd Lieut. Jan. 9, 1778.
  William Bradford, 2nd Lieut. Aug. 24, 1778.
  William Hutchins, 1st Lieut. June 23, 1779.
  Jonathan Emerson, 1st Lieut. Sept. 19, 1777 W.
  John Moore, 1st Lieut. Sept. 1, 1778.
  Peleg Williams, 1st Lieut. May 10, 1778.
  James Gould, 1st Lieut. Sept. 19, 1777 W.

Removed:
  Francies Shandonet, Ensign, July 1777. A.D.Q.M. General.
  Caleb Stark, Adjutant, Aug. 28, 1778 or before Brigade Major
    to General Stark.
  Robert Barnet, Lieut. Invalid Reg't. June 1, 1779.

Deceased:
  Joseph Larrance, Ensign, June 5, 1777; Joseph Lawrence,
    June 4, 1775, (AcB).
  Patrick Cogan, Quartermaster, Nov. 8, 1776.

Discharged:
  Samuel Sweat, Ensign, Sept. 26, 1777.
  David Magett, Ensign, Nov. 20, 1777.
  Samuel Cotton, Chaplain, Aug. 7, 1777.

Surgeon John Hale of Hollis is given in Greenough's Roster. We find no mention of him in any Journals (J.O.). Doctor John Hale's "Loss at Ticonderoge" is £ 46.

First New Hampshire Regiment

Date	Name	Rank
Feb. 22, 1777	Joseph Gilley	Colonel
Apr. 2, 1777	George Reid	Lt. Colonel (see 2nd N.H. Regt.)
Sept. 20, 1777	Jeremiah Gilman	Lt. Colonel
Sept. 20, 1777	Wm. Scott	Major
Nov. 8, 1776	Benjamin Kimball	Paymaster
Aug. 24, 1779	Thomas Blake	"
Jan. 1, 1778	Jeremiah Pritchard	Adjutant
Aug. 23, 1778	Josiah Munro	Quartermaster
May 2, 1777	John Hale	Surgeon
May 2, 1777	Jonathan Pool	Surgeon's Mate
Nov. 8, 1776	Amos Morrill	Captain
Nov. 8, 1776	Jason Wait	"
Nov. 8, 1776	Amos Emerson	"
Nov. 8, 1776	Ebenezer Frye	"
Nov. 8, 1776	Isaac Farwell	"
Apr. 3, 1777	Nathaniel Hutchins	"
Sept. 8 or 20, 1777	Simon Sartwell	Captain Lieutenant
Mar. 5, 1778	Moody Dustin	Lieutenant (with Captain's rank)
Nov. 8, 1776	Nathaniel McCauley	Lieutenant
Sept. 20, 1777	Josiah Munro	"
	Wm. Hutchens	" (Resigned June 23, 1779)
Mar. 5, 1778	Asa Senter	Lieutenant
Mar. 5, 1778	Jeremiah Pritchard	"
	Daniel Clapp	"
June 23, 1779	Bezaleel Howe	1st Lieutenant
Sept. 20, 1777	Simon Morrill	2nd "
Jan. 10, 1778	Jonathan Willard	2nd "
Aug. 23, 1779	" "	1st "
Mar. 5, 1778	Joshua Thompson	2nd "
	Thomas Blake	2nd "
July 29, 1777	Jonathan Pirkins	Ensign
Sept. 20, 1777	Joseph Mills	Ensign
Sept. 28, 1777	Hubbard Carter	"
Jan. 10, 1778	Samuel Thompson	"

Corrections and Comments on Greenough's Roster (Sullivan Expedition 1887, pp. 319, 320).

1. Jonathan Willard, both 2nd Lieut. and 1st Lieut. Aug. 23, 1779 but not Quartermaster until July 5, 1780.
2. Josiah Munro, 1st Lieutenant and Quartermaster.
3. Jeremiah Pritchard, 1st Lieutenant and Paymaster until May 1, 1780.

4. Joseph Mills, not adjutant until May 1, 1780.
5. Jonathan Pool, Surgeon's Mate May 4, 1777. Add to roster.
6. Bezaleel Howe, 1st Lieutenant June 23, 1779.
7. Simeon Morrill, 1st Lieutenant between June 23 - Aug. 23, 1779.
8. Jonathan Willard, 1st Lieutenant Aug. 23, 1779 - omitted in Greenough's List.
9. Joseph Mills, Ensign not Lieutenant below J. Perkins in rank.

First Company

(Colonel's Company)

Joseph Cilley   Colonel
Simon Sartwell   Capt. Lieut.
Joshua Thompson   2nd Lieut.
Samuel Caldwell   Sergeant Major
John Joiner   Quartermaster Sergeant
John Jordon   Sergeant
Ripley Bingham   Sergeant

James Cochran   Corporal
Daniel Stearns   Corporal
John Combs   Corporal
James Campbell   Drum Major
Stephen Abbott   Drummer
_____ _____   Fife Major
John Clark   Fifer

Privates

David Adams
Isaac Adams
John Allen
Nathaniel Bartlett
Thos. Bates
Samuel Boyd
Joseph Burley
Moses Chase
John Clark
John Cowdrey
Wm. Cowen
Thomas Davis
(Samuel Davis)
Philemon Ducit
William Durrah
Ralph Ellingwood
Ebenezer Hills
Thomas Kimball
Nathan Mann
Wm. Mann

John Matthew
Abel Merrill
John Millet
James Moore
Samuel Morrison
Wm. Pettigrew
Joel Royce
Thos. Sanderson
James Seils (Sceele)
Michael Silk
John Smith
Ephrem Stephens
Jacob Taylor
Loring Thompson
John Wallace (see 4th Co.)
Samuel Weir
Jonathan Wheelock
Thomas Whitlock
Eben. Williams
Joseph Wilson

Second Company

(Lieut. Col.'s Company)
(Late Capt. John House's Co.)

Lt. Col. Jeremiah Gilman   Captain
Nathaniel McCalley   1st Lieutenant
Thomas Blake   2nd Lieutenant
Isaac Gibbs   Sergeant

Samuel Hews (Hill)   Sergeant
Samuel Hews   Corporal
Stephen Jennings   Corporal
Asa Lovejoy   Drummer

Privates

Ben Barnett (Burnett)
Reuben Blood
Simeon Blood
Isaac Boynton
Nathan (or iel) Bugbee
Robert Burts
Edward Carter
Jonathan Conant
Wm. Connell (Connick)
Stephen Conray
Nathan Davis
Lemuel Dean
Ralph Emerson
Edward Evans
Daniel Fuller
David Gibbs
Joshua Gibbs
Simeon Gould
Wm. Hale

Abel Lovejoy
Robert Mason
Matthew Miller
_____ Bell (substitute for M. Miller)
Derrick Oxford
Nathaniel Patten
Thomas Pratt
Joel Proctor
Daniel Putnam
James Roese
David Sanderson
Medad Taylor
George Thomas
Seth Thompson
Wilder Willard
David Wright
Jonathan Wright
Phineas Wright

Third Company
(Major Company)

William Scott   Major
Moody Dustin   1st Lieutenant
Bazaleel Howe   2nd Lieutenant
Thomas Stickney   Sergeant
William Richardson   Sergeant

John Hillsgrove   Sergeant
William Long (Lang)   Corporal
John Hillsgrove   Corporal
Thos. Capron   Corporal (until June 7)
Thos. Witlock   Drummer
John Scott   Fifer

Privates

Aaron Adams
John Allds
Samuel Allen
Samuel Ayers (Eyers)
Samuel Bates
Abner Bingham
David Bryant
Ephraim Cross
John Cross
David Dickey
Jacob Downing
John Dorman
Noah Emery
Samuel Fugard
James Gilmore
Nathl. Glynes
Timothy Herrington
Levi Hoit
Moses Hutchins
James Lamb

Samuel Morrison
Thos. McNeal
Ebenezer Matthews
John McCoy
Saml. Miller
Nathl. Patten
Jethro Pettingill
John Reade
Reuben Roberts
Jacob Royce
Joel Royce
Thos. Severance
William Simpson
Adam Thompson
John Vance
William Walker
Abiel Walton
Wilder Willard
Abner Wise

Fourth Company

(1st Captain's Company)

Amos Morrill   Captain
Nathaniel McCauley   Lieutenant
Hubbard Carter   Ensign
Samuel Wells   Sergeant
Benjamin Cotton   Sergeant

Thomas Scott   Sergeant
Samuel Whiddon   Corporal
Theophelus Cass   Corporal
Benjamin George   Corporal
James Campbell   Drummer
Daniel Rider   Fifer

Privates

John Ash
Ben. B. Berry
Joshua Blodgett
Ben Brown
Benj. Butler
Caesar Burns
John Caldwell
Solomon Chapman
William Cook
Robert Cunningham
Joshua Danford
James Dickey
Nathaniel Dickey

Benj. Dow
Richard Drought
Philip Flanders
Benj. George
Isaac George
Thomas George
Nathaniel Grahams
Jos. Grant
Joseph Hazelton
Elijah (Elisha) Hutchinson
Levi Hutchinson
John Jennins
Daniel Kidder

Simon Knowles
Moses Lock
Samuel Lock
John Lovering
Timothy Martin
Florence (Terence) McCally
Paul McCoy
Andrew McIntire
David Merrill
John Merrill
John Moore
Nathaniel Moulton
James Orr

Ben Pettingill
Zadock Reid
Nathaniel Rendell
John Robinson
Joshua Sinclair
Samuel Sinclair
Alex Smith
Ephraim Stevens
John Wallace (substitute for
   James Rendel)
Peter Wells
Wm. Willey
Joseph York•

Fifth Company

(Second Captain's Company)

Jason Wait   Captain
Ripley Bingham   Sergeant
   (See Colo.'s Co.)
Robert Parker   Sergeant and Corporal
Richard Robinson   Sergeant and
   Corporal

Silvester Wilkins   Sergeant and
   Corporal
Joseph Hadley   Sergeant deserted
   June 5, 1779
Elijah Averill   Corporal
David Johnson   Corporal
Hezekiah Clark   Drummer

Privates

Samuel Allen
Abner Bingham (See Major's Co.)
Wm. Brown
Josiah Burton
Alpheus Butler
Ezekeel Davis
Joseph Davis
Charles Dougherty
Ebenezer Fosgate (Forgood)
Chas. Geers
Henry Harris
Solomon Harris
Eleazer Haywood
Thomas Hunt
Simon Hutchins
Francis Joiner
Alpheus Kingsley
John Lapish
John McGee

Wm. McGee
Enoch Morse
Ben Perkins
Richard Richardson
James Rider
Daniel Riter
Benj. Smith
Isaac Smith
Tyler Spafford
Henry Stevens
Nathan Tuttle
Stephen Ward
Rufus Walton
Reuben Wheeler
George Wilson
Thomas Wilson
Lewis Wisso
Joseph Wright

Sixth Company

Amos Emerson   Captain
                      Lieutenant
                      2nd Lieutenant
Jonathan Burroughs   Sergeant
Israel Ingalls   Sergeant
Wm. Richardson   Sergeant (See Major Co.)

Sanders Bradbury   Sergeant
John Manning   Corporal
Jeremiah Fowle (Towl)   Corporal
Nathaniel Batchelder   Corporal
Paul Wood   Fifer

Privates

Samuel Aiken
Samuel Barrons
Ebenezer Berry
John Berry (Perry)
Charles Bowles
Noah Buswell
Simon Butterfield
Thomas Fuller
Thomas Goush (Grush)
Duncan Grant
Reuben Hall
Charles Harrison (Hanson)
Jesse Heath
Samuel Hoit
Peter Hovey (Honey)
David Hunt

Zaccheus Hunt
John Kent
Jonathan Knox
Eliphalet Manning
John McClelan
Bernard Merrill
Jonathan Nash (Neck)
Jonathan Powers
Wm. Powell
John Rowe
Daniel Shirley
Wm. Simpson
Benj. Smith
Benj. Taylor
Henry True
Daniel Woods

Seventh Company

(Fourth Captain's Company)

Ebenezer Frye   Captain
Joshua Thompson   Lieutenant
Jere Holman   Sergeant
Thos. Stickney   Sergeant (See Major's Co.)
Robert Hodgart   Sergeant

Wm. Dickey   Sergeant
Jonas Cutting   Corporal
Joseph Marsh   Corporal
Joseph Palley   Drummer
Sam Danford   Fifer

Privates

James Boies
James Brown
Davis (d) Bryant
James Campbell
Thomas Colburn
Zebulon Colbie

Bishop Coster
Samuel Dalton
Sam Danford
Jacob Dayne (See Major's Co.)
David Dickey (See Major's Co.)
Jacob Eastman

Samuel Eyers (See 1st Co.)
Robert Forest
Samuel Fu(l)gard (See Major's Co.)
George Gault
James (Jacob) Gilmore (See Major's Co.)
Nathaniel Glines (See Major's Co.)
Thomas Haines
John Hall
John Head
Timothy Herrington (See Major's Co.)
Levi Hoit (See Major's Co.)
Peter Jenkins (See Major's Co.)
James Lamb (See Major's Co.)
John Mack
Joseph Mack
Ichabod Martin
Thomas Matthews
John (Nathan) McCoy (See Major's Co.)
Stephen McCoy
Joseph McFarland
Thomas McGlaughlin
Obed McLain
Alexander McMasters

George McMurphy
John McMurphy
James Mutchmore
Joseph Norris
Jethro Pettingill (See Major's Co.)
Nathan Plummer
John Reid (See Major's Co.)
John Riddle
James Riddle
John Sampson
Nathan Shade
Wm. Simpson
Edward Smith
Bartholomew Stevens
James Thompson
Solomon Todd
John Vance
Wm. Walker (See Major's
Samuel Walton
James Wilson
Robert Wilson
Daniel Young

Eighth Company

(Fifth Captain's Company)

Isaac Farwell   Captain
(*Wm. Hutchins   1st Lieutenant)
Hubbard Carter   Ensign
Levi Adams   Sergeant
John Joiner   Sergeant
   Quartermaster Sergt. (See Colo.'s Co.)

Gilbert Caswell   Sergeant
Nathaniel Hayes   Corporal
Joseph Burk   Corporal
Abner Preston   Drummer
Thomas Dodge   Fifer

Privates

David Abraham
Jonas Adams
Joel Andrews
John Caldwell
Bunker Clark
John Clark
Benj. Critchett
John Cross
Ira Evans
Moses Farnsworth
Thomas Gilmore
Winsor Gleason
Matthew Greer
John Grout (Grant)
Silvanus Hastings

James Hawkley
Wm. Hewitt
Page Herriman
Moses Hutchins
Jonathan (John) Kelley
Wm. Lattin (Letton)
Isaac Mitchell
Timothy Newton
Thomas Osgood
Samuel Phillips
Noah Porter
Abner Powers
Nathaniel Powers
Simeon Powers
Wm. Pritchard

Lemuel (Samuel) Royce (Rice)
Paris Richardson
Levi Simmons
Silas Simmons
John Simons

Samuel Sisco
Roger Stevens
Wm. Taggart
Joseph Tucker

Ninth Company

Nathaniel Hutchins   Captain
Daniel Clap   Lieutenant
Joseph Mills   Ensign
Eliphalet Quimby   Sergeant
Samuel Caldwell   Sergeant (Sergt. Major June 23rd)
Amos Barnes   Sergeant

John Chadwick   Sergeant
John Chadwick   Corporal
John Thing Connor   Corporal
Benj. Williams   Corporal
Enos Chellis   Corporal
Samuel Stocker   Drummer
Daniel Crecy   Fifer

Privates

Wm. Batchelder
James Boles (Bowles)
Samuel Cammett
Thomas Cammett
Joshua Church
Moses Colby
John Cosper (Cupper)
James Doude
Stephen Dusten
John Eastman
Thomas Eastman
James Edgerly
Elijah Fairfield
John Farnham
Jacob Flanders
John Flanders
Thomas George
Anthony Gilman

Windsor Gleason
Charles Greenfield
Thomas Harvy
Wm. Hodgkins
Enoch Hoyt
Jonathan Judkins
Samuel Lock
Stephen Lord
Bradstreet Mason
Colburn (Coleman) Parker
Thomas Perry
Joseph Sanborn
Jonathan Sawyer
John Sweet
Henry Thompson
Ezra Turner
Jonathan Webster

Second New Hampshire Regiment

In our account of the 1st, 2nd and 3rd New Hampshire Regiments we have permitted (in original manuscript) Topic I to remain almost as originally written and typed. In it by pre- and post-trip evidence, depreciation rolls, account books, pension records and sundry other sources minus the actual rolls of 1779 we approximated the rosters of each company. Indeed in this individual account of the 2nd Regiment we were happy to conclude the topic with the actual May 1779 roster. Had we published this paper with just topic I discussion we find we would have been just about as much astray as Greenough was with his Roster of the Officers of this trip in his 1889 paper. Therefore we appreciate his effort and hope for as much forgiveness for ourself many honest mistakes we have made. However, the discovery of these New Hampshire muster rolls, payrolls and miscellaneous records in the Adjutant General's Record Office (National Archives) has proved a clincher and a final court of decision. Rolls such as jacket 13-1 or Item 201 from the important period June, July, August and September 1779 suffice for our purpose.

Second New Hampshire Regiment

The rank, staff and other commissioned officers of this regiment.

Had we no roll for May or October 1779 the other rolls might give us a composite roll with the presumptive officers of the expedition. For example, Major Benjamin Titcomb who was accidentally killed, on the Sullivan expedition gives us "A list of the Rank and Occurrences of The Field Commissioned And Staff Officers in The Second New Hampre Regt- (Original in Department of State, Washington, D.C.)

Were we obliged to use this evidence only we would presume that all the above Captains who were promoted probably were not of this active regiment later nor those from Captain's rank to Surgeon mate who were absent, discharged, resigned, or dead. On this basis S. Bradford, James Crombee, John Colcord, George P. Frost, Josiah Meloon, might have been present on the Sullivan trip yet they all were probably absent. I am afraid Hon. Charles Greenough did not check all the extant individual rosters. For example, he includes George P. Frost, but Frost spent the period on the Hudson training summer recruits until the Sullivan party returned.

In the Depreciation Rolls to January 1, 1780 we have the names of the regiments with their officers and men and the sums due them. The names of the "(2d Regiment Officers) 2d Regt. Commanded by Col. Geo. Reid for years 1777, 1778 and 1779." The names follow.

From this list to Jan. 1, 1780 we ought to have all and more besides who were on the expedition. This was published in 1886 and no doubt was used in the roster of the Sullivan Expedition (1887). We will later discuss why George Aldrich, Nathan Taylor, Windborn Adams, Wm. Parker, William Wood, Sam Bradford, Nathan Hale, Thomas Hardy, John Drew, Geo. P. Frost, Fredk Mt. Bell, David Forsyth, Richard Brown were probably absent from the trip (see Company accounts).

We will bore you with two or three more rolls to determine who were on the trip, who couldn't have been on the trip and what had already befallen some of the 2nd regiment officers. A very useful "Return of Officers in Second Regiment" (N.H.S.P., Vol. XVI R.R., Vol. 3:4-5) is "A return of the Field, Staff & other Commission'd Officers that are or ever have been in the 2d New Hampshire Regiment with the time of their Appointments, promotions, Deaths, discharge or Resignation since the 1st Jany 1777 to 1st Jany 1780".

Second New Hampshire Regiment

	George Reid	Lieutenant Colonel
	Benjamin Titcomb	Major
	Jeremiah Fogg	Captain and Paymaster Resigned PM Oct. 17, 1779
	James Carr	Captain and Paymaster Nov. 18, 1779
	William Mdt Bell	Lieutenant and Adjutant
	Joseph Potter	Lieutenant and QM
	(Robert R. Henry	Surgeon Oct. 24, 1779)
	William Wood	Surgeon's Mate Discharged July 1779
	Ira Evans	Chaplain
Nov. 8, 1776	Caleb Robinson	Captain
"	James Carr	"
"	Elijah Clayes	"
Apr. 2, 1777	William Rowell	"
Sept. 20, 1777	Moses Dustin	"
Oct. 9, 1777	Jeremiah Fogg	"
Dec. 22, 1777	Enoch Chase	"
Nov. 30, 1779	Samuel Cherry	" (Nov. 30, 1779) and Capt. Lieut.
Dec. 22, 1777	Ebenezer Light	Lieutenant
"	Noah Robinson	"
"	Joseph Potter	"
"	Peletiah Whittemore	"
"	Wm. Mordt Bell	"
Sept. 20, 1777	Luke Woodbury	2nd Lieutenant
Oct. 9, 1777	Samuel Adams	"
Dec. 22, 1777	Wm. Taggart	"
Apr. 2, 1777	Joshua Merrow	Ensign
May 6, 1777	Daniel Gookin	"
Sept. 16, 1777	Caleb Blodgett	"
Sept. 20, 1777	George Burnham	"
Oct. 9, 1777	William Twombley	"
Dec. 22, 1777	Thomas Challis	"

Corrections and Comments on Greenough's Roster (Sullivans Journals 1887, pp. 320, 321):

1. James Carr became Paymaster Nov. 18, 1779 vice Fogg.
2. William Mordaunt Bell. Add Lieutenant.
3. Richard Brown, Quartermaster, resigned Aug. 22, 1778.
4. Joseph Potter, Quartermaster, on Sullivan trip.
5. Robert R. Henry, Surgeon, appointed Oct. 24, 1779. Was he on the trip?
6. William Wood, Surgeon's Mate. Discharged July 1779.
7. George Aldrich, Captain, not on trip.
8. Samuel Cherry, Captain, Nov. 30, 1779.
9. Micah Hoit. Not on trip.
10. James Nichols, Lieutenant, on furlough Col. Hazen.
11. George P. Frost, Lieutenant. Not on trip.
12. Thomas Lyford
13. James Butterfield — With Geo. Aldrich elsewhere.
14. Thomas Callis = Thomas Chellis.

First Company

(Colonel Enoch Poor's and Nathan Hale's Company)

George Reid	Lieutenant Colonel	
Samuel Cherry	Captain Lieutenant	
Luke Woodbury	Lieutenant	
Daniel Gookin	Ensign (Chase)	Ensigns or higher but in other companies on this trip
Caleb Blodgett	" (Clayes)	
George Burnham	" (Rowell's)	
Wm. Twombley	" (Dustin's)	
Thomas Challis	" (Fogg's)	
John Downing	" (Major's)	
Eliphalet Norris	"	
John Sanborn	"	
Daniel Horn	"	Reduced Aug. 24, 1779
Theo Colby	QM Sergeant	
Jonathan Leathers	Corporal	
Josiah Calley	"	
(John Smith	"	See Carr's Co.)
Barnabas McBride	"	
Caleb Clark	"	
(Thomas Warren	Drum Major)	
Philip Fowler	Drum Major	
(Moses Looge	Fife Major)	
Jonathan Leavitt	Fifer	

Privates

Thos. B. Ashton
Ebenezer (Edward) Bean
Thos. Blanchard
Nathaniel S. Clark
Primus Coffin (Lane)
Samuel Daniels
Edward Fyfied (Fairfield)
Simeon Haines
Wm. Haines
Uriah Hanscomb (?)
Phinehas Hodgdon
Wm. Hogg
Daniel Horn
James Kennestone (Kennison)
Nicholas Leathers
Wm. Leaver
Jonathan Leavitt
Simeon Marsh (?)
Simeon Mason
Samuel McGuin (Mequin) (?)
James Norris
John Small
(John Smith)
Moses Roberts
Caesar Wallace
Thomas Webster

Second Company

(Formerly Capt. Fred. Mordaunt Bell's Co.)
(Major Titcomb's Co.)

Benjamin Titcomb   Major
(Micah Hoit   Lieutenant)
Samuel Adams   Lieutenant
Joseph (John) Richardson   Sergeant
Stephen Noble   Sergeant
Samuel Card   Sergeant
(Joseph Jewell   Corporal)
Daniel Wyman   Corporal
Wm. Hill   Corporal   Jan. 1, 1779
Job Kennison (Kennistone)   Drummer
Francis Drew   Fifer

Privates

George Abbott
Noah Allard
Aaron Bickford
John Blazedall
Thomas Blazedell
Joseph Bunker
Joseph Burnham
Jesse Clark
Wm. Clifford
Richard Colomy (Calome) (Hollomy)
John Cook
Downing (Dependence) Colbrath
Elias Critchett
Thomas Currier
Moses Davis
Francis Drew
Samuel Davis
James Eastman
Elijah Gould
(Ephraim Ham)
John Ham
(Thomas Hanscomb)
Joath Henderson
Samuel S. Hayward (Haywood)
John Hill (Hull)
Wm. Hill
And. Johnson
Ephraim Jones
(Amos Kamp (Kemp))
John Kenney (Cenney)
Edward Leavitt
Ephram King
Joshua Lock
James McDaniel
Moses Miles (Riales)
John Norton
Daniel Richardson
Moses Runnells
John Sergeant
Moses Spencer
John Taylor
Vincent Torr
Isaac Watson
Benj. Welsh
John Welsh
Phineas Wentworth
Henry Wisdom
The four ( ) are doubtful.

Third Company

(First Capt. Company)

Caleb Robinson   Captain
Ebenezer Light   Lieutenant
Wm. Taggart   2nd Lieutenant
Wm. Mordaunt Bell   QM Sergeant
Wm. Gordon   Sergeant

Wm. Moore   Sergeant and Corporal
Eben Eastman   Sergeant and Corporal
Israel Rowell   Corporal
John Nichols   Corporal
Jona Hill   Drummer

Privates

Henry Baxter
Dennis Bickford
Moses Blake
Christopher Callis
Richard Clements
David Colby
Solomon Cole
Moses Copps
Thomas Currier
London Daily (?)
John Diamond
John Dalloff (?)
Jona S. Dudley
James Dunlap (?)
Edward Eastman
Moses Ferrin
James Dolloff
Winthrop Fox (?)
Eleazer Ferguson
Ezekiel Gilman
Joseph Gorden
Jonathan Greene
Israel Hall (Hull)
Thomas Hall
Joseph Harris
Jona Hill
John Hilton
John Hopkinson
Richard Howe
Pearson Huntress
John Jewell (?)
Wm. Jewett

John Kimball
John Merrifold (?) (Manifold)
Alex Magoon
Dudley Marsh
Hugh Matthews
Thomas Matthews
Jacob Merrill
Joshua (John) Mitchell
Elkins Moore
Isaac Morse (Moss)
John Nichols
James Norris
Samuel Norris
Jona Perkins
Elijah Pollard
Alex Patterson (?)
George Patterson (?)
Hezekiah Pollard (?)
Eliazer Quimby
David Richards (?)
Natt Richardson
Thomas Rollins
James Rowell
Elisha (Elijah) Smith
Broadstreet Taylor
John Thompson
John Ward
Melcher (Michael) Ward
Samuel Wilson
Timothy Woodall
Israel Woodbury
Wm. Woodbury

Fourth Company

(Second Capt. Co.)

James Carr   Captain
(George Pepperill Frost   Lieutenant)
   (On Hudson July 12, 1779)
Joshua Merrow   Ensign and Lieutenant
Elijah Buzzell (Bussell)   Sergeant
David George   Sergeant
Anthony Hanson   Sergeant

David Morgan   Sergeant
Charles Stanton   Corporal
Ebenezer Waldron   Corporal
(Ebenezer McElvin (McIlvain)
   Corporal)
Wm. Palmer   Corporal
Bradley (Bradbury) Greene   Drummer
Ebenezer Fletcher   Fifer

Privates

James Boyes
(Jonathan Buzzell)
Ambrose Cole
Ezekiel Demeritt (Demery)
Zaccheus Dustin (Zacharias)
John Dutton
Joshua Edgerley
George Fall
Daniel Foster
(Jonathan George)
Michael George
Jonathan Godfrey
Edward Grant
Samuel Grant
John Job
James Marden

Ebenezer McElvin
Farrar Miller
John Morgan
Simeon Moulton
Patrick Murphy
Jonathan Quimby
Thomas Quint
James Robinson
Jacob Russell
Paul Sanborn
Wm. Scott
Volent (Valentine) Sergeant
Daniel Sullivan
Ebenezer Waldron
Daniel Watson
Thomas Wills (Wells, Willis)

Fifth Company

(Formerly Capt. John Drew's Co., later (after 1779) Capt. Chase's Co.)

(Third Capt. Company)

Elijah Clayes   Captain
Joseph Potter   Lieutenant
Caleb Blodget   Ensign
David Copps   Sergeant
John Demerit   Sergeant
John Neal   Sergeant (Dustins
   after July 1)

Abel Morrill   Sergeant
Jonathan Tucker   Sergeant
Jonathan Tucker   Corporal
Paul Otis   Corporal
Samuel Williams   Corporal
   Reduced July 17, 1779
Isaac Pinkham   Drummer
Daniel Pinkham   Fifer

Privates

- Benj. Berrey
- John Babb (Ball)
- Edward Brown
- Corrydon Chesley
- Paul Cook
- John Critchet
- Ebenezer Crommett
- Ebenezer Davis
- Ephraim Davis
- Edward Dearborn
- Zebez Dow
- Robert S. Fasket (Stockets)
- Jonathan Folsom
- Philip Fowler
- Carty (Carter) Gilman
- Simon Gilman
- John Haywood
- Thomas Howe
- Richard Hunkin
- Zacharias Kelsey
- John Lander
- Stephen Meeder
- Abel Morrill
- Timothy Mosher
- John Otis
- David Page
- George Parshley
- Thomas Parshley
- Daniel Pinkham
- Robert Rawlings
- Aaron Rollings
- John Rowe
- Samuel Trickey
- Gloster Watson
- Thomas Welsh
- Sam. Williams

Sixth Company

(Formerly Capt. Elijah Clayes' (1777-1778) Co.)

(Fourth Capt. Co.)

- William Rowell   Captain
- Pelatiah Whittemore   Lieutenant
- George Burnham   Ensign
- Amos Boynton   Sergeant
- Silas Coolidge   Sergeant (See Carr's Co.)
- (James Reed   Sergeant)
- John Taggart   Sergeant
- Zadock Dodge   Sergeant
- Ebenezer Jennens   Corporal
- William Kendall   Corporal
- Joseph Taggart   Corporal Sept. 1, 1779
- Joseph Slack   Corporal Reduced Sept. 1, 1779
- John Dodge   Fifer   Reduced Sept. 1, 1779
- Snow Boynton   Drummer

Privates

- David Brooks
- Jesse (Job) Cammel
- Elias Cheney (Channey)
- John Dodge
- Zadock Dodge
- Noah Downs
- Daniel Esquire
- Jude Hall
- Jonathan How
- Jonathan Lake
- Jona Margery
- Zabez McBride
- Reuben McCallister (McCloster)
- Robert McClurgh
- John Mitchell
- Thomas Murdock
- Ebenzer Sergeant
- Joseph Slack
- Moses G. Sweet
- Joseph Taggart
- Nathaniel Taylor

Seventh Company

(Fifth Capt. Company)

Moses Dustin   Captain
Wm. Twombly   Ensign
Thomas Hutchinson   Sergeant
   May 10, 1779
John Neale   Sergeant

Jonathan Huntress   Corporal
Oliver Smith   Corporal
Edward Wade   Corporal
Edward Gotham   Drummer

Privates

Daniel Alley
John Barter (Barker)
John Buss
Robert Carson
Wm. Cutler
Jonathan Huntress
Thomas Hutchinson
James Kelley
Nathaniel Marston
Robert Craige
Wm. Cutler
David Doe

John Edwards
Samuel Godding (Gordon)
William Hilton
Jno Neal
John Rendall
John Robinson
Aaron Rollins
Oliver Smith
Eliphalet Veasey
Edward Wade
Joshua Wilson

Eighth Company

Jeremiah Fogg   Captain
Noah Robinson   Lieutenant
Thos. Challis   Ensign
William Towle   Sergeant
Abraham Greenway   Sergeant
Oliver Thurston   Sergeant

Lemuel B. Mason   Sergeant
Abraham Greenway   Corporal
Benjamin Dodge   Corporal
Ithiel Gorden   Corporal
Francis Walls (Watt)   Drummer

Privates

Philip Blazedell
John Brosbee
Enoch Burnham
Thomas Chamberlain
Ebenezer Cook
Thomas Cook
Benj. Dockam
George Downing
Lemuel Dudee
Henry Durgin
Cato Fisk

John Garland
Eliphalet Gorden
Ithiel Gorden
Theophilus Downing Lovering
  (Loring)
Edward Martin
Lemuel B. Mason
John Mitchell
Jotham Nute
Joseph Pearle
Adam Perkins

Ben Pinner
James Quimby
David Watson
Winthrop Wiggin

Daniel Wingate
Enoch Wingate
Daniel Woodman
Joseph Young

Ninth Company

(Seventh Capt. Co.)

Enoch Chase   Captain
Wm. Mordaunt Bell   Lieutenant
Daniel Gookin   Ensign
Jonathan Downing   Sergeant
   Sergt. Major June 1

David Morgan   Sergeant
Silas Coolidge   Sergeant
John Mills   Sergeant
John Mills   Corporal
Nathl. Frost   Corporal
Stephen Runnels   Corporal

Privates

Cato Baker
Josiah Blodgett (?)
Dependence Colbrath
Wm. Colby (?)
Ebenezer Crummet
James Crommet
Nathaniel Frost
Thos. Hammet
Benj. Leach
Ebenezer Palmer

Richard Presby
Edward Randall
James Rowell
Israel Runnels (?)
Stephen Runnels
John Seavey (Seamey)
Abraham Senter
John Smith
John Spring
Samuel Ward
James Young

Third New Hampshire Regiment

I Composite Evidence from all sources except A.G.O. muster rolls of 1779.

No history of the 3rd Regiment has been written. Kidder in his History of the 1st New Hampshire Regiment had one journal only for the Sullivan expedition, that of Lieut. Thomas Blake, but of the 3rd New Hampshire Regiment there are at least four (Lieut. Colonel Henry Dearborn, Sergeant Moses Fellows, Captain Daniel Livermore, Major James Norris) for the regimental history, were someone to write it.

In General Poor's Return July 1, 1779 the three New Hampshire regiments had 536 rank and file. Of these 536, 347 were fit for duty, not sick, not on command, not on extra services, not on furlough.

Muster Rolls of 1779.

Previous to Sept. 1948 we were bemoaning the absence of 1779 muster rolls. In this regiment in Topic I from New Hampshire Regiments we longed for the May 1779 and intermediate material to October 1779. The Adjutant General's Office (AGO N.H. Jacket 27-1) has such material and more.

Third New Hampshire Roster

(Alexander Scammell Colonel	Absent as Adj. Gen., Jan. 15, 1778)	
Henry Dearborn	Lieutenant Colonel	
James Norris	Major	
Joseph Boynton	Lieutenant and Adjutant	
James Blanchard	Lieutenant and Paymaster	
Nathan Hoit	Lieutenant and Quartermaster	
Jacob Hall (Hull) Jr.	Surgeon	
Isaac Smith	Surgeon's Mate	
Israel Evans	Chaplain	

Nov. 8, 1776	Daniel Livermore	Captain
Nov. 8, 1776	Isaac Frye	"
May 4, 1777	William Ellis	"
Aug. 4, 1777	David McGregore	"
(June 1, 1778	Nicholas Gilman	")
May 22, 1779	Wm. A. Hawkins	"
(May 22, 1779	Thos. Simpson	Captain Lieutenant)
July 19, 1779		" "
July 19, 1779	John Dennett	
May 1, 1778	Benj. Ellis	Lieutenant
"	Adna Penniman	"
"	Jonathan Cass	"

May 1, 1778	Joseph Boynton	Lieutenant
"	Dudley L. Chase	"
"	Nathaniel Leavitt	"
May 21, 1778	Nathan Hoit	"
May 22, 1779	James Blanchard	2nd Lieutenant
Aug. 4, 1777	Jonathan Cilley	Ensign
Sept. 20, 1777	Archibald Stark	"
Oct. 8, 1777	Nathan Weare	"
Nov. 14, 1777	Neal McGaffey	"
May 1, 1778	Bradley Richards	"
May 1, 1778	John Harvey	"
May 1, 1779	Moses Page	"
May 1, 1779	Robert B. Wilkins	"

Corrections and Comments on Greenough's Roster (Sullivan journals, etc. 1887, pp. 321, 322).

1. Nicholas Gilman, Captain and Adjutant - not on trip. Assistant Adj. General Jan. 15, 1778.
2. Joseph Blanchard, 2nd Lieutenant and Paymaster - should be James Blanchard. In one roll it appears as Amos Blanchard.
3. John Hovey, Ensign and Quartermaster. Who is he? Is Ensign John Harvey or Surgeon Ivory Hovey meant? Nathan Hoit, Lieutenant, is Quartermaster.
4. Jacob Hall, Surgeon, should be Jacob Hall, Jr.
5. Mark Howe, Surgeon. No such person in N. H. rolls.
6. Isaac Smith, Surgeon's Mate, should be added.
7. Thomas Simpson, never Captain, on trip. On May 22, 1779 he became Capt. Lieut. but resigned July 19 or 20, 1779 and John Dennett was chosen in his place.
8. John Dennett, not Lieutenant, but Capt. Lieutenant.
9. John Harvey, Ensign, to be added.
10. Robert B. Wilkins, Ensign, to be added.

First Company

(Colonel Scammell's Company)

John Harvey   Ensign
Neal McGaffey   Sergeant Major
  (See 3rd Co.)
Michael Parkes   Sergeant
Daniel Cass   Sergeant
Edward Mason   Sergeant
  (See 3rd Co.)
Moses Fellows   Sergeant
Thos. Beal   Sergeant (transferred to 9th Co.)
Thomas Powell   Drum Major & Drummer (May 28, 1779)

Noah Sinkler   Drummer & Drum Major (May 28, 1779)
John Jones   Quartermaster Sergt.
Moses Fellows   Corporal
Abraham T. Sweatt   Corporal
(John Midgett   Corporal)
  Discharged Mar. 31, 1779
Abner Fowler   Corporal
Joshua Thornton · Fife Major
John Morrison   Fifer

Privates

Heman Amy
Wm. Burley
Jona Bean
Moses Cass
David Clifford
Benj. Chase
Zaccheus Clough
Ephraim Dudley
Trueworthy Dudley
Thomas Dolloff (ph)
John Durgan
Daniel Felch
Abner Fowler
Matthew Greeley
Reuben Hoyt
Ben Howard
Humphrey Hunt
Wm. Mallen
James Marston
James Mason

Jno Morrison
Jno Piper
David Piper
Thomas Piper
Daniel Philbrook
Zach Quinby
Jno Rowen
Samuel Rowell
Joseph Sanborn
Richard Sinkler
Benj. Sleeper
Samuel Silver (Trans. to 9th Co.)
Jeremiah Smith (Trans. to 9th Co.)
Peter Smith
Joshua Snow
Enoch Thomas
Daniel Torrey (Trans. to 9th Co.)
Elijah Wadleigh (Trans. to 9th Co.)
Benj. Whittier
Nehemiah West

Second Company

(Lt. Colonel's Company)

Henry Dearborn   Lieut. Colonel
John Dennett   Lieutenant
James Blanchard   Lieutenant
Wm. Gale   Sergeant
Patrick O'Fling   Sergeant
David Hall   Sergeant

David Duncan   Corporal
John Paverly (Peverly)   Corporal
Nathaniel Waldron   Corporal
Nathaniel Brown   Drummer
  Reduced Mar. 15
Samuel Odiorne   Fifer

Privates

Peter Abbott (see 9th Co.)
Nathaniel Brown
Philip Cooper
Benj. Cross
Samuel Davis
James Edgerly
Wm. Heath (see 4th Co.)
Joseph Hodson (Hodgdon)
Benj. Hoit
Joseph Hull (Hill)
John Herrington
Simon Knowles
Richard Lock

Henry Longmaid
John Marden
John Odiorne
Daniel Rowlins (Rawlings)
Wm. Russell
Thomas Shaw
Richard Sherman
Thomas Sprown
Stephen Switcher (Sweetsar) (Swicher)
John Wait
Thomas Waters
James Worcester

Third Company

(Major's Co.)

James Norris Major
Benj. Ellis Lieutenant
Neal McCaffey Ensign
Edward Mason Sergeant
  (see 1st Co. AcB)
Moses Kelsey Sergeant

Elisha Neas Sergeant
Wm. Rundlett Corporal
John Bean Corporal
Nehemiah Leavitt Corporal
Isaac Moore Drummer
(Samuel Judkins Fifer)
  (see 4th Co.)

Privates

Ammie Andrews (Anders)
James Batchelder
Josiah Bean
Charles Burget
Josiah Chase
John Clough
Zaccheus Clouth (see 1st AcB)
John Cunningham
Simon Dearborn
Jonathan Flood
Wm. Furnell
Anthony Garoutte (Gerrott)
John Grear
Joseph Griffin

Samuel Judkins (see 4th Co.)
John Leavitt
Daniel Libby (?)
Like Libbey
Jonathan Mason
Abraham Page
Chase Page
Jonathan (John) Prescott
Jeremiah Rawlings
Samuel Runnells
John Smith
Thomas Speed
Ambrose Viccor

Fourth Company

Daniel Livermore   Captain
Nathan Hoit   Lieutenant and QMaster
Jonathan Cilley   Ensign
Robert Livingston   Sergeant
George Cooper   Sergeant

Moses Page   Sergeant
Amos Flood (Blood)   Corporal
Stephen Webster   Corporal
Samuel Judgkins   Drummer
Nathaniel Brown   (Drummer) (see 2nd Co.)

Privates

Beriah Abbott
Edward Ames (Arms)
John Boyce (Boyer)
Jacob Burkheart
John Craig
Acquila Davis
Jacob Eastman
Wm. Eastman
Jeremiah Fairfield
Ebenezer Farnham
Wm. Heath
John Hillery

Joseph (John) Orient (Ryant) (Briant)
Thomas Pitts
Wm. Rowe
Henry Seelingham
Jacob Sellingham
Benjamin Sergeant
Andrew Stone
John Straw
Hezekiah Swain
Edward Taylor
Oliver Taylor
Peter Tozer

Fifth Company

Isaac Frye   Captain
Jonathan Cass   Lieutenant
Nathan Weare   Sergeant (see 6th Co.)
Levi Lamprey   Sergeant
Samuel Barker (Baker)   Sergeant

Matthew N. Sanborn   Corporal
Benjamin Cate   Corporal
James Floyd   Drummer
Josiah Moulton   Fifer

Privates

James Allard (Artland)
Stephen Atkinson
John Blaisdell
Wm. Cotter (Cotton)
Abner Dearborn
Jonathan Eaton
Richard Green (see 9th Co.)
Nathan Greenleaf

John Ham
Stephen Hermon
Hirssa (Hussa) Hoagg
Charles Hodgdon
Philip Johnson
Simon D. Lovering
Samuel Marston
Jonathan Miller

James Moulton
Joseph Nealy
Benj. Page
Ichabod Perry (see 6th Co.)
Eliphalet Rawlins
John Rawlins
Stephen Richardson (see 6th Co.)
Jacob Seagull

Robert Simpson
Levi Stickney
Jacob Thomas (?)
Robert Thurston
Wm. Wallace
James (Wm.) Wilkins (son)
Elisha Winslow
John Youngman (see 6th Co.)

Sixth Company

Wm. Ellis   Captain
Joseph Boynton   Lieutenant and Adjutant
Nathan Weare   Ensign
Robert B. Wilkins   Sergeant (also
   1st and 5th Cos.)
Asa Wilkins   Sergeant

Richard Hughes   Sergeant
Christopher Martin   Corporal
John Godfrey   Corporal
Wm. Pettingill   Corporal
Uriah Ballard   Drummer

Privates

Jacob Blanchard
Thomas Blood
Peter Chandler
Humphrey Cram
Ebenezer Drury
Jonathan Foster
Joseph Gray
David Hasselton
Amos Hoit
Nehemiah Hoit

Reuben Hossmore
Ichabod Perry
Asa Pierce
Stephen Richardson
Benjamin Smith
Nathaniel Smith
Jonathan Wooley
John Youngman
Thomas Youngman

Seventh Company

David McGregore   Captain
Nathaniel Leavitt   Lieutenant
(James Blanchard   Lieutenant and
   Paymaster   See 2nd Co.)
Bradley Richards   Ensign
Bradley Richards   Sergeant
Benjamin Knight   Sergeant

Aaron Copps   Sergeant
Joseph Copper (s)   Sergeant
Joseph Copps   Corporal
George Shepherd   Corporal
Samuel Sargent   Corporal
George Everitt   Drummer
  (Averill)

Privates

Benj. Atwood
James Barnes
George Christopher
Joseph Chase
Ward Clark (?)
Daniel Cross
Silas Fox
Austen George
Robert Hastings
Sterling Heath
Joseph Hobart (Hubbard)
Enoch Hunt
Wm. Inglish
David Jewell
Stephen Keyes (see 9th Co.)
John Knight

Moses Knight
Daniel Messe (Moss)
John Peters (Petis)
Benj. Philips (see 9th Co.)
John Philips (see 9th Co.)
Benj. Preston
John Seshons (Sessions)
Moses Smart
Richard Smart
Isaac Smith
Joseph Smith
Henry Springer
John Whitten
Edward Wood
Gideon Wood
Thomas Wood

Eighth Company

(Nicholas Gilman   Captain)
Dudley L. Chase   Lieutenant
Archibald Stark   Ensign
Kimber Harvey   Sergeant
Amasa Parker   Sergeant

Timothy Crossfield   Sergeant
Levi Fuller   Corporal
Caleb Aldredge   Corporal
  (Deserted May 25, 1779)
John Wolley   Drummer
  (Deserted May 25, 1779)

Privates

John Balch
James Barnes (see 7th Co.)
Naboth Bettison
Peter Bebee
Samuel Britton (Deserted
  May 25, 1779)
Henry Carter
Calvin Chamberlain
Timothy Crossfield
James Eddy
Wm. Farley

Joseph Fay
Daniel Foster
Abraham Lawrence
Nathaniel Merrill
Josiah Powers
Silas Ray
Peltiah Razey (Ray)
Eliphalet Shipman
Benj. Thatcher
Jonathan Wooley (see 6th Co.)
Jonathan Woodcock

Ninth Company

William A. Hawkins   Captain
Adna Penniman   Lieutenant
Thomas Beal   Sergeant
Wm. Presson   Sergeant

Samuel Mitchell   Sergeant
Abner Stagg (Hogg, Fogg)   Sergt.
Benjamin Carr (Karr)   Corporal

Privates

Peter Abbott
Reuben Austin
John Combs
James Craige
Daniel Cross (?)
George Fishley
Joseph Green
Richard Green
Stephen Keyes
John Martin

John Miller
James Nesmith
Benjamin Philips
John Phillips
Samuel Silver
Jeremiah Smith
Daniel Torry
Elijah Wadleigh
Robert Woodward

May have been present

John Blair
Joseph Cooper
Samuel Houston
Randell McAlester
Samuel Mitchell
Benj. Putnam

David Scott
Samuel Spear
John Swan
James Taggart
James Turner

THIRD BRIGADE

(General Hand)

Fourth Pennsylvania Regiment

Shortly after the battle of Monmouth, June 28, 1778, Col. Butler was ordered to Schoharie, New York, with his regiment, and a detachment from Morgan's rifles under Major Parr, late of Fort Pennsylvania and Capt. Long of the Maryland line, to defend the frontiers of New York and to chastise the Indians (Pa. Arch. (5) II, 1026). On June 28, 1778, the 4th Regiment at Schoharie is 1 Lt. Col., 1 Major, 5 Captains, 6 Lieutenants, 1 Adjutant, 1 paymaster, 1 quartermaster, rank and file present fit for duty 122; sick 11 present; sick absent 43; on command 12, or 190 in all for rank and file. His strengths must be close to the Wm. Bradford memorandum (Papers Penn. Hist. Soc.) who had somewhat more 235 rank and file. Just before the march to Lake Otsego June 13, 1779, Colonel Butler had 194 rank and file.

We examined the different series of Penn. Archives, visited Harrisburg and perused the Penn. Hist. Society material but we have yet some uncertainty re the complexion of the various companies of the 4th and 11th Penn. regiments on the Sullivan Expedition. We have seen no positive actual muster rolls of 1779 nor general returns to secure us positively. There must be some names missing in our lists. Our lists are doubtless approximations.

Composite Published Evidence

This is compiled from many sources like Penn. Archives (5) Vol. IV: 133-138; Vol. II Continental Line; (2) X 491-537, or Certificate Books to Aug. 1, 1780 or to Jan. 1, 1781 or to War of Revolution Book 7 State of Pa. Depreciation Book (AGO) or several journals. From these we secure these men of the staff.

William Butler Colonel	George Boss Adjutant
Thomas Church Major	James Hunter Paymaster to June 1, 1779
George Tudor Captain	Erkuries Beatty Paymaster to "
Wm. Gray Captain	Peter Summers Quartermaster
John McGowan Captain	Chas. McCarter Surgeon
Adam Bettin Captain	James Jones Surgeon Mate
Henry Bicker Jr. Captain	John Pratt Ensign
Wm. Henderson Captain	Henry Henley Ensign
Wm. Sproat Captain	John Coleman Ensign
Thomas Campbell Capt. Lieut.	Andrew Henderson Ensign
Garret Stediford Lieut.	Nathaniel Smith Ensign
Erkuries Beatty Lieut.	John Allison Sergeant Major
Peter Summers Lieut.	Thomas Cook Quartermaster Sergt.
George Boss Lieut.	John Spaulding Drum Major.
Matthew Petan Lieut.	John Williams Fife Major
Wilder Bevins Lieut	

Corrections or additions to Greenough's List:

   a. Omit Wm. Cross, Captain, resigned May 14, 1779.
   b. Add John McGowan
   c. Add Wm. Sproat
   d. Add Thomas Campbell, Capt. Lieut.
   e. Add James Hunter
   f. Add James Jones
   g. Add John Coleman, Ensign.
   h. Add Adam, Capt.
   i. Make John Pratt and Henry Henley Ensigns.

Fourth Pennsylvania Regiment

Col. Butler's Co.

Wm. Butler   Colonel
John Allison   Sergeant Major
(Thos. Cook   Quartermaster Sergeant absent)
John Spalding   Drum Major
James Williams   Fife Major
Henry (John) Eaton   Sergeant

Joseph Lower (Loer)   Sergeant
Alexander Faulkner (Falconer)   Sergeant
Andrew Rodgers (Rogers)   Corporal
James Stewart   Corporal
Thos. McElwain   Corporal

Privates

John Butler
Henry Davishelter
   (Davis Henry Hiter)
John Hazelhurst (Haselhurst)
John Hutchinson
Thomas Jones

Anthony Leabeck (Seabeck)
Joseph Lower
Thomas McElwain
George (Leo) McSwine
Nathan Seabrook
Wm. Wilson

Major Church's Co.

Thomas Church   Major
George Donelly   Sergeant
Michael Redman   Sergeant
Alexander King   Corporal

Matthew Hamilton   Corporal
John Ward   Corporal
Joseph Camp   Corporal
Abraham Vanbrimer   Fifer

Privates

- Christian Beagle
- Joseph Camp
- John Chickney (Chigney)
- Peter Gable (See Henderson's Co.)
- John Garvey
- Henry Harmody
- Thomas Harvey (Harbey)
- Frederick Hill
- Abraham Hood (Hodge)
- Edward Laferty
- John Martin
- John McCormick
- Stophel Mingle
- Wm. Reed
- Manus Spank (Mauns Hans)
- Casper Slicker (Shleker)
- John Ward

Capt. Tudor's Co.

- George Tudor   Captain
- Wm. Smith   Sergeant
- John Cochran   Sergeant
- James Richard (Richards)   Sergeant
- John Sloan   Sergeant
- Thomas Jones   Corporal
- Samuel Hunter   Corporal
- Nicholas Keemer   Corporal
- John Baker   Drummer

Privates

- John Devolt (Devold)
- Wm. Farrall (Tarrol)
- Patrick Hartney
- Wm. Maloney
- James McDonark (McDonack)
- Dennis McNamara (McNamard)
- John Nixon
- Daniel Patterson (Petterson)
- Sadler Roach
- Owen Sullivan
- John Wilmott (Wimot)

Capt. McGowan's Co.

- John McGowan   Captain
  (at Schoharie after July)
- Chas. Stewart   Sergeant
- Wm. Robert Howe   Sergeant
- Jno Mackay (Mackey)   Sergeant
- John Christie   Corporal
- John Evans   Corporal
- George Heft   Drummer
- Casper Shipe   Fifer

Privates

Felix Chriesman (Chrisman)
John Ellis
Edward Foster (Forster)
George Ingleth
Edward Jones
Daniel Magee (McGee)
Manus Mullen
Bernard Reily

Wm. Rogers
Wm. Rowik (Roark)
George Shaffer
Wm. Shipe
Federick (Deterich) Snyder
Andrew Socks
Thomas Sollars
Martin Warner

Capt. Fishbourne's Co.

(Benjamin Fishbourne Captain
   Aid de Camp Gen. Wayne 1779-1783 Absent)
George Ogleby Sergeant
George Knox Sergeant
James McPike Sergeant

Isaac Stett (Still) Sergeant
George Johnston Corporal
John Marz (Mease, Mean) Corporal
John Bowden (Bouden) Drummer

Privates

John Boyle
John Brown
Wm. Brown
James Campbell
John Dermand (Disman)
Hugh Divine (Devinney)
Michael Harman (Harmand)
Thomas Isanogle
James Kienan
Alexander King
Claudius Martin
James McGee

Chas. Miller
Daniel Miller
Chris'n Moser
Bernard Oldwire
Thomas Parks
Christn Patterson
Abraham Saunders
Henry Stanford (Stamford)
Caspr Stone
Martin Teats (Taits)
James (Jacob) Wise (Wice)

Gray's Co.

Wm. Gray Captain
Wm. McIntire Sergeant
Andrew Rourke (Roark) Sergeant

Wm. Prosser (Prosper) Sergeant
Michael Hundley Drummer

Privates

Henry Been
Thomas Carroll
John Hardy
John Hawkins
Richard Kermelian (Kinchan, Keenakan)
James McBride

Hugh McElroy (McIlveny)
James McIntire
Gilbert Moore
Thomas Murdoch
Wm. Patterson
Thomas Perry

Adam Bettin's Co.

Adam (Bettin) Bitten   Captain
Thos. Beggs   Sergeant

Michael Lynch   Corporal
John Lillicrop   Corporal

Privates

John Antrum (Antram)
Philip Boyer
Christian Leavitt (Lewalt)?

Samuel Lewis
James Page
Hugh Stone ?

Henry Becker Jr's Co.

Henry Becker Jr.   Captain
John Steel   Sergeant
Wm. Hunter   Sergeant

John Close   Sergeant
Jacob Deal   Corporal
James Murphy   Drummer

Privates

Mich'l Cain
Jno Cohey (Cowey)
Patrick Dempsey
George Fetrick (Detrick)
Conrad Hine
Jacob Over
Jno Owinge

Lloyd Powell
Jacob (John) Puffenbarger (Deffenberger)
James Shannon
Joseph Spencer
Hugh Woods
Jacob Moyer ?

Henderson's Co.

Wm. Henderson   Captain
Michael Kain   Sergeant
Moore Beggs   Sergeant
Thomas Clark   Corporal

John (Ira) Good   Corporal
James Dickinson (Rickinson)   Corporal
Abraham Van Brimer   Fifer (Church's Co.)

Privates

John Adams
Wm. Burchell (Bunchell)
Wm. Cady (Cody)
Jacob Crayman (Craymer)

Jonas Douglass
Robert Fair
Peter Gabel
Casper Sliker (Church's Co.)
Wm. Welsh

Eleventh Pennsylvania Regiment

I. Roll of the field and staff officers and other commissioned officers of the Eleventh Penn's Regiment, in the service of the United States, commanded by Lieut. Col. (From Hubley's Field Book) (Pa. Archives (5) III, pp. 638-641 or (2) XI, pp. 51-53).

Roster of Field and Other Officers, July 1779

Lieutenant Colonel Commandant
 Hubley, Adam, commissioned Feb. 13, 1779

Major
 Edwards, Evan, commissioned December 16, 1778

Captain-Lieutenant
 Jackson, Jeremiah, commissioned Apr. 23, 1779

Ensign
 Thornbury, Francis, commissioned Oct. 2, 1778, promoted Captain May 10, 1780

Major's Company

Lieutenant Burke, Edward, commissioned October 4, 1777, promoted Captain lieutenant May 10, 1780

Ensign Allison, Robert, commissioned Oct. 1, 1778; promoted lieutenant May 10, 1780

Third Company

Captain Bush, George, commissioned July 23, 1778; resigned March 11, 1780

Lieutenants
 Lemmon, William, commissioned July 23, 1778; resigned March 11, 1780
 Weitzel, Jacob, commissioned April 2, 1779; doing duty of ensign, rank and pay of lieutenant; promoted lieutenant May 10, 1780

Fourth Company

Captain Keene, Laurence, commissioned January 13, 1777

Lieutenant Street, Benjamin, commissioned Nov. 30, 1778, resigned May 25, 1780

Ensign Burley, Henry, resigned March 10, 1780

Fifth Company

Captain Forrester, James, commissioned November 12, 1777; died Mar. 16, 1780

Lieutenant Mahon, John, commissioned June 1, 1778

Ensign Reed, Samuel, promoted lieutenant Oct. 2, 1780

Sixth Company

Captain Walker, Andrew, commissioned January 23, 1778

Lieutenant Pettigrew, James

Seventh Company

Captain Claypole, Abraham George, commissioned June 10, 1778
       Morrison, Samuel, February 13, 1779

Eighth Company

Captain Sweeney, Isaac, commissioned July 23, 1778

Lieutenant Davis, Septimus, commissioned July 7, 1777; resigned Feb. 24, 1780

Ensign Huston, William, commissioned June 2, 1777; doing duty as adjutant, with rank and pay of lieutenant; promoted lieutenant, May 10, 1780

Ninth Company

Captain Carberry, Henry, November 30, 1778

Lieutenant McCurdy, William, November 12, 1777; promoted Captain lieutenant October 2, 1778

Paymaster, Bush, George

Quarter-master, Mahon, John

Adjutant, Huston, Wm.

Surgeon, Wiggins, Thomas, July 1, 1779; resigned January 23, 1780

Surgeon's Mate, Wharrey, Robert

Lieutenant Colonel's Company

1346 Adam Hubley, Lieut. Colonel	134 Marmaduke McCann, Private
H (James Forrester, Captain)	134 Samuel McClellan (McCalling), Prt.
P (Edward Burke, Capt. Lieut.)	145 Wm. Meadows, Private
P13456 Francis Thornbury (Thornburg), Ensign	346 Jacob Miller, Private
13456 Terrence Duffy, Sergeant	13456 John Morgan
13456 Edward Denny, Sergeant	1346 David Murray
1346 Michael Ashley, Sergeant	1345 Wm. Murray
1346 John Burgess, Corporal	14 Michael Notieo
124 Henry Mitchell, Corporal	134 Isaac Parker
P1345 Thomas Cunningham, Drummer	14 Philip Pendle
P13456 George Shively, Fifer	1346 Wm. Pillmore
134 Wm. Burney (Barney), Private	134 Wm. Porter
134 Martin Bloomenshine, Private	134 George Seager
14 Stephen Boyles, Private	14 Wm. Seprile
P13456 John Brown, Private	1346 Peter Shoemaker
H1346 Patrick Connally, Private	134 Joseph Smith
13456 Benjamin Cox (Cos), Private	124 Wm. Steel
134 John Goldsberry, Private	14 John Sweeney
134 Daniel Harris, Private	14 Henry Trimler
1346 Patrick Kirken (Kerking), Private	1246 John Trookey (Torguy, Sorguy)
134 John Linkamore, Private	134 Garret Welsh
134 Bartholomew Longstreet, Private	4 Robert Taylor

If we count our entire list of privates, it is 33, the exact number of the June 15, 18 or 26, 1779 report for the rank and file of the Lt. Colonel's Company.

1. Penn. Archives 5th Ser. III, pp. 644-646.
2. Penn. Archives 5th Ser. III, pp. 621-628.
3. War of Revolution Book 7, Pa. against U.S.A. Deprec. Pay. Adj. Gen. Off. (Nat. Archives).
4. Penn. Archives 2nd Ser. XI, pp. 57-59.
5. Penn. Magazine 27, pp. 455+ Deprec. Pay.
6. Penn. Archives Fifth Ser. IV, 176, Deprec. Pay.
P. From Patton's Regiment

Major's Company

H25 Evan Edwards, Major (Hartley's)	H345 John Wright, Corporal
P25 Edward Burke, Lieutenant	345 David Williams, Drummer
P4 (Jeremiah Jackson, Lieutenant)	P2345 George Reese, Fifer (Reas, Reesie)
P (Jacob Weitzel, 2nd Lieutenant)	P12345 Israel Austin (Ashton), Private
H235 Robert Allison, Ensign	P2345 Peter Beatty
P12345 Wm. George, Sergeant	P2345 Joseph Boyd
H2345 Robert Pendergrass, Sergeant	P2345 Philip Boyer
345 Wm. Dingley, Sergeant	HP2345 John Brown (Bryan)
P2345 Edward Coyle, Corporal	P2345 Michael Campbell
H2345 Ephraim (John) Donaly, Corporal	P2345 Charles Dickey (Dickrey)

P243 Simon Flynn, Private
P12345 Wm. George
 P2345 Archibald Gordon
 H2345 Robert Hadlock
 P2345 John Hamige(r)
 H2345 Wm. Hastings
 P2345 Cornelius Hopper
  1345 Thomas Johnston
P(2345 John Kenny, prisoner
   P34 James Lewis
    34 Wm. Lock
  2345 Arthur McCullough

 H2345 Andrew McNabb
 P2345 Wm. Maypowder
 P2345 Robert Oldis
P12345 James Quickley (Quigley)
  2345 John Reynolds
  P243 Allan Rogers
   P34 John Ryan
  2345 Samuel Shaw
 P2345 Edward Stain (Stains)
  P243 James Todd
  2345 John Unbehand
   234 James Winters

Same references as for Lieut. Colonel's Company.

Third Company

I. Composite Published Evidence

   H24 George Bush, Captain
    H2 Wm. Lemmon, Lieutenant
  P124 Jacob Weitzel, Ensign
  1234 Daniel (David) Connell, Sergeant
  P124 Samuel Gothrop, Sergeant
  1234 Thomas Connor, Sergeant
 H1235 James Byrnes, Corporal
   H12 Thomas Newgent, Corporal
   123 Jos. Daily, Corporal
  P124 Benjamin Jefferies, Drummer
    12 George Hughes, Fifer
  H124 John Barr, Private
   124 James Bradley
     2 Daniel Callahan
  1245 Phineas (Philip) Cartwright
   125 John Clack
    H2 Adam Clandenan
  H124 John Clare (Cleare)
   124 Richard Conden (Couden)
   124 Wm. Dean
 P1234 Robert Douglass
  1234 George Foster
   124 George Fullerton
    12 Ralph Gadsby
   124 Henry Gardner

    P2 John Gilbert, Private
H12345 Joel (John) Gray
   P12 George Hawke
    P2 Jacob Lute
  H124 Thomas McCalvin (McCelvey)
  H124 Forest McCutchun (McCullion)
 H1234 John McDowell (McDonnald)
  H124 John McElroy
    H2 James McNanamy
  H124 Daniel Newingham
   P12 Martin Ricker
    H2 Wm. Russell
  1245 John Scott
  1234 Nicholas Seppull (Sipprill)
 P1234 Samuel Shannon
 P1245 Wm. Sherter (Shorter)
  1234 Thos. Slautry (Slatry)
     2 Wm. Smith
   124 Robert Stubbs
   124 Daniel Sullivan
     2 Andrew Susong
    24 Laurence Terrill
   124 James Thompson
 12345 Abraham Woodside (Wood)
   P24 Daniel Wilger (Wilker, Welgar)

1. War of Revolution Vol. 7 A.G.O. Penn. D.P.
2. Penn. Archives Second Series Vol. XI, pp. 61-63.
3. Penn. Mag. Hist. Biog. Vol. 27, 455+.
4. Penn. Archives Fifth Series, Vol. 5: 176.
5. Penn. Archives Fifth Series 4:621-628.
6. H - From Hartley's Regiment
   P - From Patton's Regiment

Fourth Company

P2356 Lawrence Keene, Captain
P36 Benj. Street, Lieutenant
P36 Henry Burley, Ensign
M23456 Wm. Gilbert, Sergeant
M356 Wm. Shaw, Sergeant
2346 Wm. Davidson (Davison), Sergeant
M23456 James Beatty, Corporal
23456 James Robeson (Robinson), Corpl.
2356 John Allan, Corporal
23456 Phillip Reemer (Reymer), Drummer
36 Laurence Fry, Drummer
13456 James (Wm.) Raddock (Reddick), Fifer
H236 John Alexander, Private
23456 Robert Bohannon
M23456 John Byens (Burns)
136 John (Patrick) Calahan (Caloghan)
236 Richard Carman
36 Nathaniel Coulter (Colter)
2356 John Conner
36 Jacob Crow
12346 John Foster (Forgery)
M2356 Michael Fry
123456 John Hanley (probably Lengley), P
36 John Hunter
3456 Richard Hutchinson (Hutcheson)
H23456 Jacob Kinch (Kink, Kuich)
236 Abraham Louke
H2356 John McClahan (McClelland)
H1236 Edward McHenry (McKinney)
M2356 Michael McMullan
236 John Mulvany
36 James O'Neal
H236 Nicholas O'Neal
H36 John Rea
36 Elijah Rippey
H36 Patrick Rodey
36 Robert Rossett
M2356 Wm. Scott
23456 James Stewart (Stuart)
23456 John Sullivan
236 John Tupley (Tapley)
236 James Weir
236 Robert Willson

1. Penn. Archives Fifth Series III, pp. 621-628.
2. War of Revolution, A.G.O. Book 7, Penn.
3. Penn. Archives Second Series XI, 63-65.
4. Penn. Mag. Hist. Biog. Vol 27, p. 455+.
5. Penn. Archives Fifth Series, 4, 176+ D.P.
6. Penn. Archives Fifth Series III, 650-652.
   H - From Hartley's Regiment; P - From Patton's Regiment;
   M - From Malcolm's Regiment.

Fifth Company

(9th Co. per Pa. Archives (5) Vol. III, 660 or (2) XI, 72-74) (McAllister's Company)

James Forrester, Captain
P236 (Jeremiah Jackson, Captain)
H25 John Mahon, Lieutenant
25 Samuel Reed, Ensign
1236 Jeremiah Terrell, Sergeant
123456 John Barber, Sergeant
H36 Thos. Judge, Sergeant
236 Matthew Pearson, Corporal
H23456 John McDonald, Corporal
H2356 Thos. Harrington, Drummer
23456 Wm. Stephenson, Fifer
2356 James Holmes, Fifer
2356 James Allen, Private
3456 James Bell
23456 John Borrage (Burridge, Burges)
3456 George Brett (Britt)
36 Walter Burke
H6 Wm. Chambers
H12356 Robert Clark
2356 Thomas Connor
H1236 Jas. Crangle (Crange)
H36 Lewis Dempsey (Dimpsey)
36 James Dorran
36 James Emly

    36 James Farewell, Private
 23456 Daniel Frazer
 H1356 Peter Gichan (Gehen, Gecher)
  2346 Adam Glaze (Glazer)
   236 Chas. Gordon
 23456 John Goudy
123456 John Croigill (Grasgill)
 H2356 Richard Harper
    36 Chas. Hickey
   356 Adam Hines (Himes)
   236 Neal McCatheran
    36 George McCooney

H23456 Wm. McGinnis (McGinnet), Prvt.
 H2356 Henry McGill
 H2356 Samuel McManamy (McManime)
   356 John Manson (Mahon, Mansion)
 23456 Wm. Marquiss (Marguis)
  H236 Benj. Messam (Missum)
    36 Wm. Miles
    36 Daniel Morgan
 H2356 Thomas Morrow
   H36 Patrick Roach (Rach)
  H236 Andrew Webb

1. Penn. Archives Fifth Series Vol. III, 621-628.
2. War of Revolution Book 7 A.G.O. Penn.
3. Penn. Archives Second Series Vol. XI, 72-74.
4. Penn. Mag. Hist. Biog. Vol. 27, p. 455+.
5. Penn. Archives Fifth Series Vol. 4, 176+.
6. Penn. Archives Fifth Series III: 660-662.
   H - From Hartley's Regiment; P - From Patton's Regiment

Sixth Company

(Fifth Co. Pa. Archives 5th Ser. III, 653+ or 2nd Ser. XI, 65-67)

I. Composite Published Evidence.

   H36 Andrew Walker, Captain
 H2356 James Pettigrew, Lieutenant
H23456 James Johnston, Sergeant
  1356 Barnet Carny (Bartley), Sergeant
  2356 James Robeson (Robinson), Sergeant
  H236 Robert Jefferies, Corporal
   H36 Patrick Limerick, Corporal
    36 Wm. Wiley, Corporal
  H356 James Thurston (Thornton), Drummer
   H36 Frederick Wolfe, Fifer
  2356 James Benson, Private
   236 Wm. Boe
  2356 Wm. Brown
  2356 Philip Buckley (Brickley)
 H2345 Wm. Byrns
    36 Robt. Caseboit (Casebolt)
   236 James Coleman
 23456 Wm. Douglass
  2356 James Gallacher
  2356 Robert Grant
 H2356 Alexander Gray

 H2356 James Grier (Greer), Private
 H2356 Isaac Herrington
  2356 John Horner
  H236 Edward Keating (Keaton)
 H2356 Nicholas (Michael) McCoy
H12356 Robert McCullough (Roger)
 H2356 Jas. McDonough
 H2356 James McEntire
  2356 Neal McGeary (McCucheson)
 H2356 John McKimins (McCummings)
    36 Wm. Mimmaert
   356 Daniel Murray
    36 Marion (John) Nixon
  H236 Wm. O'Bryan
  1356 Anthony Patton
  H236 Henry Peters
    36 Wm. Savage
  H236 Francis Shaffner
H12356 Wm. Simmonds
    36 Edward Smith
   H36 Wm. Williams

83

1. Penn. Archives Fifth Series III, 621-628.
2. War of Revolution Book 7 Penn. A.G.O.
3. Penn. Archives Second Series XI, 65-67.
4. Penn. Mag. Hist. Biog. 27: 455+.
5. Penn. Archives Fifth Series IV, 174.
6. Penn. Archives Fifth Series III: 653-654.
   H - From Hartley's Regiment

Seventh Company

(Sixth Company Pa. Archives (5) III, 656-657 or (2) XI, 67-69.)

I. Composite Published Sources

An unpublished Patton Regiment roll (A.G.O. Jacket 147) will help for an understanding of the New Eleventh Company of Capt. Claypole. It is a "Muster Roll of Captain Abraham George Claypoole's Company in the Regiment of Foot...Feb. 1779.

Commission'd Captn. A. G. Claypoole

1st Lt. Edw'd Burke

Sergeants	Corporals	Drum and Fife
1. Sam'l Gaulthrop	None	1. Sam'l Nightlinger
2. John Alexander		2. John Brown Com'd at Peekskill

Privates

Henry Carrel, Com'd
Jacob Cook
Sam'l Dickey
John Denny
Michael Darr
Richard Dalvins Gd.
Hugh Duff, Com'd at Phila.
James Frost Gd.
Jas. Fitzgibbons
Jno. Harrington

Hans Hagabough Gd.
George Hawke
Henry Harpole, Com'd
James Kearney
Peter Kishimer
Geo. Rictmaker
Jno. Shaw
Nichs Struble Gd.
Dan'l Welgar
Haverstraw, Mar. 3, 1779
Henry Rulgus Jun. D.C.M.

Item 19 (345) Payroll for Apr. 1779 has Richard Dolphin; has same people.
Item 17 Payroll for Feb. 1779 has Geo. Rytimire, has Hugh Duffy.

From the above roll one can see that of the 25 people in his company Feb. 1779, 16 were in his company from July 1779 onwards. In fact by this time nine more Patton men from other companies also were in his company making 24 Patton recruits in his total company of 39 men. It was distinctly a Patton company only three or four distinctly Hartley men were in it.

II.

P36 Abraham George Claypole, Captain	P23456 James Frost (Trost), Private
P (Edward Burke, Lieutenant)	P356 Hans Hagabough (Bagaboe)
356 Samuel Morrison, Lieutenant	P36 Henry Harpole
P236 John Alexander, Sergeant	P346 John Harrington
1236 Thomas Curtis, Sergeant	H36 Horatio Harrison
2346 Allan McLane (McClean), Sergeant	P36 Peter Kisheimer
P2356 Jacob (James) Cable (Kabel), Corpl.	123456 John Lewis
H2356 Christian Shockey, Corporal	H36 George McCalla
2356 John Reily (Reiley), Corporal	H2356 Thomas McCulla (McCelvy)
P2456 Samuel Nightlinger, Drummer	2356 James McAllister
P23456 John Brown, Fifer	2356 Felix McLaughlin
P2356 Nicholas Bergenhoff (Bergahoff), Pt.	P236 John Mansfield
236 James Boden	P356 George Rightmyer
P356 James Burke	1236 Wm. Salmond (Solomon)
P236 Henry Carroll	P2356 John Shaw
12356 John Coleman	P2356 Daniel Sheyfey
P123456 Jacob Cookson (Cook)	123456 John Stoner (Stone)
236 Patrick Dagney	P236 Nicholas Struble
P236 John Denny	12356 Edward Wheelan (Whelon)
P36 Michael Dero (Darr)	
P236 Richard Dolver (Dolvin, Dolphin)	
P2346 James Fitzgibbons (Fitzsimmons)	

1. Penn. Archives Fifth Series III, 621-628.
2. War of Revolution Book 7, Penn. A.G.O.
3. Penn. Archives Second Series, XI, 67-69.
4. Penn. Mag. Hist. Biog. 27, p. 454+.
5. Penn. Archives Fifth Series IV, 174.
6. Penn. Archives Fifth Series III: 655-657.
    H - From Hartley's Regiment; P - From Patton's Regiment

Eighth Company

(Seventh Company Pa. Archives (5) III, 657-658 or (2) XI, 69-70.)

H346 Isaac Sweeny, Captain	1236 George Carman, Private
P36 Septimus Davis, Lieutenant	36 John Edgar
H2356 Wm. Huston, Ensign	2356 Wm. Fields (Michael) (Field)
2356 Thos. Willson, Sergeant	36 Hugh Forsythe
H2356 John Gray, Sergeant	2356 James Hines
346 Patrick Clemens, Sergeant (McLean)	2356 Andrew Kelley
236 Andrew Miller, Corporal	H236 Roger O'Brien
2356 Edward Blake, Corporal	12356 Valentine Stickle (Steigle, Steigh
H36 John Smith, Corporal	23456 Hugh Swords (Sword)
2356 Robert Hunter, Drummer	236 Wm. Wilson
H356 John McElroy, Fifer	

1. Penn. Archives Fifth Series Vol. III, 621-628.
2. War of Revolution Book 7, A.G.O. National Archives.
3. Penn. Archives Second Series Vol. XI, 69-70.
4. Penn. Mag. Hist. Biog. Vol. 27, p. 455+ Deprec. Pay.
5. Penn. Archives Fifth Series IV, 176+.
6. Penn. Archives Fifth Series III: 657-658.
   H - From Hartley's Regiment; P - From Patton's Regiment

Ninth Company

(Eighth Co., P.A. Fifth Ser. III, 658 or Second Series XI, 70-72).

H356 Henry Carberry, Captain	236 James McGinnis, Private
H2356 Wm. McCurdy, Lieutenant	236 Cornelius McMuling (McMullen)
12346 John Campbell (Cambel), Corporal	2346 Edward Mealey (Meally)
H1236 Matthew Cusick, Fifer	2356 George Miller
H1236 Daniel Anthony, Private	356 Mc D. Morrison
236 John Barker	2356 Joseph Murphy
36 Wm. Barden	12356 Geo. Nicholson (Nichols)
36 -- Black	1346 Joseph Noles (Knowles)
H2356 Wm. Caldwell (Calwell)	H236 Thomas Nugent
36 James Everett	36 John Pry
3456 McD. (Michael) Grew	2356 John Renall (Reynolds)
36 Samuel Harrison	2356 Peter Riley (Reyle, Ryle)
H2356 John Harris	36 Daniel Robinson
36 Jacob Horine	236 John Romander
236 Matthew Keller	36 Robert Sharer
136 -- Kitwell (Kisbal)	H2356 John Smith
36 David Lipey	2356 Frederick Snyder
H1236 Andrew (Arthur) McCluskey (McClaskey)	236 Wm. They (Tye)
H36 Edw. McDonald (McDonal)	36 Jacob Vandiver
H1236 James (John) McElroy	H36 Thomas Woods
36 Arthur McGarity	126 Wm. Tyerman (Turman)

1. Penn. Archives Fifth Series III, 621-628.
2. War of Revolution Book 7, Penn. A.G.O.
3. Penn. Archives Second Series XI, 70-72.
4. Penn. Mag. Hist. and Biog. 27: 465+.
5. Penn. Archives Fifth Series IV, 176-182.
6. Penn. Archives Fifth Series III, 658-660.
   Reprint of 3 above with Wm. Tyerman added.
   H - From Hartley's Regiment

GERMAN BATTALION

(4 Md. companies, 5 Pa. companies)

Of this regiment we have the best evidence of any Pennsylvania group. It was made up of 4 Md. and 5 Pa. companies. They were the biggest group of the Pa. forces. Some journals accused them of desertion, e.g., "Wednesday July 14th. Last night thirty-three of the German regiment deserted under the plea of their time being out. They went off properly armed with drum and fife." Their time was up. They were not deserters. They used bad judgment in going off with drum and fife. They had given 3 years <u>old line</u> service not <u>militia</u> and their time was up. Besides most of the Md. troops (120 men) had their time up.

With much effort we labored hard on the evidence of the presumptive lists of the 4 Maryland and 5 Pennsylvania companies of this regiment. They were quite accurate. We let them stand as formerly written with the corrective sections from muster and payrolls. We chose 7 pertinent items from the Adjutant General's Records Office holdings for the corrections.

First Company

Michael Boyer   Captain
Jacob Low   Sergeant
Jacob Alexander   Sergeant
John Ladder   Sergeant
Christian Sandley   Sergeant
Thomas Hutchcraft   Drummer
Henry Ferrins   Drummer
Thomas Polehouse   Corporal
Fredk. Shoemaker   Corporal
Andrew Robinson   Corporal
John Hoshield   Corporal
John Shotz   Corporal

Privates

Thomas Mahoney
George Kepphard
Peter Kuntz
Abraham Kettle
Henry Fisher
Owen Curley
Charles Fulham
James Johnson
John Wade
John Malady
Levy Arrand
John Timlin
Thos. MacKrell
Michael Hartman
John Smetard
John Dalton
Edward Robinson
Ludwig Wessinger
Rudolph Marolf
Jacob Miller Jr.
John Able
Adam Ganter
Jacob Miller Sr.
Jacob Cramer
Leonard Ludwick
Michael Shoemaker
Peter Emmerick
Henry Herring
Michael Masson
Henry Cronise
Philip Fisher
John Snider
John Wachtel
Philip Strider
Jacob Reggnagle
Caseman Hill
Conrad Houserman
Michael Stoner
William Taylor
Jona Zimmerman
John Cline
Peter Hoover
Bart Engle

From payrolls 1779 (A.G.O. 185-2) July - Oct. 1779, Nov. 1778 - Feb. 1779, Nov. 1779 - July 1780. Also 3 Penn. Archives, 3 Maryland Archives and one Penn. Hist. Society paper.

II. Payrolls of 1779 (A.G.O. 185-2)

    a. July - October 1779. Item 23

    a. Payroll of Captn. Michael Boyer's Company of the German Regt. of the Continental Forces in the United States Commanded by Lt. Colo. Ludwick Weltner For the Months of July, August, Septr. and October 1779."

Michael Boyer   Captn.
Jacob Low   Sergeant
Jacob Alexander   Sergeant
John Ladder   Sergeant
Christn. Sandley   Sergeant
Thos. Polehouse   Corporal
Fredk. Shoemaker   Corporal
Andrew Robinson   Corporal
John Hoshield   Corporal
John Shotz   Corporal
Thos. Hutchcraft   Drummer
Henry Ferrins   Drummer
Thos. Mahoney   Private
George Kepphard
Peter Kuntz
Abraham Kettle
Henry Fisher
John Folliot
Owen Curley
Charles Fullem
James Johnson
John Wade
John Malady
Levy Arrand
John Timlin
Thos. Mackrell
Michael Hartman
John Smetard

John Dolton   Private
Edward Robinson
Ludwick Wessinger
Rudolph Marolf
Jacob Miller Junr.
John Able
Adam Gantner
Jacob Miller Senr.
Jacob Cramer
Leonard Ludwick
Michl Shoemaker
Peter Emmerick
Henry Herring
Michael Masson
Henry Cronise
Philip Fisher
John Snider
John Wachtel
Philip Strider
Jacob Reggnagle
Caseman Hill
Conrad Houseman
Michael Stoner
Wm. Taylor
Jno. Zimmerman
Jno. Cline
Peter Hoover
Bartle Engle

    b. Nov. 1778 - Feb. 1779

The payroll for Nov., Dec. 1778 and Jany. and Feby. 1779 has Marcus Young, Lieut., Henry Hains, Ensign, has Sergt. John Lether for John Ladder, Corporal Andrew Roberson for Andrew Robinson, has Joseph Miller, private, John Alexander, private, Christopher Keplinger priv., Martin Watkins priv., Thomas Polehouse private, John Smaller for John Smetard, Philip Hinkle private, Bernard Ritewaner priv., James Dier priv.

c. Nov. 1779 - July 1780

In Nov., Dec. 1779 and Jan. - July 1780 payroll there are only Capt. Boyer and Capt. Jacob Grometh, Sergeants Low and Alexander, Corporals Polehouse and Shoemaker, Drummers Hutchcraft and Ferrins and 19 privates.

a. Item 23 "Pay Roll of Lt. Colo. Ludwick Weltner's Company in the Germany Regt. - - - July, August, Septr. and October 1779."

Philip Shrawder Capt. Lieut.	John Gropp Private
Wm. Lewis Sergeant	George Gitting
Jono Danl Jacquet Sergeant	John Hatfield
Jacob Hose Sergeant	Henry Michael
James Smith Corporal	Thomas Clifton
Jno Michael Corporal	John Craft
Jno Breecher Corporal	Francis Gavin
Adam Stonebraker Corporal	Jacob Kline
Bernard Frey Corporal	John Kebler
Moses McKinsey Drummer	Mathias Kiser
Joshua McKinsey Drummer	John Armstrong
Michael Gambler Private	John Elnier
James Ashley	Jacob Bishop
Wm. Pointer	Christn Raver (Raybird)
Jacob Mosers	Philip Fisher
Jonathan Hackett	Fredk Locher
Henry Stroam	Alexr. Taylor (Sailor)
James Duncan	Patrick Fleming
Geo. Wilhelm	George Rigleman
Melcher Benner	Henry Statler
Fredk Shwietzer	Christn Waggoner
Michael Yockley (Yackley)	John Smith
Conrad Hoyle	Henry Painter (Panther)
Jona. Flick	Philip Smithly
Fredk Filler	Jacob Heffner
Michael Weaver	John Smithly
James Forney	Jacob Hoover
Jacob Beltzhover	Henry Quier

b. The payroll for Mar. - June 1779 has James Smith as private, John Altnire for John Elnier, Jacob Messon, James Smith private.

a. Pay Roll of the 1st Vacant Company in the German Regiment of Foot - - - July, Augt. and Sept. and Octr. 1779.

John Weidman Lieut.	Francis Burginam Fifer
Fredk Lindaman Sergeant	Peter Fortner Fifer
Michel Hantz Sergeant	Michel Rumel Private
Jno Winand Sergeant	Jno Bruner
Fredk Seperal Corporal	Mark Miller
George Fagundus Drummer	George Strough

Philip Myers   Private
Jno Kochenderfer
George Smith
Jno Hapeny
Adam Stall
Henry Shoup
Adam Hawke
Thobias Hess
Michel Hess
Henry Hergood
Patrick Hegans (Higgans)
Andw Hagger

Henry Fifer   Private
Peter Myers (Mayer)
Henry Swedge
Jno Sain
Adam Specht
Philip Clime
Thos. Keen
Ditrich Banig
Casper Waggoner
Fredk Brininger
Philip Helter

    b. Tye Pay Roll of Majr Danl Burchard's Company in the German Regt. - - - March, April, May and June 1779 has Capt. Lieut. Phil Shrawder. Fifer Peter Fortner enlisted May 11, 1779.

II. Pay Rolls of 1779 (A.G.O. 186-2)

    a. Payroll of Captain Bunner's Company German Regiment - - - July, Augt., Sept. and Octor 1779 (A.G.O. 186-2 Item 23)

Jacob Bunner   Capt.
David Morgan   Lieut.
David Diffenderfer (Deffenderfer)   Ensn.
George Francis   Sergt. Majr
David Levy   QrMr Sergt   Discharged July 24, '79
Peter Gabriel   Sergt.
Jacob Wisert   Sergeant
Henry Winkler   Sergt.   Died Oct. 26, '79
Jno. Harris   Dm. Majr   Pd R B.
Joseph Alexander   Fife Majr
Andrew Deel   Corporal
Philip Shreader   Corporal
Henry Moser   Corporal
Fredk Multz   Drummer   Discharged Aug. 14, 1779
Jno Brown   Fifer   Joined Sept. 1, 1779

Fredk Hersh   Private
Titmor Bantze
Martain Hidler
Jacob Sheapert
Henry Hamrick
Jacob Myers
Henry Snyder
George Oeldenberger
Niclous Stober
Wm. Leaman (Leyman)
Fredk Deats
Jno. March
Theodore Hardman
Jno Kyser
Conrad Rough   deducted
Philip Shearer
Fredk Ranky

    b. The payroll Item 22 for March, April, May, June 1779 has the same officers (without Jno Brown fifer), has Conrad Rouch absent, and also has the same 17 privates.

c. Pay Roll of Capt. Peter Boyer's Company - - - July, August, Septbr and Octbr 1779." (A.G.O. 182-2 Item 23)

Peter Boyer   Capt.
Jacob Grometh   Lt.
Geor Luft   Sergt.
Jacob Wentz   Sergt.
Jacob Myers   Corpl.   deserd. July 13, 1779

James Gohoon   Corpl.   killd. Sept. 15, 1779
Chn Riffit   Corpl.
John Hart

Privates

F. Rively
Henry Shuler
F. Kerls
Martin Shudy
Peter Coppus
Cond Gerhart
Jno Wideman
H. Lear
Jacob Harper
Michl Ferrick
Chn Leidy
Jos. Kittle
Geo Kerstetter
Ths Whealer
F. Delinger
Jacob Botomer
P. Lash

Davd Drexler
Chn Fleisch
Davd Bloom
P. Cook
Wm. Kerls
John Fismire
Jacob Grumly
Chn Christman
Jno Sunliter
Heny Deberwing
R. Brookhouse
Godfried Lowry
James Eniey
Wm. Neving
James Champness
Cornelius Quinlin
Hugh McCaw

b. The payroll for Mar. - June 1779 (Item 23) has not Jacob Kiser nor Charles Jones as Sergeants, nor John Rouch as drummer, has a Robert Porter, Peter Krein, Jacob Keiser, John Spenck.

c. The payroll for November and Dec. 1779, Jany. - July 1780 has only 19 privates, and the one for Aug. - Dec. 1780 has 15 privates.

a. Pay Roll of Captn. William Rice's Compy - - - July, August, Sept. and October '79 - Item 24.

Wm. Rice   Captn.
Godfried Swartz   Lieut.
Christian Cleackner   Ensign
George Price   Sergt.
Francis Multz   Sergt.
Frederick William   Corpl.
Jacob Levi   Drummer
Abraham Price   Private

John Smith   Private
Michael Brodbeck
Jacob McClain
Everhard Mayers
Henry Yeable (Yaple)
Joseph March
Philip Gillman
Henry Sypert

b. The payroll for Nov., Dec. 1779 - July 1780 (Item 25) has only Capt. Wm. Rice and Ens. Clickner & 7 privates.

c. The payroll for Mar. - June 1779 Item 23 has the same 7 privates.

    a. "Pay Roll of Captn. Charles Baltzell's Compy. - - - July, August, Sept. and Octr. 1779."

Charles Baltzell Captn.	Jacob Wink Private
Jacob Cramer Lt.	James Hughes
Jacob Rayboll Ensign	Adam Musler
John Cole Sergt.	John Kendrick
John Herring Sergt.	Michl. Groch
John Trucks Sergt.	Stephen McGraw
Jacob Kisers Sergt.	Wm. Vinsent
Charles Jones Sergt.	George Boogh
Philip Boem Corpl.	Wm. Mummer
Patrick Kelly Corpl.	Thos. Wolferd
John Burk Corpl.	John Binnet
Benj. England Drummer	John Miller
John Brown Fifer	Lewis McCollough
John Rouch Drummer	John Broer
John Franklin Private	Jacob Waggener
Jacob Haflick	Daniel Baylor
Christian Smith	Peter Gun
John Stanton	Conrad Boem
Benj. Ellet	Peter Engler
John Emereley	Fredk Mongausl
Richd Haselip	Conrad Keyley
Francis Kerns	Christn Settlemeyer
Robert Porter	Jacob Shitz
James Tite	Adam Shaffer
	Matthias Shryer

    a. Pay Roll of Captn. Berd Hubleys Compy in the German Regt. Commanded by Lieut. Col. Weltner for the months of July, August and October 1779.

Berd Hubley Captn.	Jno Grane Private
Marcus Young Lieut.	Christpr Mencher
Jno Johnston Sergt.	Adam Noble
Lewis Brownsberry Corpl.	George Hantzell
George Funck Corpl.	Christn Baker
Israel Jenkins Drummer	Jacob Herricke
Lewis Reishley Private	Henry Dominick
Christn Hague	Jno Leonard
Jacob Visler	Maths Flach
Jno Keppard	Thos. Turner
Jno Kuhn	Maths Leaf
Geo. Linn	

b. The pay roll for March, April, May and June '79 has in addition to the above

John Weidman   Lieutenant
Henry Schrupp Ensign Resigned June 20, '79
Lewis Reishly Sergeant
No other changes

c. The pay roll for Nov., Dec. 1779 - Jan., Febr., March, April, May, June, July 1780 has Lewis Reishly back again as Sergeant.

d. The last muster roll we have seen, namely for Oct. 1778, has 22 privates--the following not in the above pay rolls of 1779 namely Jacob Shirk, Casper Israelo, John Ryebecker, Philip Stroud, Robert Donochon, John Snyder, Burchardt Hand.

II. Pay Rolls of 1779 (A.G.O. 188-2)

a. July - Oct. 1779 Item 23

a. "Pay Roll of Capt. Christ Myers Compy - - - July, August, Septr and October 1779." Item 23

Christ Myers   Capt.
Martin Shugart Lieut.
Wm. Runnelson   Sergt.
Fredk. Sollers Sergt.
Geo. Stouffer   Sergt.
Wm. Johnson   Sergt.
Joseph Hoock   Corpl.
Jacob Etter   Corpl.
William Krafft Corpl.
Michael Smith   Drummer
William Rider   Private
Thimothy Cahill
Robert Smith
John Fennill
Richd Gaul
George Grethorn
Mathw Smith
Christn Castner
Benj. Cole
John Shively
Jacob Kauffman
John Welty
Cornelius Vaughan
Thomas Procter
Thomas Halfpenny
John Shaffer
Geo. Lightheiser
Jno Shryack
Joseph Streiter
Jacob Myers

Henry Smith   Private
David Finck
Joseph Williams
John Smith
John Dycke
Thomas Laromor
Geo. Rittlemyers
Godlieb Danroth
Martin Lantz
Peter Baker
John Eysell
Fredk Wm. Haller
Michael Crowley
Wolfgang Elzberger
Vendel Lorentz
Jacob Morley
Philip Kantz
Paul Esling
John Slife
Ferdinant Lorentz
Henry Rumfelt
John Harley
Jacob Frymiller
Michael Kersner
Abraham Frantz
Davis Muma
Jacob Ruppert
Jacob Kentz
Rudolph Crower
John Richards
Edward Gould

FOURTH PENNSYLVANIA ARTILLERY

Early in 1947 and 1948 we considered our roster of this organization as quite satisfactory. Almost all the soldiers and officers alike served from enlistment (mainly 1777) to the end of the war or at least to March 1780. When in 1949 we found in Adjutant General's War Office (A.G.O. 58-1 Item 2) a general return of the whole regiment (6 or 8 feet x 1½ feet) we became quite certain of the completion of the 4th Pa. Artillery roster. In May - Oct. 1779 we have not muster rolls, payrolls nor general returns. There is a very slight measure of uncertainty re the makeup from Sergeants downward. From Mar. 19, 1779, Apr. 3, 1779 and other evidence the command seems to be as follows:

Thomas Proctor   Colonel
Thos. Forrest   Lieut. Colonel
Matthew Maguire   Paymaster
George Hoffner   Adjutant
John B. Webster   Quartermaster
(Wm. Adams   Surgeon   Absent Feb 9 - Oct 1, 1779)
John Morton   Surgeon's Mate
Isaac Craig   Captain
Amos Wilkinson   Captain
Joseph Rice   Captain
Francis Proctor, Jr.   Captain
Patrick Duffy   Captain
John Brice   Captain
Robert Coltman   Captain
Worsley Emes   Capt. Lieutenant
Laurence Allman   Capt. Lieutenant
Thos. Douglass   Capt. Lieutenant
James Loyd   Capt. Lieutenant
Robt McConnell   Capt. Lieutenant
John Shute   Lieutenant
Jesse Crosby (Crossley)   Lieutenant
Geo Hoffner   Lieutenant
Matthew Maguire   Lieutenant
John Stricker   Lieutenant
John B. Webster   Lieutenant
Samuel Story   Lieutenant
Shubert Armitage   2nd Lieutenant

Non Commissioned Staff and Musicians

Jno Molony   Clerk
Dan Hawthorn   Sergt. Major
James Patterson   QrMr. Sergt.
Thos. Gray   Fife Major
Wm. Norton   Drum Major
Chars Hoffman   Musician
Wm. Shippen   Musician

Peter Calkhoffer   Musician
Jacob Snell   Musician
Thos. Mingle   Musician
Geo. Weaver   Musician
Samuel Hockukoi   Musician
Michl Thurston   Musician
Wm. Moore   Musician
Conrad Grapingeiser   Musician

In the Penn. Archives (Second Series XI, p. 217) list of Band of Procter's Regiment appear the following names - Daniel Cross, Casper Ebener, Henry (Anthony) Hoover, Wm. Mayberry, Robert Patterson, George Thompson, George Chace, John Clark. These appear in various company lists. There are missing from the above Penn. Archives list the following drummers and fifers. Were they absent? Quite surely Wm. Tatten was absent and quite likely the following six: John Graff, Abisai Lary, John Mitchell, Francis Moore, Joshua Pike, and Wm. Snead.

First Company

(Isaac Craig's Co.)

Isaac Craig   Captain
Laurence Allman   Lieutenant
James Loyd   Lieutenant
John Stricker   Lieutenant
Elias Williams   Sergeant
Samuel Blackwood   Sergeant
Thomas Wiggans   Sergeant
Wm. Clark (Clock)   Corporal
Wm. Rushworm (Rushmore)   Corporal

Wm. Clark   Bombardier
Jno Harris   Bombardier
Jno Wilks   Gunner
Jas Fitzsimmons   Gunner
David Broderick (Brodwick)   Fifer
Michael Clinger (Clingin)   Fifer
George Thompson   Drummer
Anthony Hover   Drummer
Patrick Crafford   Mattross
(Matt)   (Crawford)

Jonathan Trickle Mattross
    (Treakle)
Timothy Lane Mattross
James Burns Senr. Mattross
Chas. Kitts (Katts) Mattross
Wm. Blair Mattross
Barney (Barry) Cunningham Mattross

John Tarne Mattross
John Steer Mattross
Peter Olinger Mattross
Fred Shubert Mattross
Benj. (Bennet) Daly Mattross
Shoebert Armitage Cadet

Second Company

(Capt. A Wilkinson's Co.)

Amos Wilkinson Captain Resigned June 7, 1779
Thomas Douglass Lieutenant
Lewis Sewalt Sergeant
Jno Bell Corporal
Patt Smith Gunner
Thos. Jennings Gunner
John Young Mattross

Wm. Clare (Clark) Mattross
David Reed Mattross
Robert Young Mattross
Richard Sweetman Mattross
Edward Toole Mattross
Ben Farnham Mattross
Jos Johnson Mattross

Third Company

(Capt. Joseph Rice's Co.)

Joseph Rice Captain
Robert McConnell Lieutenant
John Shute Lieutenant
Joseph Morgan Sergeant
Daniel Forbes Sergeant
Robert Davidson Corporal
Robert Pauper Gunner
Martin Miller Gunner
Daniel McCoy Gunner
George Keller Fifer

Thos. Connelly Drummer
Michael Ring Drummer
Jno Malony Mattross
Geo Godfrey Mattross
Howard Knight Mattross
Wm. Talbott Mattross
Wm. Ford Mattross
Wm. Syms Mattross
Jno Van Ostrand Mattross
Daniel Murphy Mattross
Isaac Sebey (Sevey) Mattross

Fourth Company

(Capt. Francis Proctor, Jr's Co.)

Francis Proctor, Jr. Captain	Jno Thornton Mattross
James Norris	Jno Mohony Mattross
Daniel North Sergeant	(Malony)
Richard Evitt Sergeant	Leonard Branson Mattross
Jno Stafford Bombardier	(Brown)
Wm. Hays Gunner	Hugh McDonald Mattross
John Coony Gunner	Thos. Mullen Mattross
Jno Clark Drummer	Wm. McCoombs Mattross
Geo Chase Drummer	Wm. Crowley Mattross
Wm. Campbell Drummer	Wm. Mooney Mattross
Dan'l Cross Drummer	Herms Thornton Mattross
	Jno Hill Mattross

Fifth Company

(Capt. Patrick Duffy's Co.)

Patrick Duffy Captain	Chas. Young Mattross
Wm. Stuart Sergeant	Jno Evans Mattross
Philip Wetzell Corporal	Jno Gibbons Mattross
Frederick Smalts Gunner	Peter Deeter Mattross
Jacob Bryan Fifer	Joseph Craft Mattross
Robert Patterson Fifer	Chrisn Miller Mattross
Wm. McDaniel Drummer	Michael Joice Mattross
Casper Ebenard Drummer	Jno Stewart Mattross
John Conrad Vercloss Mattross	Chas Schaffer Mattross
Wm. Baker Mattross	Jno Toplin Mattross
	Jno Rogers Mattross

Sixth Company

(Capt. John Bryce's Co.)

John Brice Captain	Henry Gavan Bombardier
James Bennett (Benner) Sergeant	Samuel Butler Bombardier
George Henderson Sergeant	Henry Conckle (Conchet, Conele) Gunner
Casper Shane Corporal	Daniel Fennell Gunner
Wm. McMullen Corporal	Henry Love (Lose) Mattross
Benj. Lovett Drummer	Wm. Emberson Mattross

Thomas Howell   Mattross
Ed Callahan (Gallahan)
John Dunn
John Lisk (Lirk)
James Carter
Wm. McMahon

Robt McNeal   Mattross
Jas Gill
Jno (Joel) Redman
Christ'r McDonell
Geo. Farrell

Seventh Company

(Capt. Robt Coultman's Co.)

Robert Coltman   Captain
Jesse Crosby (Crossley)   Lieutenant
Philip Lower   Sergeant
Benj. Whitlow (Whittow)   Corporal
Fred Byerly   Corporal
Reynard Smith (Smick)   Corporal
Jno Spade   Drummer
Henry Guger (Guiter, Gaiter)   Drummer
Thos Mayberry   Gunner

Wm. Mayberry   Mattross
John Gutzelman
Fred Redhair
Jacob Fager (Degan)
Christn Hubart
Nicholas Sailheimer
   (Michl) (Seilheimer)
Michl Bowers
Thos Johnson

Eighth Company

(Capt Lieut Worsley Emes' Co.)

Worsley Emes   Capt. Lieutenant
John Martin Ludwick   Sergeant
Joseph Adams   Sergeant
Francis Donelly   Sergeant
Peter Burkett   Corporal
James (Jacob) Grimes   Corporal
James Say (Toy)   Corporal
Glover Hunt   Bombardier
Wm. Henderson   Bombardier
Thos. Tweedy (Tiverdy)   Gunner
Michael McNulty (Patrick)   Gunner
Wm. Hannah (Hannon)   Gunner
Jno Snell   Gunner
Jacob Smith   Fifer
James Crutcher   Fifer
Hugh Fegan (Tegan)   Drummer
John Craig (Creag)   Mattross

Thos. McCook   Mattross
Patt Diver (Dever)
Laur. Lowerman
Jno Storts (~~Stortz~~)
Wm. McMullen
Thos. Lange (Luge) (Logue)
John Miller
Geo. Hutheson
Jon'an Sturges
G. L. Feighter
Fred Winkler
Archey Hannah (Archibald)
Chas Conrade (Conrad)
Matths Camph (Camp)
Wm Wilkerley (Weatherby)
James McCracken
Fred Orne

Morgan's Riflemen

(Col. Daniel Morgan)

James Parr Major
John Coleman Adjutant
Henry Henly QrMr.
Benj. Ashby Pay Master
Daniel Shute Surgeon Left June 15
Michael Simpson Captain
(Gabriel Long Captain
  Resigned May 13, 1779)

(Philip Slaughter Capt. Lieut.
  Nov. 1, 1778; Capt. May 13, 1779)
Thomas Boyd Lieut.
Wm. Stephens Lieut.
Elijah Evans Lieut.
Benj. Ashby Lieut.
Reuben Long Ensign
John Howe Sergeant Major

Corrections or additions to Greenough's (1887) Roster

1. Benj. Chambers, Ensign absent
2. Add:
    a. John Coleman, Adjutant (until Aug. 1)
    b. Henry Henly, QrMr.
    c. Benj. Ashby, Pay Master
    d. Daniel Shute, Surgeon (until June 15)
    e. Wm. Stephens, Lieut.
    f. Elijah Evans, Lieut.
    g. Benj. Ashby, Lieut.
    h. Reuben Long, Ensign
       "   "   Lieut. (May 10, 1779)
    i. John Howe, Sergt. Major

A Pay Roll of Captn. Simpson's Company of Detached Rifle Men for the Month of August 1779.

Michael Simpson Captn.
Thomas Boyd Lt.
Wm. Stephens Lt.
Stephen Sims Sergt.
Jon. Armstrong Sergt.
Jon. McMahon Sergt.
Jon Watson Sergt.
Benj Custard Sergt.
John Ray Corpl.
Thos Benston Corpl.
John Kelly Corpl.
John Ryan Corpl.
Michael Parker Private
Albert Weaver
William Linn

William Kerr Private
Anthony Granad
Michs Chocer
Alexr Thompson
Petr Condon
David Davis
James Elliott
Patrick McCaw
Felix Hoover
Phillip Potter
John Yost
John Solomon
John Curry
Saml Poarter
Jas Hambelton

Edward Lee Private
John Casper
Edwd Huselen
Robt Shepherd
Timothy Murphy
Isaac Heselton
James Crage
John Erwin
Jedh Tuffs
Willm Rabb
John McCreery

John McKenny Private
John Williber
Joseph King
Robt McDonol
Dan Hidden
Wm English
John Tidd
Daniel McMullen
Benjn Wheeler
Ml Simpson
   Captn Rifle Corps

2. June 1779
John Allen, Thomas Burk, Samuel Falling, and Thomas Davis deserted June 16, 1779
Has Felix Pitter instead of Philip Potter
Has Samuel Parker instead of Samuel Poarter
Has no Benjn Wheeler

3. July 1779 (Item 204)
Has John Clark discharged July 25, 1779

4. Sept. 1779 (Item 206)
Has Thomas Boyd Lt. killed Sept. 13, 1779

2. "Payroll of the late Capt. Gabriel Long's Company of Detach'd Rifle Men formerly commanded by Colo. Daniel Morgan for the month of July 1779."

Elijah Evans Lieut.
Benjamin Ashby Lieut.
Reuben Long Ensign
John Howe Sergeant Discharged July 25
Nicholas Long Sergt. Discharged Aug. 1
Elias Tolland Sergt.
Thomas Coleman Sergt. Discharged Aug. 1
Joseph Evans Sergt.
Jeremiah Samuel Sergt.
Samuel Burks Sergt.
Smith Kent Sergt.
Rowley Jacobs Corpl.
John Gazaway Corpl.
Wm. Suddeth Corpl. Discharged July 23
Vincent Howell Corpl. Discharged July 23
Elijah Hendricks Corpl.
Duncan McDonald Corpl.
Wm Loyd Private

Jacob Smith Private
James Wilson
James Harris
Jesse Wilhite
Patrick Howracan Discharged Aug. 1
Henry Holdaway Discharged Aug. 1
Chas Morgan
Daniel Grant Discharged Aug. 1
Mack Robinson
John Straughan Discharged July 24
John Grant Discharged Aug. 1
Thomas Dermott
John Colman Discharged Aug. 1
John McJohnson Discharged Aug. 1
Moses Spencer
Samuel Davis Discharged Aug. 1
John Hopewell
Benjamin McKnight
Wm. Castle
Reuben Long
Thomas Wright
David Allison
   (Ellison)

Christopher Rooney   Private
Joseph Vance
John Smith   Discharged Aug. 1
John Lyon
Wm. Jacobs
Daniel Davidson (Davis)
John Robinson
John Austin
Wm Bartlett
Samuel Middleton

Richard Roundsiver   Private
James Jiles
John Adams
Wm. Haddle   Discharged Aug. 1
Wm. Barby   Discharged Aug. 1
Andrew Elder
James McGuire
Daniel Dunnegan
Chas Witt
Richard Skeggs

Capt. J. P. Schotts Rifle Corps

Capt. A. Selin's Corps of Pioneers
(Major, Count, Nicholas Ottendorf's Corps)
(Sometimes given under Armand's Legion)

John Paul Schott   Captain
Antoni (Anthony) Selin   Captain
Lawrence Myers   Lieutenant
Christian Frolich   Lieutenant
Frederick Lebe (Lube, Leibe)   Sergt. Major
Francis McGarran   Q.M. Sergeant
Henry Lieders   Sergt. (later Q.M. Sergt.)
Henry Singer   Sergt.

John Stynehiser   Sergeant
Jacob Hilfe   Sergeant
John Geedecke   Sergeant
George Marks   Corporal
Andrew Reaburg   Corporal
Daniel Sheetz   Corporal
Samuel Hewlett   Corporal
Wm. Marx   Drummer

Privates

John Bengel
Jonathan Boswell
Adam Brandhefer
Martin Breckhall
John Brecker
Owen Cooley
Peter Corback
Hugh Cromwell
Wm. Dorn
John Eurach
Michael Eurach
Christopher Felts
Henrich Frantcher
Jacob Frey
Wm. Gennis
Henry Keck

John Kepler
George Kerse
Valentine Keyser
Gabriel Kline
Martin Lantz
John Levering
Basil Lewis
John Poorham
Jacob Reynard
James Ridgway
Tobias Ritter
John Roch
Christian Swanhiser
Adam Sypert
Henry Till
Samuel Ulett (Hewlett)

Wyoming Company

(Capt. Spalding's Independent Company)
(Capts. Ransom's & Durkee's Cos. united)

(Approximate roster)

Simon Spalding   Captain
John Jenkins   Lieutenant
Obadiah Gore   Lieutenant
   (see end of this list)
Thomas McClure   Sergeant
Peregrine Gardner   Sergeant
Thomas Baldwin   Sergeant
Thomas Williams   Sergeant

Lemuel Whitman (Witman)   Sergeant
Frederick Eveland   Sergeant
Thomas (Oneill) Neal   Sergeant
John Hutchinson   Sergeant
Azel Hyde   Corporal
Jeremiah Coleman Jr. (Clemen)   Corpl.
Benj. Clark   Corpl.
Thomas Parks   Corpl.

Privates

Mason F. Alden
Amos Amesbury
   (Ormsbury, Armstrong)
____ Austin
Waterman Baldwin
(Walter Baldwin)
Thomas Bagley (Bagby)
Jeremiah Baker
(Nathan Beach)
   (Boatman to Tioga Pt.)
Isaac Benjamin
Charles Bennett
Isaac Bennett
Oliver Bennett
Rufus Bennett
David Brown
James Brown Jr.
Moses Brown
Asabel (Asa, Asel) Burnham
John Carey
Wm. Cornelius
Wm. Carroll (Corrial)
Gurdon (Gideon) Church
John Church

Nathaniel (Nathan) Church
Benj. Cole
Benj. Cole Jr.
____ Colton
Wm. Conover
Wm. Concles
Price Cooper
   (Copper, Prior or Pierce)
Jediah Corning
David Crouch (Crutch)
Douglass Davidson
Wm. Davidson
David Denton
Robt. Dorrance (Durrance)
Samuel Ensign
Frederick Follett
Michael Foster
Wm. French
Elisha Garrett
Ambrose Gaylord
Justus (Justice) Gaylord Jr.
Barzelt Guarney
   (Bezaleel Gurney)
John Halstead
Richard Halstead

Henry (Harry, Harvey) Harding
Israel Harding
Timothy Hopkins
Wm. Kellogg
Lawrence Kenney (Kinney)
Rufus Lawrence
Constant Loits
Elisha Matthewson
Wm. McClure (McCluer)
Asabel Nash
Israel Nording
John Oakley
John O Neill (Neal)
Nehemiah Patterson
Josiah Pell
Thomas Peckett
(Thomas Porter)
George Palmer Ransom
Elisha Saterlee
Constant Searles Jr.
Elisha Noyes Sill
Shadrick (Sills) Sill
Stephen Skiff
Asa Smith
Azariah (Ezeriah) Smith
Isaac Smith Jr.

James Smith
Wm. Smith Jr.
John Spalding (Simon Spalding's son, not in any muster but on trip)
James Stark Jr.
John Stark
Nathaniel Stark
Roswell Stephens
Ira (Fra, Francis) Stevens
Stephen Still
John Swift
Wm. Terry
Samuel Tubbs
Thomas Tucket (must be Thomas Pickett above)
Ephraim Tyler
Isaac Underwood
Elijah (Edward) Walker
Obadiah Walker
Caleb Warden
(Cabel Worden)
James Wells Jr.
Nathaniel Williams
Richard Woodstock (Woodcock)
John Worden

Obadiah Gore   Lieutenant

Asa Chapman   Sergeant

Thomas Park   Corporal

Privates

Deliverance Adams
Joshua Farnum
Turner Jackson
Crocer (Croker) Jones
John Oakley

Ebenezer Parks
John Platner
Benj. Potts
David Shaw
Lemuel Whitman

FOURTH BRIGADE

(Gen. Clinton)

2nd New York Regiment

The composite evidence from published sources from which we made our presumptive list of officers for this trip came from 4 sources.

(A) Archives of the State of New York Vol. I.
(C) Calendar of New York Historical Manuscripts..
(G) Greenough's Roster of Officers Sullivan Expedition.
(J.O.) Mention in journals, orderly book, diaries, etc.

Greenough's Roster (G) lists all the officers we chose except (1) Israel Evans and (2) Lt. Christopher Codwise. The journals etc. (J.O.) mention 17 of the list of 29.

Speaking of journals, narratives, no regiment on this expedition has yielded more than the 2nd New York Regiment. We have Van Cortland's autobiography written in 1825 and published in 1878 and Chaplain Israel Evans' sermon at Easton, Pa.

If Quartermaster Sergeant Wm. Rogers of Malcolm's Regiment be credited to the 2nd New York Regiment we have 4 journal accounts of this expedition in Conover's (1887) Centennial volume; namely, Lieut. John Hardenburgh (7th Co.), Capt. Lieut. Chas. Nukerek (8th Co.), Quartermaster Sergeant Wm. Rogers and Sergeant Major Nathaniel Webb (1st Co.). Since 1887 two more journals from this regiment have appeared, making 6 in all for the regiments: Lieut. T. Beekam's (2nd Co.) (1888) and Lt. James Fairlee's (3rd Co.) (1929). Should we hope for journals from the other Lieutenants of the battalion? There was also the lost journal of Kimball Prince of the 3rd Company, i.e. 8 extant and 1 extinct accounts.

From several sources the officers and company rosters have been constructed (Clinton Papers, muster and payrolls of 1779). Again Adjutant General's Office (AGO) solves our difficulties.

2nd New York Regt.

Philip Van Cortlandt   Colonel
Pierre Regnier de Roussi   Lt. Colonel
Nicholas Fish   Major
Charles Nukerck   Adjutant and Captain
  Lieutenant
Robert Provoost Jr   Paymaster and Ensign
Wm Munday   Quartermaster
  1st Lieutenant
Tunis Van Wegenan   Quartermaster
  2nd Lieutenant
Charles F. Weissenfels   Quartermaster
  (Oct. 19, 1779)   and 2nd Lieutenant
Daniel Menema   Surgeon
Israel Evans   Chaplain
  (See 3rd N. H. Regt.)
Nathaniel Webb   Sergt. Major
Abner Griffith   Sergt. Major
Alexander Dunn   Quartermaster Sergt.
Isaac Morrell   Drum Major

Charles Graham   Captain
Samuel T. Pell   Captain
Jacob Wright   Captain
Jonathan Hallett   Captain
Abner French   Captain
Chas Nukerck   Capt. Lieut.
Elihu Marshall   1st Lieut.
James Fairlee   1st Lieut.
John L. Hardenburgh   1st Lieut.
Wm Munday   1st Lieut.
Christopher Codwise   1st Lieut.
Charles F. V. Weissenfels   1st Lieut.
Tjerck Beekman   1st Lieut.
Gilbert I. Livingston   1st Lieut.
Andrew White   1st Lieut.
Wm Glenny   2nd Lieut.
Tunis Van Wagenen   2nd Lieut.
Bernardus Swartout   Ensign
John Brown   Ensign
Robert Provoost Jr   Ensign

First Company

(Abraham Rikers 1776, 1777 Co.)

(Colonel's Co.)

Philip Cortlandt   Colonel
Charles Nukerck   Capt. Lieut.
(Gilbert I. Livingston   Lieut. on comd.)
(Barnardus Swartout   Ensign)
Nathaniel Webb (Wood)   Sergt. Major
Alexander Dunn   Quartermaster Sergeant
Isaac Morrell   Drum Major

David Mitchell   Fife Major
James Kipp   Sergt.   Reduced July 16, 177
David Morrison   Sergeant
Isaac McCartney   Corporal
Isaac Wilsey   Corporal
John Gavine (Gabine)   Drummer
James Scott   Fifer

Privates

Joseph Beely
Peter Cashody
Andrios Christopher
Henry Elliott
Wm Knight
James Kipp
Christopher Krom
Jacob Levi
James Ready
Jonathan Robert

Caleb Smith
Christopher Smith
Stanley Thompson
Joel Tuthill
John Wilhele
Abraham Weeks
Patrick Hamilton   )   Deserted
John Hendrick Leek)   May 29,
James Molley   1779

2nd Company

(Lieut. Colonel's Co.)

Frederick Weissenfels Lieut. Col.
   Transferred to 4th N.Y. Regt.
Peter Regnier Lieut. Colonel
Christopher Codwise Lieut.
John Brown Ensign
John Wilcox Sergeant

John Jaquish Sergeant
Thomas Gray Corporal
James Sherwood Corporal
James Newcomb Corporal
James Knapp Drummer
(John Weissenfels Fifer Discharged
   May 1, 1779)

Privates

Stephen Barber
Samuel Barnham
Andrew Bradt
Edward Cassidy
David Cole
(Francis Flood (Hood))
Christopher Horton
Nicolas Hudsal

Caleb Knapp
(Isaac Knapp)
John Olmstead
Psalter Pulman
Caleb Roberts
Nathan Sherwood
Thomas Teatsworth
Cornelius Vances

3rd Company

(Major's Co.)

Nicholas Fish Major
James Fairlie Lieut.
Andrew White Lieut.
George Douglas Sergeant
Wm Occurman Sergeant

Tobias Waygant Corporal
(John Robinson Corpl. deserted May 16)
(Stephen Robinson Drummer
   deserted May 16)
John Cherry Drummer
Michael Trout Fifer

Privates

Ebenezer Bailey
Robert Battersby
Mynt Bogart
Michl Gabbatson
Samuel Ferguson
Matthew Freebush
(Nath'l Foster deserted May 16)

John Lusk
Thomas Mason
John Rider
Wm Smith
John Steel
Abner Timmons
Richard Wheeler

4th Company

Charles Graham   Captain
Wm Munday   Lieut. (QrMaster to Regt.)
(Wm Nottingham   2nd Lieut
   resigned May 4, 1779)
Prince Kimble   Sergeant

John Smith   Sergeant
Jonas Brown   Sergeant
Jonas Brown   Corporal
Noah Hopkins   Fifer

Privates

Jacob Albright
Matthew Bell
John Braden
Andrew Bradner
George Claxton
Joseph Conklin
(Philip Corter)
Jacobus Countryman
Abraham Devere
(Thos Dickens)
John Grogan
Joseph Horsford

Wm Hunt
Robert Jensen (Jensing)
Evan Jones
Andrew Knickabacer
Kady Lary
Peter Maheu
Peter Rose (Ross)
John (Jesse) Sherman
Abraham Springstead
John Vergan (Verrian)
(Cornelius Woodman (Woodamore))
Nathan Whipple   d. June 24th

5th Company

Samuel T. Pell   Captain
William Glenny   Lieut.
(Robert Provoost Jr   Ensign)
James Carson   Sergeant

John Shucraft   Sergeant
Wm Campbell   Corporal
Wm Sarjesson   Drummer
Jacob Jones   Fifer

Privates

Caleb Chase
(Shubl Cunningham)
(Herman Davis)
James Dickens
Robert Ellison
John Garrison
Moses Graham
Joseph Hadley
John Hopper
(Wm Layton)

Noah Mott
John Peterson
Stephen Powell
Joseph Randals
John Runnels
John Simon   Transferred to 1st N.J.
Lazarus Spriggs
Caleb Steves
Philip Steves

6th Company

Jacob Wright   Captain
Tunis Van Waganen   Lieut.
Moses Harris   Sergeant
John Lester   Sergeant
Andrew Dunlap   Sergeant

Uriah Travis (James)   Corporal
David Fashee   Corporal
Abram Depew   Corporal
Barrack Wright   Drummer
Jacob Hollenbeck   Fifer

Privates

Thomas Brooks
Henry Burdick
Tunis Cole
John Cristoon
Isaac Dean
Francis Depew
Henry Depew
Frederick Dolton
Thomas Dolton
Benjamin Griffin
James Griffis
Samuel Hitchcock
James Johnson

Wm Kenyon
John Ledore
Isaac Martin
James McKinney
Wm Mute
Peter Ousterhout
Jonathan Palmer
James Sertain
Thomas Stillwiel
Samuel Street
Henry Thomas
Cornelius Van Tasel
John Yourns (Yores)

7th Company

Jonathan Hallett   Captain
John L. Hardenburgh   Lieut.
Frank Courtney   Sergeant
Chas McKinney   Sergeant
Simon Lambertson   Sergeant

James Craft   Corporal
James Rose   Corporal
John Morrell   Corporal
Chas Darby   Fifer

Privates

Oliver Arnold
John Astin
John Bennett
John Briggs
Conrad Coblar
John Collins
James Curry
Peter Donaldson
John Foster

Wm Gilbert
Samuel Griffith
Michl Havelish
Adam Himalan
James Kealy (Beayle)
Jeremiah McGowan
Charles Moore
Moses Mulliner
John Oakley

John Padden
Jacob Rose
Michael Sellars
John Shulter
Martin Simon

Peter Slutt
Richard Smith
John Venice
Wm White
Jacob Whitney

8th Company

Elihu Marshall   Captain
Charles F. Weissenfels   Lieut.
Bernard Swartout   Ensign
Thomas Duncan   Sergeant
James Stillwell   Sergeant

James Lewis   Corporal
John Conway   Corporal
Israel Walker   Corporal
George Weissenfels   Fifer

Privates

Peleg Adams
David Condon
Robert Cox
Henry Cunningham
Jacob Lomas
Michael Lyons
Hendrick May

(John McDonald   deserted May 15, 1779)
Ronald McDonald
Abraham Sherwood
Henry Stephens
Jacobus Van Atter
Zachariah Vandemark
Wm Wheeler

9th Company

(Light Infantry)

Abner French   Captain
Tjerck Beekman   Lieut.
Abraham Griffith   Sergeant
Thomas Bunting   Sergeant
Jonathan Trimmin   Sergeant

Henry Rich   Corporal
Lewis Nowse   Corporal
(Jesse Sherman   Corporal)
(Isaac Morrell   Drummer   Transferred)

Privates

Archibald Armstrong
John Bartholomew
Jonathan Benjamin
Samuel Benjamin
Jeremiah Bennett
Peter Boyce
Moses Burdick

Robt Burns
Moses Cavender
Andries Christopher
George Coble
Philip Cole
Thomas Grill
John Hitchcock

Daniel Holmes
Thos Huntley
Jacobus Ivory
Joseph Ketcham
David Lambert
Martin Mitchell
Isaac Mott

Lewis Novee
Cornelius Quick
Jacob Quick
Jesse Sherman
(John Smith   deserted May 16)
(Edward Taylor   deserted May 16)
John Ten Eyck
John Thompson

THIRD NEW YORK REGIMENT

From Composite Evidence of Published Sources

From the evidence of three sources one might closely approximate the situation in 1779, nevertheless the manuscript we constructed before we saw these 1779 lists was far astray. The Archives Vol. I (p. 209 half page) had a "Colonel's Company"(15 in all) "Lt. Colonel's Company"(5 in all) and "Officers and Men of the Third Regiment whose proper place in the same could not be ascertained"(10 in all). Of these 7 belong to the 4th Company, 5 to 5th Company, 1 to 3rd Company, 3 to the 6th. Previous to 1948 we even made the mistaken note "doubt if there was in 1779 a Colonel's or Lt. Colonel's Company". The roll shows us mistaken.

Again from the previous material we might have reasonably assigned the lieutenants and ensigns to companies yet we had before the muster rolls of 1779 appeared the following notes: "Approved except for lieutenant and ensign assignments". From May 1779 to Dec. 1779 we have musters plus examination of General P. Gansevoort's Papers (N.Y. Public Library) and we have constructed the make-up of this regiment.

3rd New York Regiment

First Company

Peter Gansevoort   Colonel
George Sytez   Capt. Lieut.
Douw T. Fonda
Robert Welden   Sergeant (see 5th Co.)
Henry Miller   Sergeant
Jonathan Hunter   Sergeant
Francis Jackson   QrMr Sergeant

Andrew Gardner   Fife Major
Samuel Gilbert   Corporal
Daniel Owens   Corporal
Nathaniel Meeker   Corporal
Coenradt Friday   Drummer
Daniel Dawson   Fifer

Privates

Peter Anthony
John Anthony
Nicholas Bovee
John Borden
John Burke
Benj. Cowdrey
George F. Cowdres
Joseph Demont
John Goodcourage

Thomas Gregg
Adam Harter
Wm. Harvey
Henry Huffner
Henry Hynes
Christian Kiesburg
Jonathan Klock
James Lighthall
Lancaster Lighthall

John McFarlin
Bartley Murray
Edward Parker
James Patterson
Eli Pixley
Chalker Pratt
Richard Robertson
John Ross
Peter Shirts
Samuel Shirts

Joseph Seevy
Solomon Smith
John Thompson
John Van Sire
Roger Wabby (Wally)
Joseph White
Francis Willet
Wm. Whitham
Michael Zeaster

Second Company

Marinus Willett Lt. Colonel
Philip Conine Lieutenant
John Burhans Ensign
Davis (David) Love Sergeant
Joseph Valentine Sergeant
Lewis Bogardus Sergeant

James Marston (Stanton) Corporal
Jacob R. Hopper Corporal
John Gadge Corporal
Isaac Palmatier Drummer
John House Fifer

Privates

David Austin
Lawrence Artwick
Thomas Allen
Jacob Bakehorn
Jeremiah Bakehorn
Joseph Clinton
Thomas Cook
Matthew Cousins
Francis Elliott
James Erwin
David Force
Gabriel Furman
Samuel Gardiner
Wm. Grite
Bishop Hadley
Jonathan Higgins
Aaron Hulbert
Seth Jones
Peter Little
Hendrix Loux

Solomon Meeker (Maker)
Robert Moore
Baltus Orr
Timothy Parks
Benjamin Preston
Othaniel Preston
Patrick Ripley (see 8th Co.)
Andrew Robinson
(John Ryley)
George Shell
Richard Sheridan
George Shift
Gideon Simpkins
Abraham Tompkins
Abraham Van Emsburg (Van Ambro)
James Van Kleck
Joseph Watson
David Weed (Wood)
Jeremiah Weldon
Arthur Williams
Wm. Wilsey

Third Company

Robert Cochran Major
Wm. Tapp Lieutenant
Josiah Bagley Ensign
Thomas Jones Sergeant
Wm. Chatfield (Catfield) Sergeant
Isaac Sturges Sergeant
James Vander Vorst Corporal

Jno Hulser (Hulson, Halser) Corpl.
John Welch Corporal
Abraham De Clark Drummer
Andrew Gardiner Fife Major (see 1st Co.)
Daniel Dorson (Dawson) Fifer
  (see 1st Co.)
John McIntosh Fifer

Privates

John Apport
John Brass
Simon Bromley
Nicholas Christman
Joseph Cornwell
Henry Ennis
Alexander Hyre
(Frederick Jansen)
John Leplink (Lupling,
John Luther
Alexander McCoy
John McIntosh
Alexander Monroe
Thos. Mott
Jacob Myers
Isaac Nostrand

Allen Nelson
Leonard Olindorf (Olmendorf)
Frederick Perkhoof (Barkhoof)
Engleis Perksmith
Simon Peters
Henry Randall
Samuel Reed
Wm. Risdal
Warren Roberts
Wm. Romer
Patrick Ryan
Abraham Sickles
John Uthest
Joseph Vessels (Wessells)
Coonradt Walter
Jacob Weeks

Fourth Company

Aaron Aorson Captain
Gerritt Staats Lieutenant
Samuel Lewis Ensign
Robert Wilkerson Sergeant
Robert Williams Sergeant
John Carlisle Sergeant

Dennis Sullivan Corporal (reduced)
John Way Corporal
Levi Sterling Corporal
Nicholas Hill Drummer
Duncan Smith Fifer

Privates

- Henry Barnes
- Henry Bass
- John Brown
- Edmund Burk
- Henry Byford
- Peter DeVaults
- Anthony Dunnivan
- Joshua English
- John Ferrigh (Frey)
- John Caspn Foor
- Coonrrad France
- Samuel Gake
- (Michael Henry)
- Thomas Herriot
- Adam Hipple
- Patrick Kelly
- Frances Lampeux
- John McClean
- John McKenzie
- Frederick Moor
- Samuel Mott
- Samuel Needer
- John Sherlock
- Lodewick Shreiner
- Levi Sterling
- Dennis Sullivan
- John Van Alta
- Adam Van Der Hayden
- Gersh Van Der Hayden
- Emanl Wagerman
- Benj. Warring
- John Wells
- John Whiley (Wylie)
- Jacob Wyschover
- James Yates
- Johan T. Yengle

Fifth Company

- Thomas De Witt   Captain
- Peter McGee   Lieut.
- John Spoor   Ensign
- John Skiffington   Sergeant
- John Smith   Sergeant
- Samuel Merricale   Sergeant
- Robert Welding   Sergeant
- George Anderson   Corporal
- Caleb Cornwell   Corporal
- Samuel Merricale   Corporal
- Hugh Fothergill   Corporal
- Degory Prout   Drummer
- Cornelius Blanck   Fifer

Privates

- Ezekiel Anderson
- George Anderson
- John Baker
- Benjn. Banks
- John Baptiste
- Stephen Barker
- John Boyce
- Kenneth Campbell
- John Class
- Caleb Cornwell
- John Dennis
- Samuel Eggs
- James Fletcher
- Hugh Fothergill
- John Freeland
- John Gall
- Wm. Grote
- Frederick Hender
- John Lambert
- (Moses Lambert   disch. June 28, 1779)
- Thos. McIntire
- Edmond Morris
- Peter Wm. Ostrander
- Adam Price

Joseph Putney
Geo. Rider
John Ross
John Joachim Schrader
Christopher Shell
John Smith
Daniel Sutherland

Laurence Van Kleef
John Wetherstine
Solomon Williams
Nathan Worden (Warden)
Frederick Wybert
(John Wright   sick)

Sixth Company

Cornelius I. Jansen   Captain
  (also given J. or T.)
Benjamin Bogardus   Lieutenant
(John Spoor   Ensign   see 5th Co.)
(Josiah Bagley   Ensign   see 3rd Co.)
(John Burhans   Ensign   see 2nd Co.)
Samuel Abbey   Sergeant

Alex McDougal   Sergeant
Jacob Sax   Sergeant
Christian Schriner (Scriver)   Corpl.
Joseph Ladd   Corporal
Albert Rose   Corporal
Nathan Upright   Drummer
Hugh McConnolly   Fifer

Privates

Henry Adams (Adomy)
Joseph Bayley
Chas. Bennett
Henry Bennett
John Black (Block)
John Buggs (Briggs, Beggs)
Timothy Canfield
Nicholas Cashady
Jno. Corragil
Joseph Edes
Joseph Evans
James Fowler
Wm. Griffis (Gifford)
John F. Hamon
Arthur Hurley (Hulley)
Leonard Leonard
John Limbaker
Moses Lent (Grant)
Corns. McDermot

John Miles
Barnhardt Minick
James Mulholland
Uriah Owens
John Pittman (Sillman)
Thomas Platts (Ratts)
Christopher Queen
Joseph Russell
Robert Ryan
Isaac Seamons
James Sheels (Shieds)
Jacob Sluyter
Geo. Upright
John Wallace
Henry Weaver
Esau Wilbur (Wilborn)
John Willis
Isaac Yeomans

Seventh Company

Leonard Bleeker Captain
Prentice Bowen Lieutenant
Benj. Herring Ensign
Wm. Vonck Sergeant
Wm. Jones Sergeant
Cornelius Maxwell Sergeant

John Beedle Corporal
John Chace Corporal
Nathaniel Ambler Corporal
Henry Hill Drummer
John Lalancet Fifer

Privates

Wm. Adams
John Beekman
George Berton
George Brady
Chas. F. Brown
Michael Burgess
John Burkdorff
James Collins
John Collins
John Cooper Senr.
John Cooper Junr.
Martin Den Warken
Frederick Deyer
Alexr. Forbes
Anthony Funna
Abraham Garrison
James Grace
John Hall
Abrm. Hopp
Isaac Isaacs

Christian Kinder
Godlieb Krack
Benj. Knapp
Wm. Maxwell
Dennis McCarty
John McFarland
John Moore
Isaac Osterhout
Wm. Patterson
Hendrick Pillgret
Richard Post
Geo. Robertson
Alexr. Smith
Hugh Somers
Peter Valentine
Wm. Vredenburgh
Geo. Waggonman
Christopher Weaver
Hendrick Wissenback
Edward Wright
(Thomas Wilson)

Eighth Company

James Gregg Captain
Wm. Colbrath Lieutenant
George I. Denniston Ensign
Wm. McLaughlin Sergeant
George Dowlar Sergeant
Joseph (Joshua) Prindle Sergeant
Henry G. Ohlin Sergeant

Henry G. Ohlin Corporal
Wm. Gallaspie Corporal
Francis Fulton Corporal
John Burroughs (Burris) Corpl.
John Wilson Drummer
Robert Wilson Fifer

Privates

Christian Alloon
Abraham Carman
Nicholas Commandine
(Joseph Conine)
   (transferred 1st N.Y. Regt.
   Nov. 14, 1779)
Samuel Deane
Hugh Deyo
Thos. Doherty
Henry Easton
Thomas Hide
Benjamin Holley
Archibald Jackson
Reuben Kellam (Kellown)
Alexander Lemmon
Francis Lovely
James Mason
John Mathers (Maitre)
William McCord
John McVey

Paul Melchior
Hendrick Minick
Richard Morrison
James Murray
Isaac Norris
Aaron Osburn
Edward Painter
Jochem Plough
Benjamin Quackbess (Quackbush)
David Raljie (Ralie)
Patrick Riley
James Robinson
John Shultz
John Spears
James Sutherland
Cornelius Swartout
George Very
John Williams
Wm. Wruns

Ninth Company

Henry Tiebout   Captain
Christopher Hutton   Lieutenant
Gerrit Lansing   Ensign
John Smith   Sergeant
Wm. Haburn   Sergeant
James Patterson   Sergeant

Mark Harr   Corporal
John Edgerly   Corporal
Robert Glen   Corporal
(Conrad Fryday   Drummer   see 1st Co.)
Charles Van Order   Drummer
John Smith   Fifer

Privates

Albert Acker
Coonrad Acker
Henry Ash
David Bagley
Wm. Barrett
John Beaumert
Christian Brant (Brent)
Wm. Bucy
Philip Burch
Godfrey Buyer
Duncan Campbell
Henry Chambers

Thomas Chickens
John Coad
John C. Corter
James Cowen
Luke Crandle
Johan Creckenbome
John Frederick
Henry Fling (Flinn)
Robert Glen
John Gray
Benjamin Geers
George Houstman

Mark Karr (Harr, Kerr)
Christian Keener
Abraham Lambert
Lockert Lewis
Peter Lowman
Joseph Lyon
Patrick Mahan
Hugh Mozure
Jno. Henry Nemire
Michael Paulsen (Poulsen)
Joseph Perchase (Purchase)
John Peters
Jonathan Pinkney

Lewis Piper
John Rynard
Peter Schriber (Schriner)
Thos. Searles (Serals, Scrals)
Jesper Stagg
James V. Blaricum
Jno. Coral V. Bonhaugle
Abraham Vanduser
Wm. Watson
Richard Welsh
Abraham Wright
Samuel Wright

FOURTH NEW YORK REGIMENT

Composite Evidence from Published Sources

Previous to the muster rolls of 1779 from the following sources we compiled a roster of the officers and file of this regiment for 1779: (1) Documents - Col. Hist. State Archives (A) Vol. I 1887; (2) Samuel Tallmadge's (T) Order Books, Albany 1932, (3) John Barr's (B) Diary Albany 1932; (4) R. Von Hovenburgh's (V) Journal 1887. These four sources were at times supplemented by Gee (G) or Bleecker (B) notes. Other papers such as E. B. O'Callaghan's Manuscript List (N.Y. Hist. Society) Clinton Papers, W. Bradford Jr. Muster Rolls (Penn. Hist. Soc.). But the two significant papers were muster rolls of 1779 and Lieut. Abraham Hyatt's unpublished orderly book (N.Y. Hist. Soc.). His volume for May 29 - Aug. 6, 1779 was especially significant. He gives more details of individuals than the three above published journals.

Fourth New York Regiment

Frederick Weissenfels Lt. Colonel
Peter Regnier Lt. Colo. and Subinsptr.
Israel Smith Paymaster and Capt.
Peter Ellsworth Adjutant and Lieut.
James Barrett Quartermaster and Lieut.
John (S) F Vasche (Vacher) Surgeon
Thomas Sibbio Surgeon's Mate
Patt Sinnott Sergeant Major (June 1, 1779)
(Joseph Morrill Sergeant Major)
Jno Dugard (Duguid) QrMr. Sergeant
Robert Ward Drum Major
Ise Penoyer Fife Major
Samuel Sackett Captain
John Davis Captain
Jonathan Titus Captain
Nathaniel Norton Captain
Theodosius Fowler Captain

Edward Dunscomb Capt. Lieut.
Silas Grey Lieut.
Peter Ellsworth Lieut.
Peter Van Bunschoten Lieut.
Thos. Hunt Lieut.
Abraham Hyatt Lieut.
Rudolphus Van Hoevenburgh Lieut.
Joseph Fraelich Lieut.
James Barrett Lieut. Nov. 9, 1779
Daniel D. Denniston Ensign
Azariah Tuthill (Turtle) Ensign
Samuel Tallmadge Ensign
Ephraim Woodruff Ensign
Joseph Morrell Ensign
John Barr Ensign
Samuel Dodge Jr Ensign
Stephen Griffin Ensign

Corrections or Additions to Greenough's Roster

a. Omit Joseph McCracken, Major
   Wounded June 28, 1778 - Resigned Apr. 1, 1780
   At Bennington May 1, 1779
b. Add Thomas Sibbio, Surgeon's Mate
   Oct. 23, 1778. Omitted Nov. 1779
c. Omit Benj. Walker, Captain Nov. 25, 1776;
   aide-de-camp to Gen. Steuben Sept. 3, 1778. Absent

d. Add Joseph Merrill, Ensign Jan. 1, 1778
e. Add John Barr, Ensign Jan. 1, 1778
f. Add Samuel Dodge, Ensign Jan. 1, 1778
g. Add Stephen Griffin, Ensign Jan. 1, 1778
   (See Tallmadge-Barr Orderly Books, pp. 125-127 for
   Regiment's Officers present)
b, d, e, f, g are also given in E.B.O'Callaghan's List (6, 6a
N.Y. Hist. Soc. for the 4th New York in 1779.

First Company

Frederick Weisenfels   Lieut. Colonel
Edward Dunscomb   Capt. Lieut.
Daniel Denniston   Ensign
Joseph Morrill   Sergeant Major
John Thompson   Sergeant
David Clark   Sergeant
John Donalds (Donnels)   Sergeant

John Duguit (Dugard)   QrMr Sergeant
Robert Ward   Drum Major
Jesse (Ise) Penoyer   Fife Major
Neal McClean   Drummer
Jesse Miller   Corporal
Daniel Conklin   Corporal
Daniel Ludlum (Ludlow)   Corporal

Privates

James Barris (Barrows)
Samuel Bernard
Reuben Brainerd
Jeremiah Brewer
Joseph Brown
Jno Bussing (Busomy)
Andrew Campbell (Campfield)
Patrick Davis
Peter Davis
John Davison
Peter Dunaven (Dunnivan)
John Elsworth
Benj. Eaton
(Upton Esston)
James Fitch
John Hiff (Kip)

Asa Hill
John Holmes
John Kelsey (Hilsy)
Daniel Ludlum
Thomas Mason
William Pangburn
Jonathan Philips
Abel Norton
Jibe Norton
Benj. Smith
Richard Thomas
Isaac Van Gelder
James Vredennurgh (Fredenburgh)
Edward Walker
John Wright

Second Company

(Major's Co. 1779)

(Joseph McCracken   Major)
Silas Gray   Lieutenant
Samuel Tallmadge   Ensign
William McCallester   Sergeant
Peter P. Van Atten (Allen)   Sergeant

Matthias Walker   Sergeant
Matthias Walker   Corporal to May 31
(James Colloney (Conelly)   Corpl.)
Aholiab Macks   Corpl. June 1, 1779
John Cherry   Drummer
William Gilchrist   Fifer

121

Privates

Daniel Bailey
Christian Blaze
John Bogg
Willm. Bunker
Christian Closs
Moses Cook
Peter Coon
George Decker
John Hubbard (Hibbard)
Wm Huff (Hoff)
John Light (Lite)
John Minks
John Myre (Mize)

Gilbert Ostrout
John H. Packall
(John H. T. Pickle)
Peter Penner
John Penney
Peter Ploss
Vinson Powell
John Strong
Ase Utley
John Van D Bogart
Gilbert Van Size
John Waner
Levi Westfall

Third Company

(Capt. Sacketts Co.)

Samuel Sackett   Captain
Joseph Froelich   Lieutenant
Simon Terboss (Terbush)   Sergeant
James Parshall   Sergeant (9th Co.)
Ezra Goldsmith   Sergeant
  (Gouldsmith)
Rynier Van Hooser (Hover)   Sergeant

Andrew Mills   Corporal
David Dickerson   Corporal
James Williamson   Corporal (5th Co.)
Barnajos (Boaning) Beebe   Corpl.
John Kader (Rider)   Drummer
Samuel Pettis (Pellet)   Fifer

Privates

Jeremiah Barnhart
Boaning Beebe
Sam'l. Buchanan (Becannan)
John Clark
Joseph Cliff (Cleeft)
Nath'l Craft
Richard Cozard (Cuviard)
Chapman Davis
Joshua Davis
Peter Denney
Zopher Hawkins
John Jones

John Joy
Jonathan Kinner
C. Norris (Maurice) Kelly
Adam Kader
John Ketcham
James Marshall (Martial)
Andrew Mills
Simon Peterson
Timothy Reynolds (Runnels)
James Smith
Jeremiah Wier
Sam'l Wilson

Fourth Company

John Davis   Captain
Peter Elsworth   1st Lieut.
Samuel C. Dodge   Ensign
(George Howell   Sergeant)
Patrick Sinnett's   Sergeant
Jacob Hicks (Hilks)   Sergeant

Joseph Talmadge   Corporal
Jonathan Russell   Corporal
Samuel Brown   Corporal
Samuel Burrows   Drummer
David Black   Fifer

Privates

James Boyles
Benj. Chapel
(Benj. Chapel Jr.)
John Chesley (Chistley)
Wm. Conn
Isaac David
Henry Dick
Thomas Halsey (Holsey)
Chas. Henry (Kinney)
Jacobus Howe (House)
Seth Howell
John Lepper

John McCollum
Benj. Miller
Wm. Morpeth
Silas Paine
Daniel Sanford
John Simmons
David Smith
Wm. Sly
Conrad Vaults
Ephraim White
Abijah Wood
Wm. Yarinton

Fifth Company

(Benj. Walker   Captain
   A D Camp to Baron Steuben)
Thomas Hunt   Lieut.
Ephraim Woodruff   Ensign
Samuel Dodge   Sergeant
Richard Davis   Sergeant
Wm McCallister   Sergeant

Abraham Dickinson   Sergeant
John Stett   Sergeant
(James) Williamson   Sergeant
Abraham Dickinson   Sergeant
Morris Bartoo   Corporal
John Snowden   Corporal
James Camby   Corporal

Privates

Jesse Adams
Frances Aymes
Jacob Backous
David Barnhart
James Cambee
Patrick Conner
Bennet Dayton
Abraham Dickinson
Michael Franks
David Greead
James Handley   War

Wm Hill
John Jeffers
Samuel Mitchell
Stephen Plum
James Robinson
George Seeds
James Scaits
(Benj. Thompson)
Nathaniel Tompkins
James Wentworth

Sixth Company

Israel Smith   Captain
Peter Van Bunschoten   Lieut.
Joseph Morrill   Ensign
John Stett   Sergeant
Samuel Higbee   Sergeant
Jacob Squirrel   Sergeant
(Stephen Buckingham   Sergeant)

John Smith   Sergeant
Wm Putnam   Corporal
Thos Jackson   Corporal
Nathan Cook   Corporal
George Gooding   Corporal
   (Godwin, Goodin)

Privates

James Anderson
John Brant
John Brown
Nathan Cook
Jacob Coon
Edmond Conklin
Isaac Crannet
Wm Dickson
John Erwin
George Gooding (Goodwin, Goodin)
Samuel Hosport
Henry Hyser
Thomas Jackson

Richard Livingston
Michael Lusk
David Moss
Wm Plumley
Simon Roe
Wm Ross
Jeremiah Scantland
John Smith
George Speed
Henry Speed
John White
Walter Willson
John Wood
Davis Worden

Seventh Company

Jonathan Titus   Captain
Abraham Hyatt   1st Lieut.
John Barr   Sergeant
Josiah Smith   Sergeant (see 9th Co.)
John Holly   Sergeant
Selah Brush   Sergeant
Timothy Bennett   Sergeant

Selah Brush   Corporal
John Howe   Corporal
Archd Cunningham   Corporal
Robert Kelly   Corporal
David Tumond   Drummer
Jesse Penoyer   Fifer (later Fife
   Major)

Privates

- Jonathan Armstrong
- Peirce Baker
- Jonathan Barker
- Jacob Bennett
- Timothy Bennett
- Richard Black
- (William Black)
- George Cooke
- Archd Cunningham
- (Gershom Curwin)
- Archd. Elliott
- Christn M. Fitzgerald
- David Gee
- Ezekiel Gee
- John Grainger
- Benjamin Hunter
- Zachariah Hawkins
- Eben James
- Robt Kelly
- Hosea Lines
- Jacob Reader
- James Reynolds
- (John Shevalier)
- (Gershom Smith)
- Jacob Spicer
- David Stratton
- Jonathan Titus
- John Tuby (Tubec, Tubu)
- Peter Tumand
- (Wm Whitehead)
- Stephen Wickham

( ) means absent because sick, on command, etc.

Eighth Company

- Nathaniel Norton   Captain
- Rudolph Van Hoevenburgh   Lieut.
- Stephen Griffin   Sergeant
- John Ellis   Sergeant
- Thomas Glover   Sergeant
- George Norton   Sergeant
- James Munday   Corporal
- John Ludlum   Corporal
- Asa West   Corporal
- Jno V. North   Drummer
- Jno M. Charlesworth   Fifer

Privates

- Cornels Ammerman
- Anthy Baker
- Stephen Benjamin
- Andw Bodley
- Menj Bogurdus
- John Canaday
- Abraham Cole
- John Curby
- Edward Curwine
- Mydert Dennis
- Saml Duall
- Jesse Gardner
- Christn Gundmyer
- Sam'l Holly
- John Huges
- John Lawrence
- Wm Lee
- Wm Linch
- Jacob Lusk
- John McDole
- Wm McIntosh
- Jack Miller
- George Morton
- Ebnezer Parker

Wm Potter
Nathan Reives
Henry Scott
Ebner B. Smith
Moses Snakeker
Henry Stringham

John Tay
John Weaver
John Williams
Saml Winchell
Elezer Yeomans

Ninth Company

Theodosius Fowler   Captain
James Barrett   Lieut.
Azariah Tuthill   Ensign
James Parshall   Sergeant
Thomas Pollard   Sergeant

Josiah Smith   Sergeant (From 7th Co.)
Andrew Rose   Corporal
Thos. Denniston   Corporal
Cato (Moulton)   Drummer
Aaron Day   Fifer

Privates

Wm Barnham (Burnham)
Jasper Blank
Francis Bredine (Budine)
Edward Collins
Obadiah Cook
Richard Cotteral
Simon Cox
Thomas Dennison
Anthony De Rouste
John Dunnivan
James Gillespie (Glasby)
Thomas Holmes
Samuel Johnson
William Johnson
Thomas Jones
Dennis Kelly

Edward Leonard
James Moody (Moddy)
Joseph Paul
Alexander Ritchie
James Robertson
Benjamin Roome
George St. Lawrence
John Sanford
Joshua Simmons
Barent Sitzer
Timothy Smalley
Adam Stagg
Joseph Welsh
John Wheeler
Jacob Whitney

FIFTH NEW YORK REGIMENT

Composite Evidence of Published Sources

Previous to the review of 1779 musters we used

A. Saffell, WT. R. Records of the Revolutionary War
   ...N.Y. 1858, pp. 161-168.
B. Fernow, B. Archives of N.Y. 1887, pp. 220-233
C. Greenough's Roster.
D. Journals, Orderly Books.
E. Calendar of N.Y. Mss.
F. Petition to legislature of N.Y. by some officers of N.Y. in 1779.
G. Clinton Papers V, 340, 367, 705.
H. Bleeker's Order Book.
I. Colls. N.Y. Hist. Soc. 1915; 474-483.

In Dec. 1779 Steuben writes "In this regiment there are six companies without any officer. A great number of men in this regiment appear to have been improperly absent a considerable time ...."

Strangely enough there is in Conover's (1887) Centennial volume not one journal from any one of this regiment and we do not recall in recent published journals any such account from this regiment. This lack, however, is more than overcome by Lieutenant and Paymaster Michael Connelly's great contribution. To him fell the task of preparing the lists of N.Y. line soldiers entitled to lands in the New York Military Tract with its townships classically named. This list is the Balloting Book.

To this regiment may be assigned some of the credit of Captain Leonard Bleecker, a Brigade Major and Inspector on this trip. His Order Book published in 1865 is an important contribution to the record of the Sullivan Expedition. True Bleecker was 2nd Lieutenant in the 1st New York line in 1775, but in 8th Co., 3rd New York regiment in 1776 per Archives (p. 207). Nevertheless in 1777 he appears as Captain of the 2nd Company in the 5th New York Regiment.

<u>Muster Rolls of 1779</u> - Again the Adjutant General's Office with April, May, June - September 1779 rolls and other evidence emboldens us to make this roster.

The May 1779 has this officer roll:

Lewis Dubois Colonel	Henry Van Denburgh Lieut.
Henry Dodge Adjutant	Henry Dodge Lieut.
Michael Connelly Paymaster	Michael Connally Lieut.
Samuel Cook Surgeon	Samuel English Lieut.
Ebenezer Hutchinson Surgeon Mate	John Furman Lieut.
James Rosekrans Captain	James Betts Lieut.
Philip D. Bevier Captain	Daniel Berdsall 2nd Lieut.
James Stuart Captain	Samuel Cook Ensign
John F. Hamshanck Captain	Bart Van Denburgh Ensign
John Johnson Captain	John Johnston Ensign
Henry Dubois Captain Lieut.	

Remember that the Lt. Col., Major, Quartermaster, 2 Captains, 3 Lieutenants, and 2 Ensigns were taken prisoners Oct. 6, 1777.

Corrections or additions to Greenough's Roster:

1. Francis Hammer absent sick at New Windsor.
2. Add 1st Lieut. Samuel English.
3. Add Ensign James Johnston.
4. Add Henry Van Den Burgh 1st not 2nd Lieut.

He gives the same as we do except for the above list.

5th New York Regiment

First Company

(Thomas Lee's Co.)
(8th Co. N. Y. Archives)
(5th Co. Saffell)

Lewis Dubois Colonel	Richard Hawkey Sergeant
Henry Dubois Capt. Lieut.	Cornelius Van DenMark Sergeant
Abraham Ferdon Sergeant Major	Francis Vantine Corporal
James Hannah Quartermaster Sergeant	Nathaniel Bonker Corporal
Joseph Glisson Drum Major	Lemuel (Samuel) Howell Corpl.
Abraham Godwin Fife Major	John Frymire Drummer
Isaac Lent Sergeant	Elijah Parker Fifer

Privates

Adam Brannon
(Jeremiah Briggs)
Josiah Bugbey
John Coleman
Samuel Currin
Michael Given
Samuel Goslin
Hezekiah Gregg
Henry Hawkey
Silas Hortain
John Hosier
Joseph Jones
Con Keef
Wm. Laon
Wm. Lawrence
John Lockwood
Ebenezer Louders
John McClamon
Robert Neuson
Jonathan Newman
Jacob Ransom
Matthias Randle
Daniel Robinson
Henry Scouten
Ezekiel Simmons
Abraham Slutt
Mervel Slutt
Wm Slutt
Peter Snyder
Seth Sprage
James Steel
Henry Strate
Wm. Strate
John Talleday
Isaac Vantine
Robert Vantine
Joseph Verrien
Edmond Warner
Samuel Weed
John Whitehead
Isaac Williams
James Wood

Second Company

(Lt. Colonel's Company)

Henry Van DeBurgh   Lieutenant
James Pride   Sergeant
Seth Stalker   Sergeant   reduced
  July 1, 1779
Cornelius Ackerson   Sergeant July 1779
James Robinson   Sergeant June 23, 1779

Cornelius Acker (Ackerson)   Corpl.
John Wilson   Corporal
John Allison (Ellison) Jr.   Corpl.
(Jasper Allen   Drummer)
John Factor   Fifer and Drummer

Privates

John Allison (Ellison)
Lawrence Bunker
Richard Cooper
Joseph Jones
Thomas Jones
Amos Kniffen (Sniffen)
Samuel Langdon
Benj. Lattimore

Roger Lattimore
George Marks
Francis McDermott
Philip Richards
John Rhodes
Francis Secus
John Secore

Joseph TenEyck
James Titus
Scott Travis
Melatiah Wilks
John Wills (Willis)
Peter Wills

Third Company

(Major's Co.)

(Samuel Logan Major Prisoner)
Henry Dodge Lieutenant
Bartholomew Van DeBergh Ensign
Wessel D. Dickinson Sergeant
   Reduced May 1, 1779
John Ferdon Sergeant

Levi Watson Sergeant
James T. Taller Sergeant
Joseph Cass Corporal
Bathnel Bonker Corporal July 1, 1779
Jonathan Oakley Corporal July 1, 1779
Griffen Jones Drummer
(Richard Dodge Fifer)

Privates

(Nicholas Avery)
Wm. Barkens
Amos Beach
(Ambrose Benedict)
John Bonker
John Cain
Wessel Dickerson
Jacob Eakley
(James Ferguson)
Thomas Gready
Christopher Harter (Hearty)
Henry House
Wm. Hughes
Prince Johnson
Daniel Loder

Jonathan Oakley
Thomas Palmerton
(John Pepper)
Gilbert Prichards (Richard)
Jonathan Rose (Roase)
James Russell
John Springstone
George Thomas
James Thornton
Vincent Vanny
Johanniah (Johanical) Weaver
Samuel Wheeler
Stephen Wheeler
Ichabod Wilbur
Jacob Wilbur

Fourth Company

James Rosekrans Captain
(5 officers - H. Dodge, R. Dodge,
  H. Pawling, H. Swartout, and
  J. McClaughry prisoners)
John Christy Sergeant
Eleazer Lucy Sergeant

Wm. Russell Sergeant
Wm. Walcott (Woolcut) Corporal
Isaac Ter Boss Corporal
John Jee or Gee Corporal
David Phillips Drummer
Griffin Jones Drummer Sept. 1779

Privates

Geo. Boulton
Jeremiah Bundy
Samuel Davis
Christopher Decker
Martin Decker
Wm. Frost
John Gibbons
Caleb Glean
Nathaniel Hollister
John Holly
Joseph Johnson
Griffin Jones
Evert Letz
John Lounsbury
Wm. Mullen
Wm. Niven (Kniver)
Kinner Newcomb

Henry Ostrander
Thomas Patterson
John Pulis
Timothy Riden
George Robinson
Wm. Russell
Harmanus Springsteen
John Storm
George Tenegar (Finegar)
John Thayer
Gilbert Utter
Isaac Utter Sen.
Isaac Utter Jun.
Matthew Van Gelder
Peter Vermiliar
Robert Waddell

Fifth Company

Philip Dubois Bevier   Captain
Michael Connoly   Lieutenant
(Ebenezer Mott   Lieutenant   prisoner)
David Birdsall   2nd Lieutenant
   (see 7th Co.)
Ebenezer Burnett   Sergeant
Henry Hornbeck   Sergeant
Jasper Pryor   Sergeant
James Robertson   Sergeant

(James Hanna)   Sergeant
Joseph Case   Corporal to Aug. 1, 1779
Nathan Tupper   Corporal
Wm. Pembroke   Corporal
James Peresonus   Corporal
(Jno. Hissam)   Corporal
   (see Capt. I Smith's Co.)
Wm. Whitehead   Drummer
Wm. Cooke   Fifer

Privates

Jonas Bartow
John Blaws
William Bloomer
Elisha Burdett
Nehemiah Cheshire
Martinus Claywater
Jacob Cline
Asa Crawford
Isaac Danielson
Moses Dimond
Wm. Dimond
Patrick Durgan

Daniel Flanagan
John Fulton
Andries Gardiner
Gideon Goodspeed
David Gregg
George Hallett
Solomon Hallett
Caleb Jewett
William Jackson
Thomas Kent
Nehemiah Kniffen
Andrew Kyser

John Kyser
John McAnarney
Joseph Mitchell
Abraham Oakey
Daniel Osten (Osburn)
Jonathan Penny
Joshua Phillips
Abraham Quick
Wm. Risten
Wm. Russell
Thomas Shirley (Shiskey, Sharkey)
George Shaffer
Markom Shay
Evert Slouter

David Smith Jun.
David Smith Senr.
Jesse Smith
Samuel Smith
Thomas Stanley
Solomon Tallady
Peter Tilton
Samuel Townsend
Abraham Traverse
Joshua Tucker
Gilbert VandeMark
Samuel Walker
Abraham Wilson

Sixth Company

James Stewart   Captain
John Lovett   Sergeant
John West   Sergeant
James Mitchell   Sergeant   (Nov. 9, 1779)

James Mitchell   Corporal
James Keeler   Corporal
John Albright   Corporal

Privates

John Albright
James Ammerman
(Walter (Wm) Brooks (Brooker))
(John Brown)
Daniel Carrigan
Wm. Carrigan
Conrad Cunite (Connight)
(Thos. Fitzgerald)
Wm. Fitzgerald
James Gillespie
Geo. Hausbrook (Holbrook)
Samuel Hopper
James Humphrey
Thomas Jones

(Abm. Kipp (Hepp))
Wm. Kipp
Jacob Lawrence
Robert Marshall
Daniel Morrison
Patrick Morrison (Morrow)
John Reed
Robert Robinson
Thomas Russell
Isaac Sampson
Thos. Smalley
Joseph Smith
Geo. Springstin (Springstead)
John Stump

Seventh Company

(Henry Godwin   Captain   Prisoner)
Samuel English   1st Lieut.
Dan Birdsell   2nd Lieut.
Joseph Morgan   Sergeant
Jonathan (James) Baylis (Bailey)   Sergt.
Henry Schoonmaker   Sergeant

Jacob Roosa (Rose)   Sergeant
John Christy   Corporal
Joseph Anderson   Corporal
Daniel Johnson   Corporal
David Godwin   Drummer
Lewis Dickson   Fifer

Privates

Stephen Albertson
Holmes Austin   (see Hamtranck's Co.)
Lemuel Bartlett
Michael Burghes (Burdje)
Jacob Craft
Prince Danford
Abraham Delancey
Nathaniel Dubois
Sutten Green

Peter Holmes
Wm. Mooney
Jeremiah Simpkins
Richard Stevens
Jacobus Terwilliger
Elias Thompson
Jacobus Van Gelder
Frederick Wemire

Eighth Company

John F. Hamtranck   Captain
Benjamin Lawrence   Sergeant
Alexander Humphrey   Sergeant
Wm. Barkens (Barker)   Sergeant May 1, 1779
Moses Gee   Corporal May 1, 1779

John Hasam   Corporal May 1, 1779
John Wandle   Corporal
John Ross   Drummer
Thomas Russell   Fifer

Privates

Nicholas Avory
Wm. Barker (Barkens)
John Battersby
Sibra (Libra) Battles
Russell Brockaway
Matthew Cain (Carm)
Joseph Carby (Carley)
John Clinton (Clintardt)
John Cornelius (Cornwell)
Martin Cort
Ebenezer Cummins
Ebenezer Curtis

Frederick Dann
Gideon Dickenson
Hezekiah Dibble
Silas Filmore
John Fluno
Moses Gee
Seth Gilbert
John Hains
John Hasam
Peter Havens (Heavens)
Wansex Hendricks
Philip Holmes

Isaac Lawraway
Elisha Millard
Henry Millard
Josiah Richmond
John Rippley
Jacob Ritterman
Sylvester Rylie
(Abraham Size)
Jonathan Skinner

James Slaven
(John Sutcliff)
Jacob Swiss
Obadiah Thorn
Peter Tofet
John Vallarey
(Joseph Van Ote (Ort, Nort))
James Wasson
John Woodward

Ninth Company

John Johnson   Captain
James Betts   Lieutenant
James Johnston Ensign
John Chamberlain   Sergeant
Henry Schoonmaker Sergeant
Wm. Willis   Sergeant

Samuel Combs   Corporal
Peter Combs   Corporal
Joseph Bouton Corporal
James Ransom   Fifer
Joshua Hunt   Drummer

Privates

Holmes Austin
James Betts
Jas Bishop
Lemuel Chapman
John Combs
Lemuel Crosby
Amos Denton
Vulker Dow
Zebry Fish
Michael Fowler
Joshua Griffin
John Hendrickson
Wm. Johnson
John McClare (McClean)
Wm. Nankerson

Wm. Nelson
John Nichols
John Peck
Jeremiah Rickey
Abrm Shear
Nehemiah Sherridon
John Slouyler
Abner Smith
Reuben Smith
Thos. Smith
Elijah Stanbury
Garret Vn Nooser
Jacob West
Richard Williams

2ND NEW YORK ARTILLERY

(Col. John Lamb's Regiment)

On this expedition at first we were puzzled to know how many of Lamb's forces were on the trip. From a study of the published journals and orderly books of the expedition (J.O.) we provisionally constructed three companies which must have been on the trip. They were:

1. Isaac Wool, Captain
1. Elisha Harvey, 2nd Lieutenant

2. Thomas Machin, Capt. Lieut.
2. Wm. Cebra, 2nd Lieut.
2. Thomas E. Gee, Sergeant

3. Andrew Porter, Captain
3. Jas. McClure, Capt. Lieut.
3. Ezra Patterson, 2nd Lieut.
3. Ezekial Howell, 2nd Lieut.
3. Robert Parker, 2nd Lieut. and Paymaster

Early we noted that Robert Parker (1929 p. 188) says in his first sentence that he marched with Capt. Wool's, Bliss's and Porter Companies of Artillery. Then we noted that _probably_ only these three companies were on the trip.

At this writing (June 26, 1948) we have worked on the rich collection of orderly books of the New York Historical Society wherein are a fine series of Lamb Orderly books.

From a few of these books we have

1. Sept. 26 - Nov. 27, 1778 Book

    Oct. 20, 1778 Lt. Cebra of Capt. Brown's Co. to join Capt. Bliss.

2. Nov. 30, 1778 - Feb. 4, 1779

3. Feb. 5 - May 30, 1779

4. June 14 - Aug. 19, 1779

    Camp near Chester with only Capts. Doughty, Fleming, Lee and Brown present.

5. Orderly Book (date unnoted by me)

    On Sept. 24, 1779 the monthly return of the five companies commanded by Col. Lamb were Capts. Lee, Doughty, Mott, Walker and Brown. But on Nov. 26, 1779 we have the significant "Monthly Returns of seven companies in the 2nd regiment of Artillery in Service of United States command by John Lamb. Esqu. with the Alterns since last Return" wherein the 157 men of the last return were supplemented by 65 joined from Wool, Bliss and Porter companies. This significant return of Nov. 26, 1779 on its end has "Last Return 159, Joined 65 ... Remarks Capts. Wool, Bliss and Porter companies joined - Capt. Lee resigned ...

2nd New York Artillery

(Capt. Porter's Company)

I. Published Sources

From Flick's The Sullivan-Clinton Campaign, 1929, pp. 191-192 or Penn. Mag. Hist. and Biog., Vol. 27, we have Robert Parker's payroll:

    Andrew Porter, Captain
    Jas. McClure, Captain Lieutenant
    Ezra Patterson, 2nd Lieutenant
    Ezekiel Howell, 2nd Lieutenant
    Robert Parker, 2nd Lieutenant and Paymaster
    Michal Royall, Sergeant (Koyal, Kyell)
    Archd McFair (McNair), Sergeant
    John McGregor, Sergeant (Abraham or Archibald)
    John Kelly, Bombardier
    John Johnston, Bombardier
    Arthur Gillas
    George Stewart, Matross
    Samuel Laughlan, Matross
    Zac Bennington, Matross (Job or John)
    Jas. (John) Rayburn (Ryburn), Matross
    John Marks, Matross
    Robert Jeff (Jelf), Matross
    Alex Martin, Matross
    Reuben Benson (Benjon), Matross
    Benjamin Phipps, Matross
    James Wilson, Matross
    John Dunn, Matross

See Penn. Archives 2nd Ser. XI, pp. 191-192 for 1778 and muster roll of June - Sept. 1779 (A.G.O. 47 - 1 Item 22). The first five officers are mentioned in Journals, orderly books, etc. (J.O.) not considering Parker's Journal. The A.G.O. 47 - 1 Item 22 muster roll has the same names as the above list.

2nd New York Artillery

(Capt. Bliss's and Capt. Lieut. Machin's Co.)

I. Published Sources

From the Machin - Doughty Return Aug. 28, 1779 (New York Col. Hist. Mss. Rev. Albany 1868 II, p. 338) we have the roster of this company on this trip. (It is part of the petition of Capt. Jno. Doughty).

Thomas Machin, Capt. Lieutenant
Wm. Cebra, 2nd Lieutenant
Thos. E. Gee, Sergeant
John Bichaman (Buchanan), Sergeant
Joseph Holstead (Halstead), Sergeant
James McBride (McGuffie), Sergeant
Andrew Sherwood, Sergeant
Daniel Thorne, Corporal
Wm. McBride, Corporal
Peter States, Bombardier
John Murphy, Bombardier
George Clark, Gunner
John Cunningham, Gunner
Wm. Ackerman (Ockemann), Matross
Samuel Woodruff, Matross
Israel Colman (Coleman), Matross
James Whitmore, Matross
Jeremiah Rundel (Randell), Matross
John Nelson, Matross
Benj. Gobell, Matross
Joseph Gobell, Matross
Weight Smith, Matross
James Moore, Matross
John Clark, Matross
Achbil Deen, Matross
Jonathan White, Matross
Amos Whittemore, Matross
Richard McCune, Matross
Hugh Waterson, Matross
Richard Smith, Matross
Oliver Hardin, Matross
Thomas Thorp, Matross

See a muster roll of Capt. Theodore Bliss Company in the Regiment of Artillery in the Service ... June, July, August and Sept. 1779 (A.G.O. 39 - 1 Item 107) and payroll Aug. 1779.

Appointed	Sergeants	Term	Remarks
	Thomas Gee		
	John Buchannan	3 yrs.	
	Joseph Halstead	3 yrs.	
	James McBride		On Command at Albany

	Corporals		
	Daniel Thorne	3 yrs.	
	William McBride		

	Bombardiers		
	Peter States	3 yrs.	
	John Murphy		

	Gunners		
	Georg Clarke		
	John Cunningham		

	Mattrosses		
	John Clark		
	Israel Colmen		
	Ashbel Dean		
	Benjamin Gable		
	Joseph Gable	3 yrs.	On Command in Albany
	James More		
	John Nelson		
	William Ockerman (Ockamin)		
	Jeremiah Randle		
	Wright Smith		On Command in Albany
	Thomas Thorpe (Tharp)		On Command in Whyimoy
	Jonathan White	3 yrs.	
	James Whitmore		

(Capt. Wool's Co.)

(Company 6 in Saffell's List)

I. Published Sources

Isaac Wool Captain	Wm. Beacon Matross
Elisha Harvey 2nd Lieut.	James Silvia Matross
Amonah (Amoreah) Vose Sergeant	Cornelius Stagg Matross
Samuel Parsons (Rearsons) Sergeant	Thomas Shullian Matross
Wm. Thomson (Thompson) Gunner	Ames Eastwood Matross
John Day Matross	Hugh Carr Matross

II. Different Lists

The above list is the Harvey-Doughty return of Apr. 20, 1779 in Capt. Doughty's petition. (Cal. Mss. Vol. II, 1868, p. 337). From the Archives of the State of New York Revolution Vol. I we secure the same list. Saffell (1858, p. 175) for Jan. 1, 1777 - Mar. 4, 1779 has the same list with these exceptions: Isaac Wool as Josiah Wool; Samuel Parsons as Pearsons and a gunner; Cornelius Stagg a Sergeant; Hugh Carr as absent; and Capt. Lieut. Wm. Stevens as present. In a list of Nov. 26, 1779 a corporal is given and Isaac Wool and Elisha Harvey are mentioned in Journals (J.O.).

See muster roll of Capt. Isaiah Wool Company in the regiment of artillery ... June, July, August and Sept. 1779 (A.G.O. 49 - 1 Item 13 or 212) also payrolls May 1779, June - Sept., 1779.

ARMAND'S LEGION

The nearest approach to the complexion of this legion at Wyoming comes in A.G.O. 16-1 - five muster rolls are especially pertinent.

A.G.O. 16-1

a. Of the Field Staff and Commissioned Officers of Colonel Armand's Independent Corps taken for the month of August 1779.

Date of Commission	Names	Rank	Remarks
1777 May 1st	Armand	Colonel	
1778 Apr. 11	John Lomogne	Major	
	J. W. Ludeman	Adjutant	
1778 Apr. 1st	Henry Ridel	Quartermaster	Sent to Boston
	Fredrik Ramke	1st Doctor	
	Gelliel Morritz	Mate	

Company of Light Dragoons

1778 Feb. 8	Charles Markle	Captain	
1778 Feb. 10	John Scharp	Lieutenant	

1st Compagnie

1778 Feb. 8	George Schaffner	Captain	
1778 July 1	F. Seguern	Lieutenant	

2nd Company

1778 Feb. 2	L. Sigougne	Captain	
1779 Feb. 6	A. Cicaty	Lieutenant	On command Boston
1779 Jan. 13	H. Ridel	Ensign	Acting Qr.M.

3rd Company

1778 June 8	Claudius deBert	Captain	
	F. W. Ludeman	Lieutenant	Acting as Adjutant

Cantito, Sept. 6, 1779

Henry Rogers
De Comy Genl Musters

b. A Muster Roll of Captain Carl Marckle Troop of Light Dragoons in the service ... November, December 1778 and January, February, March, April, May and June 1779.

Commissioned (the 8th of February Carl Marckle, Captain
           (the 10th of February 1777 John Sharp, Lieutenant

Sergeants

John Breymann
Carl Foehr, Died the 5 of July 1779
   Quarter Master Sergeant
Henry Becker (Beeker)
   Voluntairs
Chevallier De Bouveulle
Chevallier De Vaudore

Corporals

John Eidke, Reduced to Infantry July 1, 1779
Frederick Salkman
1779 Apr. 22 Martinus Lambla
   Trompeter
Georg Schemers
   Farrier
Henry Fruhling

Dragoons

1779 Apr. 9 Francois Grumout
    Mar. 29 Henry Deneoke
1778 June 11 Philip Eickhorn 3 yrs.
1779 Apr. 9 Jean Fresinar
1779 Apr. 22 Drury Fairbanck Sick in hospital
    Mar. 31 Henry Permen
    Feb. 15 Richard Gardener
    Apr. 5 Joseph Gaudart
    Mar. 21 John Hartjean
    Mar. 21 Conrad Hartmann
    Mar. 16 Wilhelm Helmithorf
    John Harboidt
    Feb. 15 John Homer deserted the 30th June 1779

Dragoons

1779 Apr. 16 Charles Laevur
    Theodeus Meisner
    Apr. 2 Louis Nette
    Apr. 15 Leger Poupon
    Mar. 21 John Reckan
    Frederick Seilecker 3 yrs.
    Frederick Smith
    John Taeger
1779 Mar. 24 Joseph Voinnards
    Feb. 15 Thomas Williams
    Apr. 20 James Wright

Wapping Creek, July 18, 1779

16-1C. A Muster Roll of Captain George Schaffner Chasser Company ... August 1779

Commissioned) the 8th of Febry 1778 George Schaffner, Captain
)
) the 1st July Frederick Segernz, 1st Lieut.

Drum Major
Cristian Findling

Fife Major
Peter Schameau

Sergeant Major
1778 Aug. Abraham Coflet 3 yrs.

Corporals
1778 Apr. 5 Henry Oppenhauser 3 yrs.
    John Helsele

Sergeants
Henry Timme
Albertus Kertel

Drummer
May 14 Martien Breitscher 3 yrs.

Privates
John Adam
Daal Burckhart
Henry Becker
Apr. 18 Henry Boeliger 3 yrs.
    Wentel Bock
    August Blumenberg
    John Drecksler
    Philip Deimer
July 7 Henry Egling 3 yrs. on Duty
Apr. 18 Henry Enttron 3 yrs.
    John Fricker
    Carll Frede
June 10 Henry Fricke 3 yrs.
    Christoph Hogsenbein
    John Huebe On Duty
    John Hopff
    John Henricks On duty
July 14 Gotlieb Lock 3 yrs.
    Henry Neuhoff
Cantito, Sept. 6, 1779

May 25 Henry Aist 3 yrs. On Duty
    Anton Wolff

14 Fife
John Schramme 3 yrs.

Privates
May 13 Rudolph Prosch 3 yrs.
May 29 Christoph Kollee 3 yrs.
    Anton Rovet On duty
    Ludewig Schelle 3 yrs.
May 10 John Schindler 3 yrs.
Appl 19 Gotlieb Stickhan 3 yrs.
Appl 18 Anton Stademan 3 yrs.
Appl 11 Henry Ulrig 3 yrs.
    John Voges 3 yrs.
June 10 Christian Verdrius 3 yrs.
July 27 Henry Voges 3 yrs. On duty
July 27 Henry Weseman 3 yrs.
May 14 John Zimmerman 3 yrs.
Aug. 20 Allosius Castor enlisted
    3 Sept 1779
Sept. 1 Henry Henneg enlisted Aug. 20, 1779
Sept. 1 Gotfried Holle enlisted
    Sept. 1, 1779
Sept. 5 Albrecht Willet enlisted
    Sept. 5, 1779

Henry Rutgers D.C. Gen. Musters

d. 16-1 A Muster Roll of Capt. Louis de Sigougne Company of ... August 1779

Feb. 9, 1778 Louis de Sigougne, Capt.

Commissioned Jan. 13, 1779 Augustin Buffant, Lieut.
              Jan. 6, 1779 Augustin de Cicaty, Lieut.
              Apr. 1, 1778 Henry Ridel, Enseigner

Sergeants
Noel du Moulin On Duty appointed
    1778, May 18
Claude Autorielli

Drummer
Jain Oliber

Corporals
Julin Augustus
Louis Curtis On Duty
Jean Quick

Fifre
Yulliams Potter

Privates
- Adriam Sambert
- Augustus frigot
- August delorme
- Guillam Tomm
- Guillam Variere
- Jean izzunus
- Oliver Hart
- --- Hall
- echard Suertity
- Jean vaille
- Jean Betz
- Jean Dennis
- Janes Pritimalan On Duty
- Jean Ellit
- Jean Frume
- Pussuy Duiore
- Jean ---
- Jean Cornel

Privates
- Jain gaintin
- Louis Kurtel
- Maturin duchesse
- Nicolas LeMay bridgear
- Nicola Shubert
- junnis Puicrel On Duty
- Jammis Bazur On Duty
- Weathetius alillins On duty
- Wilhm Job On duty
- Paul duzzuis
- Martin Bernard
- francois Tubert
- William Latta or Lottre On Duty
- hugh King
- hugh hunteley confint in Boston

Cantito Septemt the 6th ... the Capt. Louis Du Signongie Company specified in the above Roll.

Henry Rutgers
De Comy Genl Musters

The National Archives War Department Collection of Revolutionary War Records kindly made for us a photostat of this faded muster. After considerable effort we have attempted an approach to the names given on the roll. The roll is evidently not made by an American and no doubt we have made many mistakes. We had no other lists of Sigougne's Company and fear that most of the names are awry and that they should bear a (?).

e. 16-1 A Muster Roll of Capt. Claudius de Bert Compagnie of the Independent Corps in ... Mar., April, May, June 1779.

Commissioned (June the 7th 78 Claudius de Bert Capitan
(
(January the 6th 79 Berrauch de Cicaty Lieutenant

Appointed

1778   Sergeants

May 12th Diederich Grieseckus
July 12th August Fricke
         Heinrith Fiedler
           deserted May 18, 1779
         John Majer

Corporals

Apr. 23 Ludwig Knieren
May 24 August Meissner
        Adam Eckert
        David Grosse

Drumm.
Ludwig Hagemann

Fife
May 19 John Braase

1778   Privates

Conrad Brandes Deserted Apr. 9,1779
Conrad Bollman   ) On Command at
John Dollenburg   ) Headqrtrs. Calla
Friedrith Drexell) Gonivion of the
                      Mgeniers
Anton Haase
May 13th Matthias Haupt Three years
Apr. 6th Jacob Heinrichs 3 yrs.
     Fredrick Herzberg

May 22 Wilhelm Hirschelman 3 yrs.
       Philip Hall
May 22 Heinrich Huchtausa 3 yrs.
July 28 Philip Schaitner 3 yrs.
Apr. 13 Diedrich Schmidt 3 yrs.
Apr. 19 Heinrich Schmidt 3 yrs.
       Niclaus Schrampf
May 14 Frederick Vetter 3 yrs.

Wyoming July 1, 1779

Nehh. Wade D.C.M.*

Present 1 Capt. 1 Lieut. 3 Sergt. 4 Corp. 1 Drum. 1 Fife 13 Priv.

At Penn Archives, Harrisburg, we found a "General Return of the First Partisan Legion Commanded by Colonel Armand Marquis De La Roueve with alterations that happened from Jan. 1 to July 1, 1782." It is a complete list of 6 troops but there is no indication of Schott's or Selin's groups in it.

"Orderly Book June 6-July 7, 1779 Smith's Cove Headquarters July 6, 1779. A Court of Inquiry to be held tomorrow morning at 9 o'clock at the Tavern in New Windsor, the nearest to Head Quarters, to enquire into some Complaints, exhibited against Colonel Armand by Colonel James Van Denbergh of the Militia, and James Adams, both of this State, the Court will report a state of facts to the commander in Chief and their opinion of the merits of the Complaints. The court will consist of Col. Clark, Lt. Col. Brooks, Lt. Colonel Flurey, Lt. Colonel North, Major Des Espenier."

COMMENTS

I. Those with a page number were on the trip.

II. Over 7,000 names are given in the Index yet on page 4 we call the Sullivan forces slightly above 6,000.

    A. In many instances a man's name appears in three or four different forms. Many of these variants are given.

    B. Only one of a name appears, yet for John Brown there were 10 or more different individuals - John Jones 5 different persons - John Smith 9 different persons. Many were 2 or 3 - like the 2 John Whites.

    C. On musters a person's name may appear in two different ways - rarely three names for one person. In this way we counted 145 names or about 350 persons involved.
        For example - Morris Ader appears as
                Morris Akers

                or

                an Erwin may also be
                called Ewing.
Even very divergent names might be applied to one person.

    D. Names without a page number.
This index of this huge army made at several different periods and at this setting some 5 or 6 surveys of it were made by the 86 year old. After the 6th effort we found 186 names without a page number. The index was gone over a 7th time and 94 pages found. I'm satisfied without question that the 92 without pages indicated were on the trip or appeared in some muster I saw from Concord, New Hampshire to Washington, D.C.

    E. The 1,142 paged manuscript on which this is based will be placed in Cornell University's Library and the carbon copy either in Washington or some other suitable place for future scholars.

INDEX

Abbey, Samuel, 116
    Zabes, 10
Abbott, Cato, 41
    George, 58
    Peter, 67, 71
    Richard, 18
    Stephen, 48
Able, John, 88, 89
Abraham, David, 53
Acker, Albert, 118
    Conrad, 118
    Cornelius, 129
Ackerman, William, 137
Ackerson, Cornelius, 129
Ackley, John, 39
Adam, John, 142
    William, 95
    Capt, 73
Adams, Aaron, 50
    Abel, 24
    David, 48
    Henry, 116
    Isaac, 48
    Jacob, 12
    James, 144
    Jedediah, 40
    Jesse, 123
    John, 72, 102
    Jonas, 53
    Joseph, 99
    Levi, 53
    Paleg, 110
    Samuel, 56, 58
    William, 116
    Winaborn, 56
Ader, Morris, 15
Adition, Consider, 19
Adler, S.S., 1
Adomy, Henry, 116
Agar, Hugh, 26
Aiken, Samuel, 52
Aine, Frank, 41
Aire, Frederick, 41
Aires, Frederick, 41
Aist, Henry, 142
Akers, Amos, 21
Akess, Morris, 15
Albertson, Stephen, 133
Albright, Jacob, 108
    John, 132
Alden, Ichabod, 38
    Mason F., 103
Aldrich, George, 56, 57
Aldridge, Caleb, 70
Alexander, Jacob, 88, 89, 90
    John, 84, 85, 89
    Joseph, 91
Alillins, Weathetius, 143
Allard, James, 68
    Noah, 58

Allds, John, 50
Allen, Benjamin, 33
    Jacob, 32
    James, 82
    John, 34, 40, 48, 82, 84, 85, 101
    Joseph, 40
    Samuel, 54, 51
    Thomas, 113
Alley, Daniel, 62
Allison, Benjamin, 34
    David, 100, 101
    James, 34
    John, 72, 73, 129
    John Jr., 129
    Joseph, 36
    Powell, 10
    Robert, 78
Allman, Lawrence, 95, 96
Alloon, Christian, 118
Altmire, John, 90
Aman, Charles, 27
Ambler, Nathaniel, 117
Ames, Edward, 68
    Ephraim, 43
    John, 21
Amesburg, Amos, 102
Ammerman, Cornels, 125
    James, 132
Amy, David, 18
    Herman, 66
Anderson, Andrew, 27
    Daries, 28
    Elijah, 5
    Ezekeel, 115
    George, 115
    James, 124
    Joseph, 23, 28
    Samuel, 13
    William, 15, 27
Andrews, Ammie, 67
    Joel, 53
    William, 24
Anson, James, 36
Anthony, Daniel, 86
    Henry, 96
    John, 112
    Peter, 112
Antis, Henry, 2, 5
Antram, John, 76
Antrum, John, 76
Aorson, Aaron, 114
Applegate, Benjamin, 33
    Moses, 14
Appleton, Abraham, 21
    Benjamin, 33
Armand, Charles, 102, 140
Armitage, Shubert, 95, 97
Armstrong, ____, 2
    Amos, 103

Armstrong, con't.
    Archibald, 110
    John, 90
    Jon, 100
    Jonathan, 125
Arnold, Oliver, 109
Arrand, Levy, 88, 89
Artland, James, 68
Artwick, Lawrence, 113
Ash, Henry, 118
    John, 50
Ashby, Benjamin, 100, 101
Ashley, James, 90
    John, 39
    Michael, 80
Ashton, Israel, 80
    Thomas, 58
Astin, John, 109
Atkinson, Stephen, 60
Atwood, Benjamin, 70
Augur, Hugh, 25
Augustine, George, 10
Augustus, John, 142
Austin, David, 113
    Holmes, 133, 134
    Israel, 80
    James, 35
    John, 102
    Reuben, 71
Autorielli, Claude, 142
Averill, Elijah, 51
    George, 69
Avery, Nicholas, 130, 133
Ayres, Rheuben, 12
Ayrs, Samuel, 50

Babb, John, 61
Babcock, Joseph, 17
Backhoof, Frederick
Backous, Jacob, 123
Badeau, Charles, 9
Bagab, N
Bagley, David, 118
    Josiah, 114, 116
Bagnall, Richard, 39, 41
Bailey, Daniel, 122
    Ebenezer, 107
    John
Bakehorn, Jacob, 113
    Jeremiah, 113
Baker, Anthony, 125
    Cato, 63
    Christian, 93
    Jeremiah, 103
    John, 74, 115
    Peirce, 125
    Peter, 94
Balch, John, 70
Baldwin, Thomas, 103
    Walter, 103
    Waterman, 103

Ball, Cornelius, 37
   John, 61
   Justis, 26
   Stephen, 9
Ballard, Boston, 43
   Jeremiah, 27
   Uriah, 69
   William H., 38, 39
Baltsell, Charles, 93
Bandal, John, 29
Banghearb, Barney, 27
Bangs, Joshua, 43
Baning, Ditrich, 91
Banker, John, 43
Banks, Benjamin, 115
   Jemmerson, 27
   Joseph
Bantse, Titmos, 91
Baptiste, John, 115
Barber, Francis, 1, 23, 24, 25
   John, 82
   Stephen, 107
Barby, William, 102
Barkens, William, 130, 133
Barker, Ephraim, 44
   Jesse, 43
   John, 44, 62, 86
   Jonathan, 125
   Samuel, 68
   Stephen, 114
   William, 133
Barnes, Amos
   Henry, 155
   James, 70
   Oliver, 41
Barnett, Benjamin, 49
   Robert, 46
   William, 9
Barney, Peter, 26
Barnham, Samuel, 107
   William, 125
Barnhart, David, 123
   Jeremiah, 122
Barr, John, 81, 120, 121, 124
   William, 16
Barret, William, 21
Barrett, James, 120, 126
   William, 9, 118
Barris, James, 121
Barrons, Samuel, 52
Barrow, James, 26
Barrows, James, 121
Barter, John, 62
Bartholomew, John, 110
Bartlett, Joseph, 41
   Lemuel, 133
   Nathaniel, 48
   William, 102
Barton, John, 42
   William, 9, 12
Bartoo, Morris, 123
Bartow, Jonas, 131
Bass, Henry, 115

Batchelder, James, 67
   William, 54
Bates, Daniel, 50
   Edward, 41
   Samuel, 50
   Thomas, 50
Batling, James, 18
Battersby, John, 133
   Robert, 107
Battles, Libra, 133
Baxter, Henry, 59
   Jonathan, 20
Bayley, Stephen, 18
Baylor, Daniel
Bazur, Jammis, 143
Beach, Amos, 130
   James, 28
   Nathan, 103
   William, 31, 36
Beacon, William, 139
Beadle, John, 117
   Moses, 12
Beagle, Christian, 74
   James, 109
Beal, Thomas, 66, 71
Bean, Ebeneser, 58
   Edward, 58
   John, 67
   Josiah, 67
Beatty, Eskurias, 72
   James, 82
   Peter, 80
Beaumert, John, 118
Beayle, James, 109
Bebee, Peter, 70
Becker, Henry, 141, 142
   Henry, Jr., 76
Beckman, John, 117
Bedell, Benjamin, 15
   Jacob, 15
Bedunah, Moses, 43
Beebe, Barnafes, 122
   Boanning, 122
Beedle, John, 117
Beekman, John, 117
   Tjerck, 105, 110
Beely, Joseph, 106
Been, Henry, 76
Begert, James, 25
Beggs, John, 116
   Moore, 76
   Thomas, 76
Begun, Albert, 34
Behall, Caspar, 14
Belknap, Tomas, 41
Bell, Fred, Mt., 56
   James, 82
   John, 37
   Jno, 97
   Joshua, 14
   Josiah, 20
   Matthew, 108
   William M., 57, 63
Beltshover, Jacob, 90

Benedict, Ambrose, 130
Bengel, John, 102
Benham, Joseph, 25
Benjamin, Isaac, 103
   Jonathan, 110
   Samuel, 110
   Stephen, 125
Benjou, Reuben, 136
Benner, James, 98
   Melcher, 90
Bennet, Thomas, 19
Bennett, Charles, 103
   Henry, 116
   Isaac, 103
   Jacob, 125
   James, 98
   Jeremiah, 110
   John, 18, 64, 65, 66, 109
   Joseph, 20
   Oliver, 103
   Rufus, 103
   Samuel, 32
   Timothy, 124, 125
   William, 9
Bennington, Job, 136
   John, 136
   Zac, 135
Benson, James, 83
   Reuben, 136
Benston, Thomas, 100
Berdsall, Daniel, 108
Bereau, Peter, 24
Bergenhoff, Nicholas, 85
Berkins, John, 18
Berkstaler, Joseph, 19
Bernard, Martin, 143
   Samuel, 121
Berry, Ben, 50, 61
   Ebeneser, 52
   John, 32, 52
Berton, David, 9
   George, 117
   John, 42
Bertram, David, 10
Bertron, David, 9, 10
Bettin, Adam, 72, 76
Bettison, Naboth, 70
Betts, Arhab, 21
   James, 128, 133
Betz, Jean, 143
Bevier, Philip D., 128
   Wilder
Bevins, Matthew, 12
   Wilder, 72
Bichamon, John, 137
Bicker, Henry, Jr., 72
Bickford, Aaron, 58
   Dennis, 59
Bickner, Godeph, 291
Bijggar, Peter, 19
Billard, James, 14
Billings, Robert, 43
Bingham, Abner, 50, 51
   Ripley, 48, 51

Binnet, John, 93
Bird, William, 10
Birdsall, David, 31
    Daniel, 133
Birmingham, Daniel, 35
Bishop, Jacob, 90
    James, 134
    John, 9, 14
    William, 27
Black, David, 133
    John, 116
    Pompey, 17
    Richard, 125
    William, 125
    _____, 86
Blackston, John
Blackwood, Samuel, 16
Blain, James, 26
Blair, John, 23, 24, 71
    William, 18
Blaisdell, John, 68
Blake, Edward, 86
    Moses, 59
    Thomas, 45, 47, 49, 64

Blanchard, Jacob, 69
    James, 64, 65, 69
    Thomas, 58
Blanck, Cornelius, 115
Blank, Jasper, 126
    Justus, 126
Bearicum, Henry, 33
    James V., 119
Blasdell, Daniel, 42
Blaws, John, 131
Blaze, Christian, 122
Blazedell, Daniel, 42
    John, 58
    Philip, 62
    Thomas, 58
Bleckman, Thomas, 26
Bleeker, Leonard H., 117
Bleur, Daniel, 14
Bliss, Elijah, 41
    Theodore, 137
Block, John, 116
Blodgett, Caleb, 37, 59
    Joshua, 50
    Josiah, 63
Blood, Reuben, 49
    Simon, 49
    Thomas, 69
Bloom, David, 92
Bloomenshine, Martin, 80
Bloomers, William, 31
Bloomfield, Charles, 13
    Jervus, 23, 29
Blower, Robert, 11
Blumenburg, August, 142
Bocannon, Samuel, 122
Bochanon, Robert, 36
Bock, Wentel, 142
Boden, James, 85
Bodley, Andrew, 125
Boe, William, 83

Boelinger, Henry, 142, 143
Boem, Conrad, 93
Bogardus, Benjamin, 116, 125
    Lewis, 113
Bogart, John, 34
    Mynt, 107
Bogg, John, 122
Bohannon, Robert, 82
    Samuel, 29
Boies, James, 18, 54
Boiles, James, 51
Bollman, Conrad, 144
Bolton, John, 32
    Joseph, 37
Bond, William, 3, 5
Boney, Michel, 26
Bonham, Absalom, 9, 12
    Ephraim, 25
Bonhaugle, J. C. U., 119
Bonker, Bathnel, 130
    John, 130
    Nathaniel, 128
Bonnell, James, 31, 36
    Samuel, 27
Boogh, George, 93
Boom, Conrad
Boozey, Daniel, 10
Borden, Abraham, 28
    John, 112
Borham, Kendrick, 17
Borrage, John, 82
Boss, George, 72
    Isaac, 130
Boston, John, 10
Boswell, Jonathan, 102
Botamer, Jacob, 92
Bouden, John, 75
Boulton, George, 31
Bouton, Joseph, 13
Bovee, Nicholas, 112
Bowden, John, 75
    Kendrick, 17
Bowen, Kendrick, 17
    Prentice, 116
    Samuel, 118
Bowers, John, 14
    Michael, 99
    Nathaniel
    Prentice, 116
Bowles, Charles, 52
    James, 54
Bowls, George, 34
Bowman, Nathaniel, 20
Boyce, James, 60
    John, 68, 115
    Peter, 110
Boyd, John, 13
    Joseph, 80
    Samuel, 48
    Thomas, 101
Boyees, Stephen, 80
Boyer, John, 68
    Michael, 88, 89, 90
    Peter, 92
    Philip, 76, 80

Boyle, John, 75
Boyles, James, 123
    Stephen, 80
Boynton, George, 61
    Isaac, 49
    Joseph, 64, 65, 69
    Snow, 61
Bradbury, Sanders, 52
Braddock, James, 32
Braden, John, 108
Bradford, S., 55, 56
    William, 46, 72
    William, Jr., 120
Bradley, James, 81
Bradner, Andrew, 108
Bradshaw, William, 12
Bradt, Andrew, 107
Brady, Edward, 24
    George, 117
Brainerd, Reuben, 121
Brandes, Conrad, 144
Brandhefer, Adam, 102
Brannon, Abraham, 37
    Adam, 129
    Michael, 37
    Reuben, 37
Bransom, Leonard, 98
Brant, Christian, 118
    John, 124
Brass, Jeremiah
    John, 114
Brasse, John, 143
Braty, Daniel, 11
Bray, William, 37
Breant, Joseph, 68
Brearly, David, 9
Brease, Timy, 12
Breasted, Isaac, 33
Brecker, John, 102
Breckhall, Martin, 102
Bredine, Francis, 125
Breecher, Jno, 90
Breitscher, Martin, 142
Bremer,
Brenion, B., 2
Brennon, Abraham, 37
    Michael, 37
    Reuben, 37
Brent, Christian, 118
Brett, George, 82
Brewer, Jeremiah, 121
    Paul, 24
Brewster, Daniel, 26
Breyman, John, 141
Briant, Jacob, 28
    Joseph, 68
Brice, John, 95, 98
Brickly, Philip, 83
Briggs, John, 109, 116
    Jeremiah, 129
Brimigion, Thomas, 42
Brimugent, Thomas, 42
    Frederick, 91
Brink, Aaron, 37
    Henry, 37

Britt, George, 82
Brittain, Daniel, 18
    John, 37
    William, 43
Britton, Daniel, 33
    John, 33
    Samuel, 70
    William, 32
Brockaway, Russell, 133
Brodbeck, Michael, 92
Brodwick, David, 95
    James, 31, 32
    William, 27
    David, 95
Broer, John, 33
Bromley, Simon, 114
Brook, James, 10
Brooker, Walter, 132
Brookhouse, R., 92
Brooks, Almiran, 20
    Armand
    David
    Jno, 38
    Thomas, 109
    Walter, 122
    William, 131
Brosbee, John, 62
Brown, Benjamin, 50
    Charles F., 117
    David, 21, 103
    Edward, 61
    Ezekiel, 38
    James, 52
    James, Jr., 103
    Job, 26
    John, 13, 32, 34, 43, 75,
        83, 85, 89, 91, 93,
        115, 124
    Joseph, 27, 40, 121
    Lockey, 37
    Moses, 103
    Nathaniel, 67, 68
    Paul, 43
    Peter, 20
    Samuel, 23
    Thomas, 17
    William, 13, 51, 75, 83
    Zebulon, 20
Browne, John, 72
    William, 51
Brownsberry, Lewis, 93
Bruen, Bryan, 2
Bruer, John, 28
Bruner, Jno, 90
Brush, David, 37
    Davis, 52
    John, 16
    Selah
Bryan, Jacob, 48
    John, 80
Bryant, Benjamin, 15
    David, 50
    Davis, 52
    John, 14

Buchanan, John, 137, 138
    Samuel, 122
Buck, Joseph, 16, 18
Buckley, Philip, 83
Bucy, William, 118
Budd, Augustin, 142
    Buffant, 142
    Conklin, 25
Budine, Francis, 125
Buffant, Augustin, 142
Buffington, Samuel, 39, 40
Bugbee, Nathan, 49
Bugby, Josiah, 129
Buggs, Jeremiah
    John, 116
Bulbury, Wooldrick, 27
Bull, William, 31, 36
Bunchall, John, 71
Bundy, Jeremiah, 131
Bunker, Joseph, 58
    Lawrence, 129
Bunnel, Benjamin, 12
Bunner, Jacob, 91
Bunton, Able, 21
Burbrance, John
Burch, Philip, 118
Burchardt, Daniel, 2
Burchart, Daah
Burchell, William, 76
Burdeau, Charles, 9
Burdett, Elisha, 131
Burdick, Henry, 109
    Moses, 110
Burdje, Michael, 133
Burges, John, 80
    Thomas, 40
Burgess, James, 37
    John, 80
    Michael, 117
Burget, Charles, 67
Burghes, Michael, 133
Burginam, Francis, 90
Burhans, John, 113, 116
Burk, Edmund, 115
    Felley, 41
    John, 93
    Joseph, 53
    Tilley, 41
    Thomas, 101
Burkdorff, John, 117
Burke, Edward, 78, 85, 86
    Hubbard, 33
    James, 85
    John, 112
    Walter, 82
Burkett, Peter, 99
Burkhart, Daal, 142
Burkheart, Jacob, 68
Burks, Samuel, 101
Burley, Henry, 78, 82
    Joseph, 48
    William, 66
Burnett, Benjamin, 49
    Ebenezer, 131
    John, 12

Burney, William, 80
Burnham, Asa, 103
    Asabel, 103
    Asel, 103
    Enoch, 62
    George, 51, 57, 61
    John, 113
    Joseph, 58
    William, 126
Burns, Caesar, 150
    Daniel, 22
    James, 22, 96
    John, 82
    Robert, 110
Burrces, John, 26
Burrcell, Jediah, 25
    Thomas, 19
    Zachariah, 27
Burres, John, 117
Burroughs, John, 116
    Jonathan, 52
Burrows, Eban, 9
    Eden, 10
    John, 31, 32
    Samuel, 123
Burtless, William, 16, 21
Burton, John, 28
    Josiah, 51
Burts, Robert, 49
Bush, George, 78, 79, 81
Busomy, Jno, 121
Buss, John, 62
Busseny, James, 121
Buswell, Noah, 52
Butler, Alpheus, 51
    Benjamin, 50
    John, 78
    Samuel, 98
    William, 3
Butterfield, James, 40, 57
    Simon, 52
Button, Samuel
Buyer, Godfrey, 118
Buzzell, Elijah, 60
    Jonathan, 60
Byerly, Fred, 99
Byford, Henry, 115
Byrnes, James, 81
Byrns, William, 83

Cabbatson, Michael
Cable, Jacob, 85
    Robert, 74
Cagan, Solomon, 11
Cahey, _____, 76
Cahill, Timothy, 94
Cain, Francis, 11
    John, 130
    Matthew, 133
    Michael, 76
Calahan, John, 82
    Patrick, 82
Calbie, Lebulon, 52
Caldwell, James
    John, 50, 52

Cicaty, A., 140
    Berrauch de, 142
Cila, John, 43
Ciley, John
    Joseph, 3, 45, 46, 48
Cilley, Jonathan, 65, 68
Civery, John, 20
Clack, John, 81
Clandenan, Adam, 81
Clapp, Daniel, 45, 47, 54
Clare, John, 81
    William, 97
Clark, Benjamin, 103
    Bunker, 53
    Caleb, 57
    David, 121
    George, 138
    Hezekiah, 51
    Jesse, 28
    John, 37, 48, 53, 98, 101, 122, 137, 138
    Jno, 98
    Jonathan, 43
    Nathaniel S., 58
    Norris, 83
    Richard, 12
    Robert, 82
    Samuel, 28, 34
    Thomas, 76
    Ward, 70
    William, 17, 95
Clarke, Elnan, 40
    George, 138
    Michael, 17
    Samuel, 10, 34
    William, 10
Class, John, 115
Clavinger, Thomas, 32
Claxton, George, 108
Clayer, Elijah, 60
Clayhale, Abraham G., 79, 85
Clayton, Henry, 29
Claywater, Martinus, 131
Cleackner, Christian, 92
Cleaft, Joseph, 122
Cleling, Capt, 7
Clemens, John, 18
    Patrick, 86
Clements, Richard, 59
Cleveland, Enoch, 40
Clevenger, Thomas, 32
Cliff, Joseph, 122
Clifford, William, 58
Clifton, George, 13
    Thomas, 90
Clime, Philip, 91
Cline, Jacob, 131
    John, 88
    Jno, 88
    Nicholas, 10
    Philip, 91
Clinger, Michael, 96
Clinhon, Henry, 20
Clintardt, John, 133

Clinton, James, 4, 5
    John, 133
    Joseph, 113
Clock, William, 96
Close, John, 67
Clough, John, 67
    William
    Zaccheus, 66
Clouth, Zaccheus, 67
Clutch, Obadiah, 18
Coad, John, 118
Coak, Jacob, 84, 85
Coaley, Owen, 102
Coalman, John, 21
Cobb, Jeremiah, 41
    John, 41
    Thomas, 27
Coblar, Conrad, 109
Coble, George, 110
Coburn, Asa, 30, 40
Cockran, James, 48
    John, 74
Coddington, Benjamin, 10
Codius, Christopher, 105, 106
Cody, William, 77
Coffin, Primus, 58
Coflet, Abraham, 141
Cogan, Patrick, 46
Cohey, Jno, 76
Colbie, Zebulon, 52
Colbratts, Dowing, 117
Colbroth, Dependence, 63
    William, 117
Colburn, Thomas, 52
Colby, David, 59
    Moses, 54
    Theo, 57
    William, 68
Colcord, John, 55
Cole, Abraham, 33, 125
    Ambrose, 59
    Benjamin, 94
    Benjamin, Jr., 94
    David, 107
    Ebenezer, 41
    John, 93
    Philip, 110
    Samuel, 40
    Solomon, 59
    Tunis, 109
Coleman, Israel, 137
Colemen, James, 83
    Jeremiah, Jr., 103
    Job, 15
    John, 72, 73, 85, 129
    Thomas, 101
Colkhaffer, Peter, 95
Collins, Edward, 126
    James, 117
    John, 109, 117
Colloney, James, 121
Colman, Israel, 137
    John, 107
Colony, Richard, 58

Colston, John, 28
Colter, Nathaniel, 82
Coltman, Robert, 95, 99
Colton, _____, 103
    George, 35
Combs, John, 48, 71, 134
    Peter, 134
    Samuel, 134
Comfort, John, 12, 34
Commandine, Michalae, 118
Conant, Jonathan, 49
Conchet, Henry, 98
Conckles, Henry, 18
Concles, William, 103
Conden, Richard
Condon, David, 110
    James, 18
    Peter, 100
    Richard, 81
Conelc, Henry, 98
Conine, Joseph, 118
    Philip, 113
Conklin, Cornelius, 33
    Edmund, 123
    Joseph, 108
Conkling, John, 33, 36
    Jonathan, 27
Conn, Samuel, 20
    William, 123
Connell, Charles, 25
    William, 49
Connelly, Michael, 124, 128
    Patrick, 80
    Thomas, 97
Conner, John, 82
    Matthew, 17
    Patrick, 123
    Timothy, 19
Conney, John, 98
Cormick, William, 49
Connight, Conrad, 132
Connor, John, 82
    John T., 54
    Thomas, 81, 82
Conover, George S., 1
    William, 103
Conrade, Charles, 99
Conray, Stephen, 49
Conway, John, 23, 24, 25, 111
Cook, Cal, 1
    Ebenezer, 62
    Jacob, 18, 84, 85
    John, 34, 58
    Moses, 122
    Nathan, 123
    Obadiah, 126
    Paul, 61
    Samuel, 126
    Thomas, 62, 72, 73, 113
    William, 50
    _____ P., 92

Cooke, George, 125
    James, 3
    Samuel, 126
Cookson, Jacob, 85
Cooley, Owen, 102
Coolidge, Silas, 61, 63
Coon, Jacob, 124
    Peter, 122
Cooker, George, 68
    John, 54
    John Jr., 117
    John Sr., 117
    Joseph, 71
    Pierce, 50
    Price, 103
    Prior, 103
    Richard, 129
Coppa, Joseph, 69
Copper, Joseph, 69
Copps, Aaron, 69
    David, 60
    Joseph, 69
    Moses, 59
Coppus, Peter, 92
Corbeck, Peter, 102
Cornelius, John
    William, 103
Cornell, Jean, 143
Cornick, Joseph, 22
Corning, Jediah, 103
Cornish, David, 42
Cornton, Benjamin, 10
Cornwell, Caleb, 115
    John, 133
    Joseph, 114
Corragal, Jno, 116
Corrill, William, 103
Cort, Martin, 133
Corter, Philip, 108
Cortland, John C., 118
    Philip, 106
Corwine, George, 27
Cory, Ebenezer, 40
    Oliver, 40
Coryell, John, 14
Cos, Benjamin, 80
Cosgrove, Charles, 25
Coster, Bishop, 52
Cotter, William, 68
Cotteral, Richard, 126
Cotton, Benjamin, 50
    Nathaniel, 40
    Samuel, 46
    William, 68
Couchet, Henry, 98
Coulter, Nathaniel, 82
Coultman, Robert, 99
Country, Luke, 27
Countryman, Jacobus, 108
Court, Jesse M., 40
Courtney, Frank, 109
Cousins, Matthew, 113
Covert, Tunis, 14
Cowdres, George T., 112

Cowdrey, Benjamin, 112
    John, 48
Cowen, James, 118
    William, 48
Cowey, Jno, 76
Cox, Abraham, 20
    Benjamin, 80
    Cornelius, 1, 22
    John, 42
    Joseph, 25
    Limon, 126
    Richard, 27
    Robert, 110
    William, 17, 34
Coyle, Edward, 80
Cozard, Richard, 122
Crafford, Patrick, 96
Craft, David, 1
    Jacob, 133
    James, 101, 109
    John, 90
    Joseph, 98
    Nathaniel, 122
    Samuel, 40
Crage, James, 71
Craig, Isaac, 95, 96
    John, 68, 99
Cram, Humphrey, 69
Crame, Jacob, 88, 93
Cramer, Andrew, 19
    Jacob, 89, 93
Crandle, Luke, 118
Crane, Aaron, 10
    Edmund, 10
    Elijah, 10
    Ezekiel, 10
    Jno, 93
    Jona, 13
    Joseph, 11
    Stephen, 34
Crange, James, 82
Crangle, James, 82
Cranie, Daniel, 10
Crannet, John
    Isaac, 124
Craven, Joseph, 14
Crawford, Asa, 131
    Joseph, 37
    Matt, 37
Crayman, Jacob, 77
Craymer, Jacob, 77
Creamer, William, 14
Creckenboom, _____, 118
Crely, Hugh, 18
Crill, John, 27
Cristeon, John, 109
Critchett, Benjamin, 53
    Elias, 58
    John, 61
Crocer, Jones, 104
Crofat, Joseph, 37
Crofort, Joseph, 37
Croker, Jones, 104
Crombee, James, 55

Cromment, James, 63
Crommett, Ebenezer, 61
Cromwell, Hugh, 102
    Oliver, 20
Cromer, Jacob, 88
Cronise, Henry, 88, 89
Crookshank, William, 36
Crosby, Jesse, 95, 99
    Semuel, 134
Crosgill, John, 83
Cross, Daniel, 70, 71, 95, 99
    Ephraim, 50
    John, 50, 53
    William, 73
Crossfield, Timothy, 70
Crossley, Jesse, 99
Crossman, Amos, 28
Crouch, David, 103
Crow, Jacob, 82
Crowell, Daniel, 10
Crower, Rudolph, 94
Crowley, Michael, 94
    William, 98
Croy, John Du, 19
Cruikshank, E., 1
Crumell, Joseph, 43
Crummet, Ebenezer, 61, 63
    James, 63
Crump, John, 18
Crutch, David, 107
Crutcher, James, 99
Culberson, William, 41
Cummings, John N., 19
Cummins, Ebenezer, 133
Cunard, Richard
Cunite, Conrad, 132
Cunningham, Archibald, 124, 125
    Barney, 97
    Barry, 97
    Henry, 110
    John, 11, 67, 137, 138
    Robert, 50
    Shubel, 108
    Thomas, 80
Cupper, John, 54
Curby, John, 21, 125
Curley, Owen, 88, 89
    William, 20
Currier, Thomas, 58, 59
Currin, Samuel, 129
Curry, James, 109
    John, 20, 100

Curtis, Ebenezer, 133
    Jean, 142
    John, 20
    Louis, 142
    Thomas, 85
    William, 39, 43
Curwin, Gershom, 125
Curwine, Edward, 125
Cusick, Matthew, 86

Custard, Benjamin, 100
Cutler, William, 62
Cutter, Ebenezer, 12
Cutting, Jonas, 52
    Stephen, 43
Cuviard, Robert, 122.

Daberwing, Henry, 92
Dagny, Patrick, 85
Dailey, Silas, 37
    William
Daily, Benjamin, 97
    Joseph, 81
    London, 59
    Silas, 37
Dalloff, John, 59
Dalton, James, 18
    John, 88
    Samuel, 52
Dalvins, Richard, 84
Danfield, Henry, 14, 17
Danford, Joshua, 50
    Prince, 133
    Sam, 52
Danforth, Daniel, 42
Danham, Nathaniel, 10
Daniels, Jonathan, 19
    Samuel, 58
Danielson, Isaac, 131
Dann, Frederick, 133
Danoth, Godlieb
DanWarden, Martin, 117
Darby, Charles, 109
    Ephraim, 27
    William, 10
Darcy, John, 31
Darr, Michael, 84, 85
David, Isaac, 123
Davidson, Daniel, 102
    Douglass, 103
    Robert, 97
    William, 34, 82, 103
Davis, Acquila, 68
    Chapman, 122
    Daniel, 26, 36, 102
    David, 22, 100
    Ebenezer, 61
    Eliab, 37
    Eliax, 37
    Ephraim, 61
    Ezekiel, 51
    Henry Hiteo, 73
    Herman, 108
    John, 13, 33, 36, 130, 123
    Joshua, 122
    Joseph, 51
    Moses, 58
    Nathan 49
    Patrick, 121
    Peter, 121
    Richard, 123
    Samuel, 48, 58, 67, 107, 131

Davis, cont.
    Seftimus, 72, 86
    Thomas, 22, 48
    William, 40
Davishalter, Henry, 73
Davison, John, 121
    William, 82
Davy, Noathen
Dawson, Daniel, 114
    Thomas, 35
Day, Aaron, 126
    Elifeh, 39, 41
    Jere, 13
    Jesse
    Luke, 38
    Moses, 26
Dayne, Jacob, 52
Dayton, Bennet, 126
    Elias, 3, 23
    Jonathan, 1, 23, 24
Deacon, Aaron, 24
Deal, Andrew, 91
    Jacob, 72
Dean, Ashbel, 138
    Isaac, 109
    John, 14, 42
    Joseph, 25
    Samuel, 49
    William, 81
Deane, James, 2
    Samuel, 118
    William, 81
Dear, William, 13
Dearborn, Abner, 68
    Edward, 61
    Henry, 3, 5, 64, 66
    Simon, 67
Deats, Frederick, 91
DeBarr, Francis, 38
DeBert, Claudius, 140, 143
Deberwing, Henry, 92
DeBois, Henry, 128
    Lewis, 4, 128
DeBouveulle, Chevalierde, 141
DeCamp, James, 26
DeCicaty, Berrauch, 42
Decker, Christopher, 131
    George, 122
    Jacob, 37
    Martin, 131
    Samuel, 33
    Thomas, 33
Decker, Peter, 98
    Deeter, Peter, 98
Deen, Aclibil, 137
Deffenberger, David, 90
Deffenberger, Jacob, 76
DeHart, Cyrus, 9
Degan, Jacob, 99
Deimer, Philip, 142
Delancey, Abraham, 133
Delaney, James, 36
Delimore, Robert, 29
Delinger, ____ R., 98

Delorme, August, 143
Demary, Ezekiel, 60
Demerit, John, 60
Demeritt, Ezekiel, 60
DeMont, Joseph, 112
Dempsey, Lewis, 82
    Patrick, 76
Deneake, Henry, 141
Dennett, John, 64, 65, 66
Dennis, Jean, 143
    John, 115
    Mydert, 125
Dennison, John, 12
Denniston, Daniel, 13, 120, 121
    George, 3, 117
    Thomas, 126
Denny, John, 84, 85
    Peter, 122
Denton, Amos, 138
    David, 103
DenWarken, Martin, 117
Depew, Abram
    Francis, 109
    Henry, 109
Derby, Ephraim, 23
Dermand, John, 75
Dermott, Thomas, 101
Dero, Michael, 85
DeRouse, Pierre, R.
DeRouste, Anthony, 126
Derry, John, 17
Detrick, George, 76
    Laus, 142
    Sigongne, 142
Detworth, George
DeVanDore, Chevalier de, 141
DeVaults, Peter, 115
Dever, Pat, 99
Devinney, Hugh, 75
Devins, Leonard, 33
Devoid, John, 74
Devolt, John, 74
Devons, Leonard, 33
Devor, Abraham, 108
    Luke, 27
DeWitt, Thomas, 115
Deyer, Frederick, 117
Deyo, Hugh, 118
D'Hart, Cyrus, 12
    William, 16, 17
Diamond, John, 59
    Moses, 131
    William, 131
Dian, John, 42
Dibble, Hezekiah, 133
Dick, Henry, 123
Dickens, James, 108
Dickenson, Gideon, 133
Dickerman, Elijah, 43
Dickerson, David, 122
    Wessel, 130
Dickey, Charles, 80

Dickey, cont.
    David, 50, 52
    James, 50
    Nathaniel, 50
    Samuel, 83
    William
Dickinson, Abraham, 123
    Gideon
    Isaac, 13
    James, 76
Dickray, Charles, 80
Dickson, Lewis, 133
    William, 124
Didrich, John, 44
Diel, Enoch, 40
Dier, James, 89
Diffenderfer, David, 91
Dimond, Moses, 131
    William, 131
Dingley, William, 80
Disman, John, 75
Disney, John, 20
Ditman, John, 44
Diver, Patt, 89
Divine, Hugh, 75
Dixon, Ashbrook, 20
    Thomas, 24
    William, 19
Dockam, Benjamin, 62
Dodge, Benjamin, 62
    Henry, 28, 130
    John, 61
    Richard, 123, 130
    Samuel, 121, 123
    Samuel, Jr., 120
    Samuel C., 123
    Thomas
    Zaddock, 61
Doe, David, 62
Doherty, Thomas, 118
Dollenburg, John 144
Dolloff, James, 59
    Thomas, 66
Dolph, Miss, 40
Dolphen, Richard, 85
Dolton, Frederick, 109
    John, 89
    Thomas, 109
Dolver, Richard, 85
Dolvin, Richard, 88
Domnick, Henry, 93
Donalds, John, 21
Donaldson, James, 33
    John, 33
    Peter, 109
    Thomas, 35
    William, 14
Donaly, Ephraim, 80
    John, 80
Donelly, Daniel, 24
    Francis, 99
    George, 73
Donnels, John, 121

Dones, Jonas, 10
Donhan, Robert, 41
Donochan, Robin, 94
Dorman, John, 50
Dorn, William, 102
Dorran, James, 82
Dorson, Daniel, 114
Dorrence, Robert, 103
Dorry, James, 35
Dotmauth, George, 20
Dotworth, George, 20
Dorton, Francis, 20
Doude, James, 54
Dougherty, Anthony, 33
    Charles, 51
    John, 29
    Peter, 14
    Robert
    Thomas, 118
Douglass, George, 107
    Jonas, 77
    Robert, 81
    Thomas, 95, 96
    William, 83
Douw, _____, 1
Dow, Benjamin, 50
    Henry, 33
    Samuel J.
    Vulker, 134
    Zabez, 61
Dowdney, Samuel, 26
Dowlar, George, 117
Downing, Andrew, 20
    George, 62
    Jacob, 50
    Joen, 57
    Jonathian, 63
Downs, James, 37
    Noah, 61
Doyle, Jotham, 42
Drake, Cornelius, 27
Drecksler, John
Drew, Francis, 58
    John, 56, 60
    Samuel, 41
Drexell, Friedrith, 144
Drexler, David, 92
Drexhill, Daniel, 40
Drought, Richard, 50
Drury, Ebenezer, 69
Dualh, Samuel, 125
Dubois, Henry, 128
    Lewis, 2, 128
    Nathaniel, 131
Duchesse, Maturin, 143
Ducit, Philemon, 48
DeCray, John, 19
Dudee, Samuel, 62
Dualey, Ephraim, 66
    James
    Jonathan, 59
    Trueworthy, 66

Duff, Hugh, 84
Duffy, John, 17
    Patrick, 95, 98
    Terrence, 80
Dugan, Robert, 36
    William, 38
Dugard, Jno, 121
Duggen, William, 41
Duquid, Jno, 121
Duquit, John, 121
Duiore, Pursuy, 143
Dunavan, John, 28
    Peter, 121
Dunbar, David, 10
    William
Duncan, Alex, 34
    David, 66
    James, 90
Dunfield, Henry, 14, 17
    Philip, 17
Duhany, Jonathan, 22
    Lewis F., 23, 24
    Nathaniel, 10
Dunlap, Andrew, 109
    James, 59
    Thomas, 37
Dunlevi, Patrick, 26
Dunn, Alexander, 106
    Darrel, 102
    John, 136
Dunnegan, Daniel, 102
Dunninvan, Anthony, 115
    John, 126
    Peter, 121
Dunscomb, Edward, 112, 121
Durgan, John, 66
    Patrick, 131
Durges, Henry, 62
Durgin, Henry, 62
Durrah, William, 48
Durrance, Robert, 103
DuSignongie, Louis, 140, 142
Dusten, Stephen, 54
Dustin, Moody, 45, 46
    Moses, 56, 62
    Zaccharias, 60
    Zaccheus, 60
Duston, Stephen, 54
Dutton, Ephraim, 40
    John, 60
    William, 40
Duxler, David
Duzzuis, Paul, 143
DiWight, James, 27
Dwight, John, 27
Dyche, John, 94

Eakley, Jacob, 130
Ealick, Alex., 14
Earl, Israel, 12
Early, Patrick, 18
Eastman, Eben, 59
    Edward, 59

Eastman, cont.
    Jacob, 52, 68
    James, 58
    John, 54
    Thomas, 54
    William, 68
Easton, Henry, 118
    Upton, 121
Eastwood, Amos, 139
Eaton, Benjamin, 13, 121
    Jonathan, 68
Ebenard, Casper, 18
Ebener, Caspar, 16
Ebenhardt, Dolph, 18, 68
Eckert, Adam, 143
Edes, Joseph, 116
Eddy, James, 70
Edgar, David, 4
    John, 86
Edgerly, James, 54, 67
    John, 42
    Joshua, 60
Edmondson, Joseph, 35
Edsall, Benjamin, 32
    Peter, 33
Edsley, John, 42
Edwards, Evan, 98
    Jesse, 18
    John, 18, 19, 62
Eggs, Samuel, 115
Egling, Henry, 142
Eickhorn, Philip, 141
Eidke, John, 141
Eiloch, Ephairm, 12
Elder, Andrew, 102
Ellet, Benjamin, 93
Ellingwood, Ralph, 48
Elliot, Archibald, 125
    Frances, 113
    Henry, 106
    James, 100
Ellit, Jean, 143
Ellis, Benjamin, 64, 67
    Daniel, 24
    John, 75, 125
    William, 64, 69
Ellison, John, 75
    Robert, 108
Ellsworth, John, 121
    Peter, 120, 123
Elmer, Ebenezer, 16
    Moses G., 16
Elwell, Benjamin, 42
    John, 42
    Samuel, 18
Elzberger, Wolfgang, 94
Emberson, William, 98
Embly, John, 64
Emerely, John, 93
Emerson, Amos, 45, 47, 52
    Jonathan, 46
    Ralph, 49
Emerton, James, 18

Emery, Noah, 50
Emes, Worsley, 95, 99
Emly, James, 82
Emmerick, Peter, 88, 89
Emmons, John, 24
    Parker, 39
England, Benjamin, 93
Engle, Bart, 88, 89
Engler, Peter, 93
English, John, 27
    Joshua, 115
    Samuel, 128, 133
    William, 101
Eniey, James, 92
Ennis, Henry, 114
Ensign, Samuel, 103
Enthron, Henry, 142
Entret, Christian, 44
    Henry, 44
Erickson, Michael, 32
Ervin, William, 113
Erwin, James, 113
    John, 124
    Peter, 14
    William, 10, 12
Eslick, Alex, 14
    Stephen, 12
Esling, Paul, 94
Esquire, Daniel, 61
Etter, Jacob, 94
Eurach, John, 102
    Michael, 102
Evans, Edward, 49
    Elijah, 100
    Ira, 53, 56
    Israel, 64, 105, 106
    John, 74
    Jno, 98
    Joseph, 101, 116
    Thomas, 21
Eveland, Frederick, 103
Everingham, William, 20
Everitt, George, 69
    James, 86
Eviced, Henry, 39
Evierd, Henry, 39
Eving, David, 9
    Remington, 19
Eyers, Samuel, 53
Eysell, John, 94
Ezeler, Jacob, 34

Factor, John, 129
Fadden, James, 41
    John, 40
Fagan, Henry, 17
    Henry, 99
Fagener, Michael, 19
Fager, Jacob, 99
Fagundus, George, 90
Fair, Robert, 77
Fairbanck, Drury, 141
Fairchild, Jeremiah, 68

Fairfield, Edward, 58
    Elijah, 54
    Jeremiah, 68
Fairlee, James, 105
Falcomer, Alex, 73
Fall, George, 60
    Samuel, 41
Falling, Samuel, 101
Falmouth, Joseph, 40
Fanney, David, 22
Fanning, James, 19
Farewell, James, 83
Farley, William, 70
Farmer, James, 11
Farney, George, 18
Farnham, Benjamin, 97
    Ebenezer, 68
    John, 54
Farnsworth, Moses, 53
Farnum, Joshua, 104
Farr, William, 12
Farrell, George, 99
    William, 74
Farrington, Josiah, 40
Farral, William, 34
Farwell, Isaac, 45, 47, 53
Fashes, David, 29
Fasket, Robert, 60
Fassett, Joshua, 40
Faulkner, Alexander, 73
Fay, Joseph, 70
Feather, George, 33
Fegan, Hugh, 94
Feighter, G. S., 99
Felch, Daniel, 66
Fellows, Moses, 64, 66
Felts, Christopher, 102
Fennell, Daniel, 98
Fennill, Daniel, 98
    John, 94
Fenton, James, 16
Ferdon, Abraham, 128
    James, 130
Ferguson, Eleazer, 59
    James, 130
    Samuel, 107
    Thomas, 18
Ferral, John, 17
Ferrick, Michl, 92
Ferrigh, John, 115
Ferren, Lawrence, 19
    Moses, 59
Ferrens, Henry, 88
Fetrick, George, 76
Fidis, George, 28
Fiedler, Heinrith, 143
Fields, Michael, 86
    William, 86
Fifer, Henry, 91
Filler, Fredk, 90
Filmore, Silas, 133
Finch, John, 20
Finck, David, 94

Findley, Rob, 19
Findling, Christian, 141
Finegar, George, 132
Finley, John, 39
    William, 13
Finn, Thomas, 20
Fish, Nicholas, 1, 4, 106
    Zebry, 134
Fishbourne, Benjamin, 75
Fisher, David, 19
    Henry, 83, 88
    John, 32
    Philip, 88, 89, 90
Fisk, Cato, 62
Fiske, John, 20
Fishley, George, 71
Fismore, John, 92
Fitch, James, 121
Fitzgerald, Christian M., 125
    Thomas, 132
    William, 132
Fitzgibbons, James, 84, 85
Fitzsimmons, James, 96
Flach, Maths, 93
Flanagan, Daniel, 131
Flanders, Jacob, 54
    John, 54
    Philip, 50
Flaugherty, John, 21
Flavhanan, Capt, 8
Fleisch, Chn, 92
Fleming, John, 32
    Patrick, 90
Fletcher, Ebenezer, 60
    James, 17, 118
Fletchers, William, 17
Flick, A., 1
    Frederick, 90
    Jona, 90
Fling, Henry, 118
Flinn, Henry, 118
Flood, Amos, 68
    Francis, 107
    Jonathan, 67
Flowers, William, 29
Floyd, James, 68
    Joseph, 19
Flumo, John, 133
Flurey, Stcal
Flynn, John, 10
    Simon, 81
Foehr, Carl, 141
Fogg, Abner, 71
    Daniel, 17
    Jeremiah, 3, 56, 62
Follett, Frederick, 103
Folliat, John, 89
Folsom, Jonathan, 61
Fonda, Douw F., 112
Foor, John, Caspu, 115
Forbes, Alex, 117
    Daniel, 97

Force, David, 35
    Jacob, 19
    Jonathan, 10
Ford, David, 113
    William, 97
Fordice, John, 13
Forest, Robert, 53
Forgery, John, 82
Forgood, Ebenezer, 51
Forman, David, 4
    Jonathan, 9, 12
Forney, James, 92
Forrest, Thomas, 95
Forrester, James, 79
Forster, Edward, 75
    Ichabod, 2
Forsyth, David, 56
Forsythe, Hugh, 86
Fortner, Peter, 90, 91
Fosgate, Ebenzer, 5
Foster, Daniel, 60, 70
    Edward, 75
    George, 81
    John, 20, 29, 82, 109
    Jonathan, 69
    Michael, 103
    Nathaniel, 106
    Smith, 40
Fothergill, Hugh, 115
    Joseph, 41
Fowle, Jeremiah, 52
Fowler, Abner, 66
    James, 116
    Joseph, 27, 28
    Michael, 135
    Philip, 57, 61
    Robe-t, 21
    Theodosius, 120, 126
Fowls, Jeremiah
Fox, Jacob, 26
    Joseph, 22
    Silas, 70
    Winthrop, 59
Fraelich, Joseph, 120
France, Coonrad, 115
Frances, George, 91
    William, 17
Franklin, John, 2, 4, 93
Franks, Michael, 123
Frantcher, Heinrich, 102
Frantz, Abraham, 94
Fraser, Daniel, 83
Frasier, George, 12
    Persifer, 2
Frasy, Daniel, 36
    Zebedee, 36
Frede, Carll, 142
Fredenburgh, James, 12
    William, 14
Frederick, John, 118
Freebush, Matthew, 107
Freeland, John, 115

Freeman, Jedediah, 10
    Judiah, 10
    Samuel, 10
    William
Frence, Abner, 106, 110
    David, 41
    Jacob, 43
    William, 103
Fresiner, Jean, 141
Frey, Bernard, 90
    Jacob, 102
    John, 115
Fricke, August, 143
    Henry, 142
Fricker, John, 142
Fricklen, Robert, 20
Friday, Coenradt, 112
Frigat, Augustus, 143
Frolich, Christian, 102
    Joseph, 122
Frost, George, 55, 56, 5
    James, 84, 85
    John, 13
    Nathaniel, 63
    William, 131
Frubling, Henry, 141
Frume, Jean, 143
Fry, Lawrence, 83
    Michael, 82
Fryday, Conrad, 118
Frye, Ebenezer, 45, 47,
    Isaac, 64, 68
Fryfied, Edward, 58
Frymiller, Jacob, 94
Fryor, Jasper, 131
Fugard, Samuel, 50, 53
Fulgard, Samuel, 50, 53
Fulham, Charles, 88
Fulkerson, Joseph, 9
Fullem, Charles, 89
Fuller, Daniel, 49
    Levi, 70
    Thomas, 52
Fullerton, George, 81
Fullingan, Jno, 10
Fulman, John, 14
Fulton, Francis, 117
    John, 131
Funck, George, 93
Furma, Anthony, 117
Funston, James, 3
Furdon, Ab, 128
Furgason, Thomas, 18
Furman, Gabriel, 113
    John, 128
Furnell, William, 67
Fyfried, Edward, 58

Gabbatson, Michael, 107
Gabel, Peter, 74
Gabine, John, 106
Gable, Benjamin, 138
    Joseph, 138

Gabriel, Peter, 77, 91
Gadge, John, 113
Gadsby, Ralph, 81
Gage, Edward, 11
Gaintin, Jain, 143
Gake, Samuel, 115
Gale, Alexander, 32
    Joseph, 24
    Samuel
Gall, John, 115
Gallahan, Ed, 99
Gallespie, William, 117
Galliher, James, 22, 82
    William, 66
Gambertson, Charles, 12
Gamble, Michael, 90
Gannon, William, 36
Gano, John, 4
Gansevort, Peter, 4, 112
Ganson, John, 43
Ganter, Adam, 88, 89
Gardner, Richard, 141
Gardiner, Andres, 131
    Andries, 114
    Samuel, 113
Gardner, Andries, 112
    George, 37
    Henry, 81
    Jesse, 125
    Peregrine, 103
    Samuel, 113
Garland, John, 62
Garlinghouse, Benjamin, 20
Garoutte, Antyony, 67
Garrett, Elisha, 103
Garretson, Joseph, 26
Garrison, Abraham, 117
    Bennet, 26
    John, 108
Garrows, Thomas, 53
Gartenhouse, Benjamin, 20
Garvey, John, 74
Garvins, George, 28
Gary, John, 13
Gaskell, William, 18
Gaskin, Daniel
Gasright, John, 17
Gaudart, Joseph, 141
Gaul, Richard, 94
Gault, George, 53
Gaulthrop, Samuel, 84
Gaven, Henry, 106
Gavin, Francis, 90
    Henry, 106
    John, 21
Gavine, John, 106
Gaylord, Ambrose, 103
    Justus, Jr., 103
Gazaway, John, 101
Geary, John, 9
Gecher, Peter, 83
Gee, David, 125
    Ezekiel, 125

Gee, cont.
    John, 130
    Moses, 133
    Thomas E., 138
Geedecke, John, 102
Geers, Benjamin, 118
    Charles, 51
Gehen, Peter, 83
Gennis, William, 102
George, Austen, 70
    Benjamin, 50
    David, 70
    Isaac, 50
    John, 15
    Jonathan, 60
    Michael, 60
    Moses, 43
    Thomas, 50, 54
    William, 80, 81
Gerald, John, 18
Gerhart, Cond, 92
German, Jeremiah
Gerratt, Anthony, 67
Gibbons, _____, 2
    Jno, 131
Gibbs, David, 49
    Isaac, 49
    Joshua, 49
    William, 12
Gibson, James, 16
    William, 24, 28
Gicham, Peter, 83
Giddeman, John, 14
Giffens, Joshua, 17
Gifford, William Capt, 3, 23
    William, 13, 116
Gilbert, John, 81
    Samuel, 112
    Seth, 133
    William, 82, 109
Gilchrist, William, 121
Gildersleeve, Finch, 31, 32, 34
Gill, Joseph, 99
Gillas, Arthur, 136
Gillespie, James, 126, 132
Gillis, Gilbert, 36
Gillman, Jonathan, 42
    Philip, 92
Gilman, Anthony, 54
    Carter, 61
    Carty, 61
    Ezekiel, 59
    Jeremiah, 45, 47, 49
    Nicholas, 64, 65, 70
    Simon, 61
Gilmore, Anthony, 54
    David, 20
    Jacob, 53
    James, 50, 53
    Thomas, 53
Gitting, George, 90
Given, Michael, 129
Givens, Robert, 39, 40

Gladhill, Eli, 17
Glaner, Benjamin, 41
Glanis, Benjamin, 41
Glann, James, 22
Glasby, James, 126
Glasor, Benjamin, 41
    William, 41
Glazer, Adam, 83
Glazier, Benjamin
Glean, Caleb, 31
Gleason, Joseph, 128
    Winsor, 53, 54
Glen, Robert, 118
Glenn, Henry, 4
    James, 22
Glenny, Isaac, 40
    William, 106, 108
Glines, Nathaniel, 53
Glisson, Joseph, 128
Glover, Thomas, 125
Gockin, _____
    Donald, 56, 57
Godell, Benjamin, 137
    Joseph, 137
Godfrey, George, 97
    John, 69
    Jonathan, 60
Godding, Samuel, 62
Godsby, Ralph, 81
Godwin, Abr., 128
    George, 124
    Henry, 133
Goedecke, John, 102
Goggins, Phillips, 26
Gohoon, James
Goldeon, John, 19
Goldsberry, John, 80
Goldsmith, Ezra, 122
Goldsworthy, John, 35
Goldthwait, Thomas, 41
Goldy, John, 18
Gondee, John, 34
Good, Ira, 76
    John, 76
Goodcourage, John, 112
Gooden, George, 124
Gooding, George, 124
Goodspeed, Gideon, 131
Gookin, Daniel, 56, 57
Gould, Joseph, 34
Gordon, Archibald, 81
    Charles, 36, 89
    Davis, 27
    Eliphalet, 62
    Ithiel, 62
    Joseph, 54
    Samuel, 62
    William, 32, 59
Gore, Obadiah, 103, 104
Gorham, John, 41
    Josiah, 41
Goskin, Daniel, 31
Goslin, Samuel, 129

157

Gosling, Thomas, 44
Gotham, Edward, 62
Gothrop, Samuel, 81
Goudy, John, 83
Gouger, Stephen, 33
Gould, Daniel, 40
    Edward, 94
    Elijah, 58
    James, 46
    Joseph, 34
Goulde, Joseph, 28
Gouldsmith, Ezra, 122
Goush, Thomas, 52
Grace, James, 117
    John, 28
Gracey, Matthew, 15
Graff, John, 96
Graham, Charles, 106, 108
    George, 37
    Henry, 20
    James, 37
    Moses, 108
Grahams, George
    Nathaniel, 50
Grainger, John, 125
Grame, George, 37
Granad, Anthony, 100
Grant, Charles, 101
    Daniel, 101
    Duncan, 52
    Edward, 60
    George, 14, 23, 24
    John, 53, 101
    Joseph, 44, 50
    Martin, 42
    Moses, 116
    Robert, 83
    Samuel, 68
Gray, Alexander, 83
    Jacob, 19
    Joel, 81
    John, 81, 86, 118
    Joseph, 69
    Joshua, 40
    Samuel, 13
    Silas, 120, 121
    Thomas, 96, 107
    William, 70, 75
Gread, David, 123
Gready, Thomas, 130
Grear, John, 67
Gregg, Hesekiah, 129
Greeley, Matthew, 66
Green, John, 26
    Joseph, 71
    Pierson, 36
    Richard, 68, 71
    Sutton, 133
    Thomas, 19
Greene, Bradbury, 60
    Bradley, 60
    Jonathan, 59
Greenfield, Charles, 54
Greenlead, Nathaniel, 68

Greenough, Charles, 55
Greenway, Abraham, 62
Greer, James, 83
    Matthew, 53
Gregg, Daniel, 14
    David, 131
    Hezekiah, 129
    James, 117
    Thomas, 112
Gregory, Stephen, 33
    Thomas, 33
Grey, Henry, 12
    Samuel, 13
    Silas, 120
Grew, McD, 86
    Michael, 86
Grier, James, 83
Grierseckies, Drederich, 143
Griffey, Edward, 32
    Joseph, 32
    Levi, 17
Griffin, Benjamin, 109
    James
    Joseph, 67
    Joshua, 134
    Stephen, 120, 121, 125
    William, 28
Griffis, James, 109
    W. E., 1
    William, 116
Griffith, Abner, 106
    Abraham, 110
    Samuel, 109
    William, 18
Griffiths, Abner, 106
    Levi, 17
Griffoy, Edmund
    Joseph, 32
Grigg, Robert, 19
Griggs, William, 20
Grill, John, 27
    Thomas, 40
Grimes, Shepard, 21
Grite, William, 113
Groch, Michael, 93
Grogan, John, 108
Groigill, John, 80
Grometh, Jacob, 90, 92
Gromes, James
Gronad, Anthony
Grosque, John, 80
Grosse, David, 143
Gropp, John, 90
Grote, William, 115
Grotoclas, Gilbert, 36
Grout, John, 53
Grow, Michael, 35
Grumal, Francois, 141
Grumly, Jacob, 92
Grush, Thomas, 52
Guard, Daniel, 27
Guarney, Barzelt, 103
Guffy, Daniel, 20
    Levi, 17

Gugen, Henry, 99
Guinnops, Benjamin, 20
Guiter, Henry, 99
Gumnops, George
Gun, Peter, 93
Gundmyer, Christian, 125
Gurney, Bezalsel, 103
Gurrell, Jno, 17
Gursee, Edward, 32
Gutzelman, John, 99
Guy, John, 25

Haase, Anton, 144
Haburn, William
Hacket, Joshua, 18
Hackett, Jeremiah, 28
    Jonathan, 90
Haddle, John, 11
Hadley, Bishop, 113
    Joseph, 51, 108
Hadlock, Robert, 34, 81
Haflick, Jacob, 93
Hageboughs, Hans, 84
Hagemann, Ludwig, 143
Hagen, Francis, 2
Hagerty, Michael
Hagger, Andrew, 91
Hague, Christian, 73
Hails, Cato, 43
Haines, John, 26
    Simeon, 58
    Thomas, 53
    William, 58
Hains, Henry, 89
    John, 133
Haldron, Henry, 20
Hale, John, 45, 46,
    Nathan, 56
    William, 45, 49
Halfpenny, Thomas, 14, 9
Hall, David, 66
    George, 10
    Isaac
    Israel, 59
    Jacob, 20, 65
    Jacob, Jr., 64
    James, 17
    Joem, 117
    John, 53, 117
    Jude, 61
    Nathan, 10
    Philip, 144
    Reuben, 52
    Silvanus, 43
    Thomas, 59
    ____, 143
Haller, Frederick, 94
Hallett, George, 131
    Jonathan, 106, 109
    Salomon, 131
Halliday, James, 37
Halls, Cato, 43
Halser, Jno, 114

Halsey, Luther, 18
    Thomas, 123
Halstead, John, 103
    Joseph, 137
    Josiah, 25
    Richard, 103
Ham, Ephraim, 58
    John, 58
Hambelton, James, 100
Hamigs, John, 81
Hamilton, Andrew, 14
    Matthew, 73
    Patrick, 106
    Thomas, 17
    William, 9
Hammer, Francis, 128
Hammet, Thomas, 63
Hamon, John, 116
Hampstead, Joseph
    Robert
Hamranck, John, 128, 133
Hambrick, Henry, 91
Hanaddy, William, 29
Hance, John, 12
Hancock, William, 42
Hancomb, Urich, 58
Hand, Burchardt, 94
    Edward, 3
Handley, James, 123
    William, 43
Hanes, John, 26, 133
Hanley, John, 82
Hanmer, Francis
Hanmet, Thomas, 65
Hanna, James, 131
Hannah, Archey, 99
    James, 128
    William, 99
Hans, Mauns, 74
Hannum, William, 40, 99
Hanscomb, Thomas, 58
    Uriah, 58
Hanson, Anthony, 60
    Charles, 52
Hantz, Michael, 90
Hantzell, George, 93
Hanyost, ___, 2
Hapenny, Jno, 91
Harbey, Thomas, 74
Harboidt, John, 141
Hardcastle, John, 13
Hardenbough, John S., 105, 106, 107
Harding, Henry, 104
    Israel, 104
    John, 26
Hardman, Theodore, 91
Hardy, Amos, 41
    John, 76
    Thomas 56
Harley, John, 94
Harmad, James, 25
Harman, Michael, 75

Harmody, Henry, 74
Harmum, Michael, 75
Harper, Jacob, 92
    John, 26
    Richard, 41, 83
Harpole, Henry, 84, 85
Harr, Mark, 118, 119
Harrington, Abner
    Alexander, 37
    Jno, 84
    John, 37, 42, 85
    Thomas, 82
Harris, Daniel, 19, 80
    Henry, 57
    Jacob, 9
    James, 101
    Jno, 91, 92
    John, 86
    Joseph, 59
    Moses, 109
    Solomon, 51
    William, 10
Harrison, Charles, 52
    Horatio, 85
    Jacob, 37
    Samuel, 86
Hart, John, 92
    Oliver, 143
Hartbridt, John
Harter, Adam
    Christopher, 130
Hartjean, John, 141
Hartman, Conrad, 141
    Michael, 88
Hartney, Patrick, 74
Harvey, Elisha, 1
    John, 65, 66
    Kimber, 70
    Thomas, 74
    William, 112
Harvy, Thomas, 54
    William, 112
Harwell, George, 75
Harwood, Thomas, 19
Hasam, John, 133
Hasbrooks, John, 70
Haselton, David, 69
Hasslip, Richard
Hassmore, Reuben, 69
Hastings, Robert, 70
    Silvanus, 53
    William, 81
Hatchett, William, 14
Hatfield, John, 90
    Stephen, 38
Hathaway, Theo, 27
Haupt, Mathias, 144
Hausbrook, George, 132
Havelish, Michael, 109
Havens, Peter, 133
Haw, Jonathan, 43
Hawes, Jonathan, 43
Hawke, Adam, 91
    George, 81, 84

Hawkey, Henry, 129
    Richard, 128
Hawkings, Edward, 22
Hawkins, John, 76
    William R., 64, 71
    Zachariah, 125
    Zopher, 122
Hawkley, James, 53
Hawthorn, Dan, 96
    William, 35
Haycock, David, 37
Hayes, Michael, 13
    Nathaniel, 53
Hayning, George, 29
Hays, Dennis, 13
    William
Hayward, Moses, 43
    Rufus, 43
    Samuel, 58
Heywood, Eliazer, 51
    John, 61
    Samuel, 58
Hazelhurst, John, 73
Hazelton, Abram, 26
    Joseph, 50
Head, John, 53
Heald, Oliver, 40
Healey, Hugh, 29
Heasley, Christopher, 130
Heath, Jesse, 52
    Sterling, 70
    William, 67, 68
Heavens, Peter, 13
Hedger, Joseph, 33
Heffner, Jacob, 90
    Patrick, 42
Heft, George, 74
Heinrichs, Jacob, 144
Helmenthorf, Wilhelm, 141
Helms, William, 21
Helsole, John, 141
Helter, Philip, 91
Hender, Frederick, 115
Henderson, Andrew, 72
    George, 98
    Isaac, 35
    Joath, 58
    Patrick, 12
    Thomas, 58
    William, 72, 76, 99
Hendricks, Elijah, 101
    Wansex, 133
Hendrickson, John, 134
Hendry, Samuel, 16
Henley, Henry, 72
Henly, Henry, 100
Hennag, Henry, 142
Hennis, William, 36
Henricke, John, 142
Henry, Charles, 123
    Michael, 115
    Robert R., 56, 57
Heppe, Abm, 117

Herbert, Eliphalet, 29
Hergood, ____, 91
Hermon, Stephen, 68
Herrick, Zebulon, 40
Herricke, Jacob, 93
Herriman, Page, 53
Herring, Benjamin, 117
    Henry, 88, 89
    John, 93
Herrington, Isaac, 83
    John, 67
    Timothy, 50, 53
Herriot, Thomas, 115
Hersabery, Frederick, 144
Heselton, Isaac, 101
Hess, Michael, 91
    Thobias, 91
Hewett, Benajah, 19
    William, 53
Hewins, William, 43
Hewlett, Samuel, 102
Hibbard, John, 122
Hickling, William, 38
Hickman, Jonathan, 22
Hidden, Dan, 101
Hide, Thomas, 118
Hidler, Martin, 91
Hiff, John, 121
Higbees, Samuel, 124
Higgins, John, 24
    Jonathan, 113
    Michael, 10
    Patrick, 91
Hildreth, Jonathan, 40
Hiley, John, 121
Hilfe, Jacob, 102
Hill, Asa, 121
    Cazeman, 88, 89
    Frederick, 74
    Henry, 117
    James, 17
    Jno, 98
    John, 27, 58
    Jonathan, 59
    Martin, 21
    Matthew, 35
    Nicholas, 114
    Samuel, 141
    Silvanus, 43
    William, 58, 123
Hillabout, Henry, 17
Hillabrant, Henry, 17
Hillery, John, 68
Hillgrove, John, 49
Hilliard, Thomas, 26
Hillings, William, 34
Hills, Ebenezer, 45
Hillsey, Joseph, 12
Hilton, John, 59
    William, 62
Himclan, Adam, 109
Himes, Adam, 83
Hinds, Dennis, 18
    Peter, 28

Hine, Conrad, 76
Hines, Adam, 83
Hines, James, 86
Hinkle, Philip, 89
Hipple, Adam, 115
Hirschelman, William, 144
Hissam, Jno, 131
Hitchcock, Daniel, 4
    John, 110
    Samuel, 109
Hitchcraft, Thomas
Hite, Christopher, 37
Hixson, Elkanah, 43
Hoagg, Hisac, 68
Hobart, Joseph, 70
Hobb, Elisha, 29
Hobbs, William
Hobble, George, 12
Hockukal, Samuel, 96
Hockuker, Samuel, 96
Hadyart, Robert, 52
Hadgdon, Charles, 68
    Joseph, 67
    Phinehas, 58
Hodge, William, 74
Hodgkins, William, 54
Huffman, Charles, 96
Hoffner, George, 95
Hogg, Abner, 71
    William, 58
Hogsenbein, Christopher, 142
Hoit, Amos, 69
    Benjamin, 67
    Levi, 50, 53
    Micah, 58
    Nathan, 64, 65, 68
    Samuel, 52
Holbrook, George, 132
    William, 11
Holdaway, Henry, 101
Holden, Joseph, 42
Holland, Thomas, 24
Holle, Gottfried, 142
Hollenbeck, Jacob, 109
Holley, Benjamin, 118
Hollenshead, John, 16, 18, 25
Hollister, Nathaniel
Hollman, George
Holly, John, 124, 131
    Samuel, 125
    William, 34
Holman, Daniel, 111
    Jere, 52
Homer, John, 141
Holmes, James, 82
    John, 9, 14, 121
    Peter, 133
    Philip, 133
    Thomas, 126
Holsey, Thomas, 123
Holstead, Joseph
Homer, John, 141
Hon, Christian, 44

Honey, Peter, 52
Hoock, Joseph, 94
Hood, Abraham, 74
    Francis, 107
    William, 28
Hoofman, Aaron, 36
Hoolden, Thomas, 21
Hooper, John, 25
Hoops, Adam, 1, 2
Hoover, Anthony, 96
    Felix, 100
    Henry, 96
    Jacob, 90
    Peter, 88, 89
Hoovy, John, 22
Hopewell, John, 101
Hopff, John, 142
Hopll, Abram, 117
Hopkins, John, 10
    Timothy, 104
Hopkinson, John, 59
Hopner, John, 2
Hopp, Abram, 117
Hopper, Christian
    Christopher
    Cornelius, 81
    Jacob, 113
    John, 25, 108
    Robert, 2
    Samuel, 132
Hopsiker, Powles, 14
Hopson, Jerdon, 17
Horam, Moses, 14
Horine, Jacob, 86
    John, 86
Horn, Benjamin, 20, 23, 29
    Daniel, 58
    Simon, 13
Hornbeck, Henry
Hornblower, Joseph, 13
Horne, Benjamin, 24
    James, 26
Horneforth, Andrew, 29
Horner, John, 83
Horeford, Joseph, 108
Hortain, Silas, 129
Horton, Christopher, 107
    John, 37
Hortwick, Barney, 17
    Matthias, 17
Hoshield, John, 88, 89
Hosier, John, 129
Hosport, Samuel, 124
Hossmore, Reuben, 69
Hottman, George, 28
Houck, Joseph, 94
Hourcran, Patrick, 101
House, Henry, 130
    Jacobus, 123
    John, 45, 49, 113
Houserman, Conrad, 88, 89
Houstman, George, 118

Houston, Samuel, 71
Hover, Anthony, 96
    Regnier
Hovey, Ivory, 65
    John, 65
    Peter, 52
How, Joseph, 44
Howard, Benjamin, 66
    Ebenezer, 41
    Eliha, 27
    Ephraim, 24
    Ezekiel, 15
    John, 24
    Joseph, 10
Howe, Bezaleel, 45, 47, 48, 49
    Jacobus, 123
    John, 27, 100, 124
    Jonathan, 61
    Mark, 65
    Richard, 74
    Samuel, 49
    Thomas, 61
    William R., 74
Howell, Ezekiel, 136
    George, 123
    Jean, 25
    John, 9, 15
    Lemuel, 128
    Samuel, 128
    Vincent, 101
    William, 35
Howard, Joseph, 25
Howlett, Samuel, 102
Hoyle, Conrad, 90
Hoyt, Enoch, 154
    Reuben, 66
    Thomas, 36
Hubbard, John, 122
    Joseph, 70
Hubart, Christian, 99
Hubble, John, 11
Hubley, Adam, 3, 78
    Bernard, 92
    John, 3
Huchtauve, Hinrich, 144
Huckukor, Sambel, 96
Hudsal, Nicholas, 107
Hudson, Abram, 13
    Enos, 42
Hueba, John, 142
Huff, Lopher
    William, 122
Huffman, Henry, 112
Huges, John, 125
Hughes, George, 81
    James, 93
    Richard, 69
    William, 130
Hulbert, Aaron, 113
Hull, Israel, 59
    Jacob, Jr., 64
    Jehiah, 25
    Joseph, 67

Hulley, Arthur, 116
Hulser, Jno, 114
Hulson, _____, 114
Humphrey, Alexander, 133
    James, 132
    Joseph, 29
Hundley, Michael, 75
Hunkin, Richard, 61
Hunt, David, 52
    Enoch, 70
    Glover, 99
    Humphrey, 66
    Josiah, 36
    Thomas, 51, 123
    William, 108
    Zaccheus, 52
Hunter, Adam, 42
    Andrew, 3
    Benjamin, 125
    Huston
    James, 72, 73
    John, 82
    Jonathan, 112
    Joseph, 42
    Robert, 86
    Samuel, 74
    William, 76
Huntley, John, 20
    Thomas, 111
Huntress, Jonathan, 62
    Nathaniel
    Pearson, 59
Hurd, Jehiel, 46
Hurlburt, Aaron
Hurley, Arthur, 116
Huselen, Edward, 101
Huston, William, 79, 86
Hutch, John, 26
Hutchcraft, Thomas, 88, 89, 90
Hutheson, George, 99
Hutchings, Gab, 13
Hutchins, Moses, 50, 53
    Nathaniel, 45, 54
    Simon, 51
    William, 45, 46
Hutchinson, Ebenezer, 128
    Elijah, 50
    Elisha, 50
    John, 73, 103
    Levi, 50
    Richard, 35, 82
    Thomas, 62
Hutton, Christopher, 118
Hyatt, Abraham, 120, 124
Hyde, Azel, 103
Hynds, Peter, 30
Hynes, Henry, 112
Hyre, Alexander, 114
Hyses, Henry, 124

Ingalls, Israel, 52
Inglish, William, 70
Insell, John, 19

Ireland, John, 19
    Thomas, 26
Irwin, James, 20
    William, 20
Isaacs, Isaac, 117
Isanogle, Thomas, 75
Israel, Casper, 94
Ivory, Jacobus, 111
Izzunus, Jean, 143

Jack, Robert, 42
Jackes, Thomas, 36
Jackson, Archibald, 118
    Travis, 112
    Jeremiah, 80, 82
    Richard, 13
    Thomas, 104, 124
    Turner, 104
    William B., 131
Jacobs, David, 37
    Davis
    Joseph, 35
    Rowley, 101
    William, 102
Jacquet, Jona D., 90
James, David, 19
    Eben, 125
Jansen, Cornelius J., 116
    Frederick, 114
Jaquish, John, 107
Jee, John, 130
Jeff, Robert, 136
Jefferies, Robert, 83
Jeffers, John, 123
Jeffrey, Humphrey, 32
Jehoickum, Capt, 2
Jelfs, Robert, 136
Jenkins, Israel, 93
    James, 34
    John, 2
    Peter, 53
Jennings, Stephen, 49
    Thomas, 97
Jennens, Ebenezer, 61
    John, 50
Jensing, Robert, 108
Jenson, Robert, 108
Jewell, Andrew
    David, 70
    John, 59
    Joseph, 58
    Robert
    Seth, 36
Jewett, Caleb, 131
    Phenix, 14
    Seth, 36
    William, 59
Jie, John, 130
Jiles, James, 102
Job, John, 60
    Willeem, 143
Jobes, John, 27
Jobs, Ezekiel, 21

Jobs, cont.
   John, 21
   Samuel, 21
Johnson, Andrew, 33, 58
   Daniel, 133
   David, 57
   Gato, 36
   George, 75
   Henry, 32
   Jacob, 35, 44
   James, 88, 109
   John, 14, 33, 128
   Joseph, 24, 37, 131
   Lewis, 33
   Martin, 18
   Matthew, 35
   Philip, 68
   Prince, 130
   Samuel, 24, 126
   Seth, 23, 29
   Thomas, 81
   William, 126, 134
Johnstone, Cato, 36, 43
   George, 27
   Isaac, 19
   James, 83, 88, 89, 128, 134
   Jno, 93
   John, 17, 18, 128, 136
   Thomas, 81, 99
   William, 28, 94
Joice, Michael, 51
Joiner, Francis, 51
   John, 48, 53
Jones, Abraham, 37
   Alexander, 26
   Amber, 29
   Armstrong, 27
   Asay, 21
   Charles, 93
   Cocer
   Crocer, 104
   Croker, 104
   Ebenezer, 12
   Edward, 75
   Ephraim, 58
   Griffin, 130, 131
   Jacob, 108
   James, 72, 73
   John, 12, 66, 122
   Joseph, 15, 37, 43, 129
   Michael, 10
   Seth, 113
   Thomas, 73, 74, 114, 126, 129, 132
Jonson, Ira, 43
Jordan, John, 48
   Peter, 42
   William, 43
Joy, James, 27
   John, 122
Judge, Thomas, 82
Judgkins, Samuel, 68

Judkins, Jonathan, 54
   Samuel, 67
June, Thomas, 41

Kader, Adam, 122
   John, 122
Kain, Nicholas, 76
Kaits, Philip, 19
Kamp, Amos, 58
Kanto, Jacob, 97
Karr, Benjamin
   Mark, 119
Katts, Charles, 97
Kauffman, Jacob, 94
Kautz, Philip, 94
Kealy, James, 109
Kearney, James
Keating, Edward, 83
Keaton, Edward, 83
Kebler, John, 90
Kecher, John, 36
Keck, Henry, 102
Keef, Con, 109
Keeler, Edward, 37
   Jacob, 34
   James, 32
Keemer, Nicholas, 74
Keen, Jacob, 20
   Thomas, 91
Keenahan, Richard, 76
Keenan, Jame
Keene, Lawrence, 78, 82
Keener, Christian, 119
Keip, Abraham
   William
Keiser, Jacob, 92
Keith, Philip, 19
Kelcher, John, 36
Keley, Barton, 29
Kellarn, Reuben, 118
Keller, Matthew, 86
   George, 97
Kelley, Andrew, 86
   James, 62
   John, 53
   Jonathan, 53
Kellogg, William, 104
Kellown, Reuben, 118
Kelly, C. Norris, 122
   David, 34
   Dennis, 126
   Edward, 35
   John, 35, 100, 121, 136
   Patrick, 115
   Robert, 124, 125
Kelsey, John, 121
   Moses, 67
   Zacharias, 61
Kemp, Amos, 58
Kenchan, Richard, 76
Kendall, William, 61
Kendrick, John, 93
Kennedy, Charles, 17
   William, 29, 30

Kenney, Lawrence, 104
Kennestone, James, 58
   Job, 58
Kennison, Job, 58
Kenny, John, 58, 81
Kent, Jacob, 27
   John, 52
   Jonas, 15
   Smith, 101
   Thomas, 131
Kentz, Jacob, 94
Kenyon, William, 109
Kepler, John, 102
Keplinger, Christopher,
Keppard, Jno, 93
Kepphard, George, 88, 89
Kerls, F., 92
Kermahan, Richard, 76
Kerns, Francis, 93
Kerr, Mark, 119
   William, 100
Kerrell, William, 18
Kerse, George, 102
Kersey, John, 24
   William, 24
Kersner, Michael, 94
Kersteller, George, 12
Kertel, Albertus, 142
Keston, Edward
Ketcher, John, 36
Ketchum, John, 122
   Joseph, 111
Kettle, Abraham, 88, 89
Keyes, Stephen, 70, 71
Keyley, Conrad, 93
Keyser, Valentine, 102
Kibbe, Ephraim, 29
Kidder, Daniel, 50
   John, 43
   Wieder, 34
Kieman, James, 55
Kiesburg, Christian, 112
Kilpatrick, James, 25
Kimball, Benjamin, 45, 4
   David, 42
   John, 59
   Thomas, 48
Kimble, Nathan, 26
   Prince, 108
Kinch, Jacob, 34, 82
Kinder, Christian, 117
Knear, John, 90
King, Alexander, 73, 75
   Anthony, 12
   Ephraim, 58
   Hugh, 143
   Joseph, 13, 101
   Michael, 97
Kingman, Loring, 41
Kingsley, Alpheus, 51
Kink, Jacob, 82
Kinner, Jonathan, 122
Kinnerly, William, 3

Lacey, Joseph - 12
  " , Jacob - 12
Long, Joseph 12
Lee, David, 12
Lay, William, 11
Leonard, Enoch, 11
Linwood, John, 11
Lennington, Henry, 13
Lewis, Benjamin, 13
Loyns, Luvring, 13
Levi, Asher, 13
Logon, Robert, 13
Leonard, Stephen 13
Losey, Abraham 13
Lott, Peter, 13
Lane, Michel, 14
Lyal, Thomas, 14
Legur, Benj..N, 15
Little, Robert, 15
Lane, Derrick, 16
Lloid, John, 17
Lowing, Peter 17
Lynch, Wm. 17
Lock, Philip, 20
Lye, Wm. 20
Luwry, Vincent, 20
Little, Jacob, 20
Lounsberry, Walker, 20
Kinsey, James, 18
  " , Shedrick, 18
Lykins, Andrew, 18
Land, Joseph, 19
Long, Richard, 19

Loper, Abram, 19
Lambert, Lanet 19
Lovelott, Lot, 21
Lyons, John 21
Lane, Derrick 21
Laudon, Samuel, 21
Loring, Ephriam, 24
Lorce, " , 24
Likens, Jacob, 24
Lyons, William 24

Maloney, Jno, 97, 98
    William, 74
Mam, Richard
Manfield, Joem, 85
Manifold, John, 59
Mann, Nathan, 48
    Richard, 34
    William, 48
Manning, Eliphalet, 52
    John, 85
Manson, John, 52
Mapes, Frederick, 32
    Phinehas, 34
    William, 27
March, Jno, 91
    Joseph, 92
    Philip, 20
Marden, James, 60
    John, 67
Margery, Jonas, 61
Markle, Charles, 140, 141
Marks, George, 102
    George, 130
    John, 136
Marolf, Rudolf, 88, 89
Marquise, William, 83
Marsh, Dudley, 59
    Joseph, 52
    Simon, 58
Marshall, Elisha, 3, 106, 110
    James, 36, 113, 122
    Robert, 132
Marston, James, 66
    Nathaniel, 62
    Samuel, 68
Martial, James, 122
Martin, Absalom, 9, 13
    Alexander, 136
    Christopher, 69
    Claudius, 75
    Daniel, 14
    David, 26
    Ichabod, 53
    Isaac, 109
    James, 29
    John, 27
    Thomas, 27
    Timothy, 51
Marx, William, 102
Marz, John, 75
Mason, Andrew, 18
    Bradstreet, 54
    Edward, 66, 67
    George
    James, 66, 118
    Jonathan, 67
    Lemuel, 62
    Robert, 4
    Simeon, 58
    Thomas, 107, 121
Masson, Michael, 88, 89
Masters, Stephen, 17

Mathers, John, 118
Mathew, John, 48
Matthews, Ebenezer, 50
    Hugh, 59
    James, 27
    Thomas, 53, 59
Matthewson, Elisha
Maule, Nicals, 26
Maxwell, Anthony, 31, 34
    Cornelius, 117
    William, 3, 7, 8, 117
May, Andrew, 10
    Hendrick, 110
    John, 43
Mayberry, Thomas, 99
    William, 96, 99
Mayers, Everbardt, 92
Maypowder, William, 81
Maze, Edward, 17
McAlester, Randall, 71
McAllister, James, 85
McAnally, Patrick, 18
McAnarney, John, 32
McBride, Barnabas, 57
    James, 76, 137, 138
    William, 137, 138
    Zabez, 61
McBurney, James, 17
McCabs, Henry, 26
McCalla, George, 85
McCallen, John
McCallester, Aholiab
    Reuben, 71
    William, 121, 123
McCalling, Samuel, 80
McCallum, John, 22, 133
McCally, Florence, 51
    Torrence, 51
McCalvin, Thomas, 81
McCalvy, Thomas, 81, 85
McCann, Henry, 10
    Marmaduke, 80
McCarter, Charles, 72
McCartney, Isaac, 106
McCarty, Dennis, 117
McCatherson, Neal, 83
McCauley, Nathaniel, 45, 47
McCaw, Hugh, 92
    Patrick, 100
McCawley, Alexander, 20
McCelvey, Thomas, 85
McClahan, John, 82
McClain, Jacob, 92
McClamon, John, 129
McClare, John, 134
McClaskey, Andrew, 56
McClean, Allen, 85
    Hugh, 21
    John, 15, 134
    Neal, 121
McClehan, John, 52, 82
McClellan, Samuel, 30

McClelland, John, 52, 82
    Samuel, 30
McClure, Andrew, 14
    James, 135
    Thomas, 103
McClurey, James, 136
    Thomas, 103
    William, 104
McClurg, Robert, 61
McCluskey, Andrew, 86
    Arthur, 86
McCoaklin, Hugh, 29
McColley, Florence
McCollum, John, 22, 133
McCombs, William, 93
McCondrey, William
McConnel, Hugh, 36
    Robert, 95, 97
McConnolly, Hugh, 116
McCook, Thomas, 99
McCooney, George
McCord, William, 110
McCork, Thomas, 99
McCormick, John, 74
    Stephen, 32
McCourt, Jesse N., 40
McCowen, Const, 20
McCowly, Alexander, 20
McCoy, Alexander, 114
    Daniel, 97
    John, 50, 53
    Michael, 83
    Nathan, 53
    Nicholas
    Paul, 51
    Stephen, 53
McCracken, James, 99
    Joseph, 121
    Philip, 33
McCray, Philip, 11
McCrea, Philip, 13
    Stephen, 4
McCreary, John, 101
McCucheson, Neal, 83
McCulla, Thomas, 85
McCullian, Forest, 81
McCullough, Arthur, 81
    James, 17
    Lewis, 93
    Robert, 83
    Roger, 83
McCully, John, 24
McCummings, John, 83
McCune, Richard, 134, 137
McCurdy, William, 79, 86
McCutchum, Forest, 81
McDade, William, 18
McDaniel, Darrel, 41
    James, 58
    William, 98
McDermott, Cornelius, 116
    Francis, 130
    Thomas, 101

McDole, John, 18, 125
McDonack, James, 74
McDonal, Robert, 101
McDonald, Benjamin, 25
    Daniel, 29
    Duncan, 101
    Edward, 86
    George, 16
    Hugh, 98
    James, 20
    John, 82, 110
    Ronald, 110
McDonark, James, 74
McDonnell, John, 35, 81
McDonel, Robert, 101
McDonaugh, James, 83
McDougal, Alex, 116
McDuffy, Randle, 17
McElroy, Hugh, 76
    James, 86
    John, 81, 86
McElvin, Ebenezer, 60
McElwan, Thomas, 73
McEntire, James, 83
McEwen, John, 31, 33
    Jno, 31
McFair, Archibald, 136
McFarland, John, 117
    Joseph, 53
McFarlin, John, 113
McGaffey, Neal, 65, 66, 67
McGanon, Francis, 102
McGariby, Arthur, 86
McGarran, Francis, 102
McGeary, Neal, 83
McGee, James, 75
    John, 51
    Peter, 115
    William, 21, 51
McGerther, John
McGill, Henry, 83
    William, 36
McGinnis, James, 86
McGinnta, James, 27, 85
McGinter, Timothy
McGlaughlin, Thomas, 53
    William, 2
McGlocken, Charles, 11
McGonegal, George, 17
McGowan, Jeremiah, 109
    John, 72, 73, 74
McGraw, Stephen, 93
McGregor, Abraham, 136
    Alexander, 20
    Archibald, 136
    John, 136
McGregore, Daniel
    David, 64, 69
McGuffie, James, 137
McGuin, Samuel, 58
McGuire, James, 102
McHenry, Edward, 34, 82
McHughes, Edward, 25

McIntire, Andrew, 51
    James, 76
    Joseph, 25
    Thomas, 15
    William, 73
McIntosh, John, 114
    William, 125
McIlveny, Hugh, 76
McJohnson, John, 101
McKendry, William, 38, 39
McKenny, John, 101
McKensie, John, 115
McKey, Thomas, 34
McKinnis, John, 83
McKinney, Edward, 82
    Malcolm, 35
    Richard
    Timothy, 28
McKinsey, Charles, 109
    James, 109
    John, 37
    Joshua, 90
    Moses, 90
McKinzie, John, 37
McKnight, Benjamin, 101
McLain, Obed, 53
McLane, Allan, 85
McLane, Michael, 33
McLaughlin, Felix, 85
    Hugh, 30
    John, 15
    William, 117
McLean, Allen, 85
McMahon, Jeremy, 20
    Jon, 100
    William, 99
McManere, John, 42
McMarris, William, 11
McMannoa, John, 42
McManus, Christ, 13
McMasters, Alexander, 53
    John, 34
McMellon, John, 29
McMelton, John, 29
McMillan, Charles, 19
    John, 29
McMuling, Cornelius, 86
McMullen, Daniel, 101
    Michael, 82
    William, 98, 99, 131
McMullin, William, 11
McMurphy, George, 53
    John, 29
McNabb, Andrew, 81
McNair, Archibald, 136
McNamara, Dennis, 74
McNanamy, James, 81
McNeal, Hector, 33
    Robert, 99
    Thomas, 50
McNulty, Michael, 99
    Patrick, 99
McPherson, Joseph, 33

McPike, James, 75
McQuag, John, 20
McSwine, George, 73
McUay, John, 118
Mead, Giled, 9
    Michael, 41
Meade, James, 10
    William, 27
Meadows, William, 80
Meads, James, 10
Mealy, Edward, 86
Mean, John, 75
Mease, John, 75
Medaugh, Ernans, 20
Medden, John, 44
Medock, Emons, 20
Meeder, Stephen, 61
Meeker, Michael, 33
    Nathaniel, 112
    Solomon, 113
    Thomas, 11
    Uzel, 35
Meese, Daniel, 70
Megonegal, George, 17
Meiner, Theodeus, 141
Meisner, August, 143
Melcheor, Paul, 118
Mencher, Christopher, 93
Mendall, Amos, 44
Menema, Daniel, 106
Menges, Moses, 37
Mequin, Samuel, 58
Merriam, Joseph, 20
Merricule, Samuel, 115
Merrill, Abel, 48
    Amos, 47
    Bernard, 52
    David, 51
    Jacob, 59
    John, 51
    Joseph, 121
    Nathaniel, 70
    Stephen, 42
Merrison, Daniel, 132
Merritt, Daniel, 42
    Stephen, 42
    William, 42
Merrow, Joshua, 56, 60
Mesely, James, 42
Messam, Benjamin, 83
Messon, Jacob, 90
Metcalf, Ralph, 44
Michall, Jno, 90
Midaugh, Emons
Middleton, Joshua, 27
    Samuel, 102
    Thomas, 20
Midgett, John, 66
Midjeo, Conrad, 11
Miels, Israel, 14
Mier, Adam, 44
    John, 47
Mighells, Asbell, 41

Miles, John, 116
    Moses, 58
    William, 35, 83
Millard, Elisha, 134
    Henry, 134
Miller, Andrew, 86
    Benjamin, 123
    Charles, 75
    Christian, 98
    Cornelius, 10
    Daniel, 75
    Farrar, 60
    Frederick, 18
    George, 86
    Henry, 112
    Jack, 125
    Jacob, 80, 125
    Jacob, Sr., 88, 89
    Jacob, Jr. 88, 89
    Jesse, 121
    John, 25, 71, 80, 93, 98
    Joseph, 18, 49, 89
    Mark, 90
    Martin, 97
    Matthew, 49
    Samuel, 50
Millet, Abraham, 42
    John, 48
Mills, Andrew, 122
    George, 41
    John, 63
    Joseph, 45, 47, 48, 54
    Reuben, 20
    Richard, 20
    William, 41
Millson, James, 33
Millspaugh, Christopher, 37
Millwood, Nathan, 42
Mimmaert, William, 83
Mingle, Stephel, 74
    Thomas, 96
Mimick, Barnhardt, 116
    Hendrick, 118
Minks, Joem, 122
Minthorn, John, 10
    Philip, 13
    William, 13
Minton, John, 10
Mitchell, Alexander, 9, 13
    David, 44, 106
    Henry, 80
    Isaac, 53
    James, 132
    John, 40, 44, 59, 61, 62, 96
    Joseph, 132
    Joshua, 59
    Martin, 111
    Richard, 32
    Samuel, 71, 123
Mitting, David, 44
Mize, John, 122
Moake, William, 44

Moddy, James, 126
Mogrew, Michael
Mohony, Jno, 98
Molloy, James, 106
Molong, Jno, 96
Monhart, Isaac, 34
Mongaual, Frederick, 93
Monroe, Alexander, 114
    Josiah, 45, 47
Monson, Salomon, 27
Montgomery, Alexander, 28
Moody, James, 126
Mooney, Barnet, 16
    Barney, 36
    John, 12
    William, 98, 133
Moonly, Barney, 36
Moor, Frederick, 114
Moore, Charles, 109
    Francis, 96
    Isaac, 67
    James, 48, 137
    John, 51, 117
    Joseph, 25
    Robert, 113
    William, 59, 96
Moorehouse, Jacob, 25
Morgan, Charles, 26, 101
    Daniel, 83
    David, 60, 91
    John, 60
    Joseph, 97, 138
    Samuel, 33
    Thomas, 10
    William, 22
Morley, Jacob, 94
Morpeth, William, 123
Morrell, Isaac, 106, 110
    John, 109
    William, 33
Morrill, Abel, 60, 61
    Amos, 45, 47, 50
    Joseph, 24, 120
    Simon, 45, 47, 48
Morris, David, 27
    Edmond, 115
    Gilbert, 76
    James, 24
    Thomas, 24
Morrison, Daniel, 132
    David, 106
    John, 44, 66
    Major, 2, 5
    McD, 86
    Patrick, 132
    Richard, 118
    Samuel, 48, 50, 79, 85
Morritz, Galliel, 140
Morrow, Joshua, 56, 60
    Patrick, 132
    Thomas, 83
Morton, George, 125
    John, 95

Morse, Enoch, 51
    Isaac, 59
    Philip, 33
Moser, Benjamin
    Christian, 75
    Daniel
Mosers, Jacob, 90
    Jonathan
Mosher, Timothy, 61
Mosier, Christian, 75
    John, 34
Mosley, James, 42
Moss, Daniel, 70
    David, 124
    Isaac, 59
    Philip, 33
Mott, David, 13
    Ebenezer, 131
    Ezekiel, 35
    Isaac, 111
    Noah, 108
    Samuel, 115
    Thomas, 114
Maulin, Noeldu, 142
Moulton, Cato, 126
    James, 69, 126
    Josiah, 68
    Nathaniel, 57
    Simeon, 60
Mount, George, 32
Mozure, Hugh, 119
    John, 34
Mulatt, Abram, 10
Mulholland, James, 116
    Patrick, 37
Mullen, Manus, 75
    Thomas, 98
    William, 131
Mullmer, Moses, 109
Multz, Francis, 92
    Frederick, 91
Mulvany, John, 36, 82
Muma, Davis, 94
Mumford, David, 13
Mumner, William, 93
Munday, William, 106, 108
Munrar, Josiah, 45, 47
Murdoch, Thomas, 76
    William, 14
Murray, Bartley, 113
    Daniel, 83
    David, 80
    James, 118
    Louise W., 1
    William, 80
Murphy, Daniel, 97
    James, 76
    John, 28, 137, 138
    Joseph, 86
    Patrick, 60
    Timothy, 101
Musler, Adam, 93
Muster, Adam, 93

Mustie, Stephen, 28
Mutchmore, James, 53
Mute, William, 109
Myers, Christian, 94
    David
    Jacob, 91, 92, 94, 114
    Lawrence, 102
    Martin, 32
    Peter, 91
Mynear, Jacob, 40
Myre, John, 122
Myres, John, 122

Nagler, Samuel, 17
Nankerson, William, 134
Nash, Asahd, 104
    Jonathan, 52
    Martin, 41
Nathan, James, 44
Neal, Thomas, 19, 103
Nealey, Abraham, 31
Neale, John, 62
Neals, Jno, 62
    John, 60, 104
Nealy, Joseph, 69
Neas, Elisha, 67
Neason, Robert, 129
Neck, Jonathan, 52
Needer, Samuel, 115
Neill, John, 32
Neilly, John O., 104
Neilson, _____, 2
Nelson, Abraham, 42
    Allen, 114
    John, 137, 138
    William, 134
Nemire, Jno, 119
Nency, Samuel, 35
Nesmiller, James, 71
Ness, Elisha, 67
Nette, Louis, 141
Neuhoff, Henry, 142
Neuson, Robert, 129
Neving, William, 92
Newcomb, James, 107
    Kinder, 131
    Robert
Newgent, Thomas, 81
Newingham, Daniel, 81
Newman, Elias, 36
Newmon, Jonathan, 129
Newton, John, 12
    Silas, 20
    Thomas, 14
    Timothy, 53
Nicholls, John, 10
Nichols, George, 86
Nichols, Isaac, 20
    Isaiah, 20
    James, 57
    John, 59, 134
Nicholson, George, 86
    Luke, 42

Nickles, Jonathan, 25
Nightlenger, Samuel, 84, 85
Nimnough, Neal, 20
Niven, William, 131
Nixon, Isaac, 19
    John, 74, 83
    Marion, 83
    Thomas, 38
Noble, Adam, 93
    Stephen, 58
Noel, Luis, 29
Noles, Joseph, 86
Nolt, Philip, 19
Norcross, Benjamin, 24
Nording, Israel, 104
Norris, Eliphalet
Norris, Isaac, 118
    James, 59, 64, 67, 98
    Joseph, 53
    Peter, 29
    Samuel, 59
North, Daniel, 98
    Jno U., 125
    St. Cal
Northend, George U., 14
Norton, A. T., 1
    Abel, 121
    George, 125
    Jabe, 121
    John, 58
    Nathaniel, 120, 125
    William, 96
Nosler, John, 29
Nostrand, Isaac, 114
Notieo, Michael, 80
Novee, Lewis, 111
Nowse, Lewis, 110
Nugent, Thomas, 86
Nukerck, Charles, 105, 106
Nute, Jathram, 62

Oakey, Abraham, 132
Oakley, John, 25, 104, 109
    Jonathan, 130
O'Brian, John, 29
O'Briant, Patrick, 21
O'Brien, Roger, 86
O'Bryan, William, 83
Occurman, William, 137
Ockamen, William, 137, 138
Ockerman, William, 138
Odiorne, John, 67
    Samuel, 66
Ogden, Aaron, 3, 9
    Eliakim, 25
    Ludlow, 33
    Matthias, 3, 8, 9
    Moses, 36
    Noah, 17
Ogleby, George, 75
Ohlen, Henry G., 117
Oldenberger, George
Oldis, Robert, 81

Oldwire, Beernard, 75
O'Fling, Patrick, 66
Oliber, Jain, 142
Olindorf, Leonard, 114
Olinger, Peter, 97
Olmendorf, Leonard, 114
Olmstead, John, 107
Omack, Thomas, 26
Oman, Charles, 27
O'Neal, Arthur, 12
    Henry, 19
    James, 82
    John, 22, 104
    Neal, 18
    Nicholas, 82
O'Neill, John, 32
Oppenhauser, Henry, 141, 144
Organ, John, 36
    Matthew, 37
Orient, Joseph, 68
Ormsbury, Amox, 103
Orne, Fred, 99
Orr, Baltus, 113
    John, 25, 31, 37
Osborne, Joseph, 15
    Luke, 12
    Stephen, 15
Osburn, Aaron, 118
    Benjamin, 11
    Daniel, 132
Osgood, Thomas, 53
Osman, Benapah, 21
    Charles, 27
    John, 18
Osmun, Charles, 27
    Nathaniel, 11
Osten, Daniel, 132
Osterhout, Isaac, 117
Ostrander, Andrew, 48
    Henry, 131
    Peter, 115
    William, 115
Otis, John, 61
    Paul, 60
Ottendorf, Nicholas, 102
Otto, Charles, 40
    John, 44
Ousterhout, Peter, 109
Over, Jacob, 76
Owens, Daniel, 112
    Uriah, 116
Owinge, Jno, 76
Oxford, Derrick, 49

Packall, John, 122
Packard, Abisha, 42
Padden, John, 110
Page, Abraham, 67
    Benjamin, 69
    Chase, 67
    David, 61
    James, 76

Page, cont.
    Moses, 65, 68
    Simeon, 4, 43
    Thomas
    Toss, 40
Paine, Silas, 123
    Thomas, 42
Painter, Edward, 118
    Henry, 90
Palden, Jonathan, 42
    William, 42
Palchouse, Thomas
Palley, Joseph, 52
Palmatus, Isaac, 113
Palmer, Ebenezer, 63
    Jonathan, 109
    William, 60
Palmerton, Thomas, 130
Palmth, Joseph, 40
Pangburn, William, 121
Panther, Henry, 90
Parcell, Anthony, 32
Park, Thomas, 104
Parker, Amasa, 70
    Colburn, 54
    Coleman, 54
    Ebenezer, 125
    Edward, 113
    Elijah, 128
    Gershom, 25
    Isaac, 80
    Jesse, 43
    Jonas, 39, 44
    Levi, 39
    Michael, 100
Park, Robert, 51, 136
    Samuel, 101
    William, 56
Parkes, Michael, 66
Parks, Ebenezer, 104
    Thomas, 36, 75, 103, 164
    Timothy, 113
    Lebulon, 25
Parr, James, 3, 100
    Silas, 11
Parrett, Adameram, 27
Parralt, Silas, 9, 11
Parshall, James, 122, 126
Parshley, George, 61
    Thomas, 61
Parsons, Samuel, 139
Partig, Nathan, 42
Partridge, Nathan, 42
Patch, John, 40
Patten, Nathaniel, 49, 50
Patterson, Alexander, 2
    Andrew, 35
    Christian, 75
    Daniel, 74
    Ezra, 136
    George, 59
    James, 96, 113, 118
    John, 16

Patterson, cont.
    Nehemiah, 104
    Robert, 96, 98
    William, 117
    Zechariah, 17
Patton, Anthony, 83
Paul, After, 36
    Arthur, 36
    Benjamin, 32
    Jesse, 16
    Joseph, 126
Paulsen, Michael, 119
Pauper, Robert, 97
Paverley, John, 66
Pawling, H., 130
Peabody, Eben, 39
    Ebenezer, 42
Pearles, Joseph, 62
Pearson, Matthers, 82
    Nicholas, 13
Pearsons, Samuel, 139
Pease, Ebenezer, 43
Peck, David, 20
    John, 16, 18, 134
    William, 35, 37
Peckett, Thomas, 104
Peeler, George, 16
Peirce, John, 44
Pell, Josiah, 104
    Samuel, 106, 108
Pellet, Samuel, 122
Pellie, Samuel, 122
Pemberton, Robert, 2, 22, 34
Pembroke, William, 131
Pendergrass, Robert, 80
    Thomas, 10
Pendle, Philip, 80
Pennell, Clement, 42
Penner, John
    Peter, 122
Penney, John, 122
Pennman, Adna, 64, 71
Penny, Jonathan
Penoyer, Ise, 120, 121
    Jesse, 121, 124
Penton, James, 16
Pepper, John, 130
Pepperill, George, 60
Perchase, Joseph, 119
Perdon, James, 11
Perisonius, Jesse, 131
Perkhoff, Frederick, 114
Perkins, Adam, 62
    Benjamin, 51
    Jonathan, 59
Perksmith, Engleis, 118
Perry, Henry, 27
    Ichabod, 69
    John, 22
    Thomas, 13, 54, 76
Persons, Harmon, 17
Petan, Mathew, 72
Peten, Henry, 83

Peten, cont.
    John, 119
    Levi, 26
    Philip, 19
    Simon, 114
Peterson, Abram, 24
    John, 70, 108
    Peter, 32
    Simon, 122
    Zechariah, 17, 108
Petis, John, 70
Petterson, Daniel, 74
Pettingall, Elkanale, 43
Pettingill, Benjamin, 51
    Jethro, 50
    William, 48
Pettigrew, James, 79, 83
Pettis, Samuel, 122
Peverley, John, 66
Philbrook, Daniel, 66
Phillips, Benjamin, 70, 71
    David, 130
    Francis, 21
    John, 70, 71
    Jonathan, 121
    Joshua, 132
    Samuel, 53
Phipps, Benjamin, 136
Piatt, Daniel, 9
    Jacob, 8, 9
    John, 11
    William, 9, 11
Picket, Thomas, 104
Pickett, Robert, 27
Pickle, John, 122
Piene, John, 42
Pierce, Asa, 69
    James, 44
    John, 14
    William, 1
Pierson, Harman, 17
    Matthew, 37
    Samuel, 37
Pies, Michael, 42
Pike, Joseph, 40
    Joshua, 96
Pilegret, Hendrick, 17
Pillmore, William, 80
Pincell, Clements, 42
Pine, John, 42
Pinkham, Daniel, 60, 61
    Isaac, 60
Pinkney, Jonathan, 119
    William, 27
Pinner, Benjamin, 63
Piper, Jno, 66
    Lewis, 119
    Thomas, 66
Pirce, Frank
Pitter, Felix, 101
Pittman, John, 116
Pitts, Thomas, 68
Pixley, Eli, 113

Plase, Peter, 122
Platner, John, 104
Platts, Thomas, 116
Ploss, Peter, 122
Plough, Jochen, 118
Plum, Stephen, 15, 123
Plumley, William, 124
Plummer, Nathan, 53
Poarter, Samuel, 100
Poiden, Jonathan, 42
    William, 42
Pointer, William, 90
Polden, Jonathan, 82
    William, 82
Polehouse, Thomas, 88, 89, 90
Polk, Joseph, 18
Pollard, Elijah, 59
    Hezekiah, 59
    Thomas, 17, 126
Pool, Jonathan, 45, 47, 48
Poole, John, 22
Poor, Enoch, 3, 4
Poorham, John, 102
Porter, Andrew, 136
    Noah, 53
    Robert, 93
    William, 80
Post, Richard, 117
Poten, John, 21
Potter, John, 13
    Joseph, 56, 57, 60
    Nathaniel
    Philip, 100
    Samuel, 26
    Thomas, 18, 104
    William, 142
    Yulliams, 142
Potts, Benjamin, 104
    Jasper, 24
Poulson, Michael, 119
Poupon, Seger, 141
Powell, Lloyd, 76
    Peter, 21
    Stephen, 108
    Thomas, 66
    Vinson, 122
    William, 52
Powers, Abner, 53
    George, 29
    Josiah, 70
    Nathaniel
    Simon, 53
Pratt, Chalker, 113
    John, 2, 4
    Thomas, 49
Presby, Richard, 63
Prescott, John, 67
    Jonathan, 67
Presson, William, 71
Preston, Benjamin, 70
    Othaniel, 113
Price, Abraham
    Adam, 115
    Benjamin, 29
    George, 92

Price, cont.
    Isaac, 12
    John, 27
    Stephen, 27
    Thomas, 33
    William, 21
Prichards, Gilbert, 130
    Jeremiah, 3, 45, 47
    William
Prickett, Azariah, 11
Pride, James, 129
Prince, John
    Kimball, 105
    William, 18
Prindle, Joseph, 117
    Joshua, 117
Prisson, William
Pritchard, Jeremiah, 2, 45, 47
    William, 53
Pritchards, Gilbert, 130
    Richard, 130
Pritimalan, James, 143
Proctor, Frances, Jr., 95, 98
    Isaac, 40
    Joel, 49
    Robert, 18
    Thomas, 3, 94, 95
Prosch, Rudolph, 142
Prosper, William, 75
Prosser, William, 75
Prout, Degory, 115
Provost, Robert, Jr., 106, 108
Prudden, Adamiram, 27
Pry, John, 86
Pryor, Jasper, 131
Psandler, Joshua, 20
Puffenbargle, Jacob, 76
    John, 76
Puicree, Junnis, 143
Pulis, John, 131
Pulman, Psalter, 107
Purchase, Joseph, 114
Purity, William, 21
Putman, Psalter, 107
Putnam, Benjamin, 71
    Daniel, 49
    Gerritt, 1
    William, 124
Putney, Joseph, 116

Quackboss, Benjamin, 118
Quackbush, Benjamin, 118
Queen, Christopher, 116
    Samuel, 40
Quick, Abraham, 132
    Cornelius, 111
    Jacob, 111
    Jean, 142
    John, 33
    Moses, 11
Quickley, James, 81
Quier, Henry, 90
Quiet, Henry, 90
Quigley, David, 20
    James, 81

Quimby, Eliazer, 59
    Eliphalet, 54
    James, 63
    John, 11
    Jonathan, 60
Quinby, Zach, 66
Quinlin, Cornelius, 92
Quint, Thomas, 60

Rabb, William, 101
Rach, Patrick, 83
Radley, William, 28
Ralfe, David, 118
Ranka, Fredrik, 140
Randall, Edward, 63
    Henry, 114
Randals, Joseph, 108
Randel, Jeremiah, 137
    John, 42
Randle, Matthew, 129
Randolph, Rufus, 10
Rankins, James, 22
Ranky, Frederick, 91
Ransom, George, 104
    Jacob, 121
    James, 134
    Palmer, 104
Rarity, John, 13
Rass, John
Ratts, Thomas, 116
Rawlings, Daniel, 67
    Jeremiah, 67
    Robert, 61
Rawlins, Eliphalet, 69
    John, 69
Ray, James, 26
    John, 34, 100
    Peltiah, 70
    Silas, 70
Raybird, Christian
Rayboll, Jacob, 93
Rayburn, James, 136
    John, 126
Raymond, James, 27
Raze, Abram, 21
Razey, Peltiah, 70
Rea, John, 82
Reabury, Andrew, 102
Read, Abijah, 40
    Eliar, 40
    Elnathan, 40
    Jesse, 41
    John, 50
    Samuel, 79
Reade, George, 15
    John, 50
Reader, Jacob, 125
Reading, Samuel, 20, 3
Ready, James, 106
Rearsons, Samuel, 139
Reckan, John, 141
Redhair, Fred, 99
Redlon, Daniel, 42
Redman, Joel, 99

Redman, cont.
    Jno, 99
    John., 28
    Michael, 73
Rednet, Henry, 40
Redwood, Prince, 42
Reed, Amos, 21
    David, 37, 38, 97
    Elias
    Giles, 25
    Henry, 32
    Isaac
    Isaiah, 28
    James, 61
    John, 18, 28, 33, 36, 38,
        42, 132
    Joshua, 32
    Lewis, 33
    Samuel, 44, 82
    Thomas, 21
    William, 37, 74
Reese, David, 80
Reggnagle, Jacob, 88, 89
Regnier, Peter, 120
    Pierre, 2, 106, 107
    George, 3, 45, 47, 55
    Jno, 31, 56, 57
    John, 53
    Zadock, 57
Reilly, Bernard, 75
Reily, John, 35
Riese, David, 80
Reives, Nathan, 126
Reishley, Lewis, 93, 94
Riesmer, Philip
Renall, John, 86
Rencastle, John, 23
Rendall, John, 62
Rendell, James, 51
    Nathaniel, 51
Reynard, Jacob, 102
Reynolds, James, 125
    John, 81, 86
    Thomas, 33
    Timothy, 122
Rhea, Aaron, 9, 12
    Jonathan, 17
Rhodes, John, 130
Riales, Moses, 58
Ribbetts, William, 12
Rice, James, 14
    Joseph, 95
    Semuel, 54
    Thad, 13
Rich, John, 36
    Jonas, 44
    Lewis, 112
Richards, Bradley, 65, 69
    David, 59
    John, 94
    Philip, 130
Richardson, Daniel, 58
    David, 59
    Jonas, 43

Richardson, cont.
    Nott, 59
    Paris, 54
    Richard, 51
    Stephen, 69
    William, 49, 52
Rickenson, James, 76
Ricker, Jacob, 13
    John, 25
    Martin, 81
Rickey, Jeremiah, 134
Rictmaker, George, 84
Ridaley, John, 53
Ridel, Henry, 140, 142
Ridgway, James, 102
Ridley, Daniel, 42
Ridlon, Daniel, 42
Riedal, William, 114
Riffit, Chn, 92
Rigleman, George, 90
Rightmyer, George, 85
    Tiley, James, 28
    John, 35
    Patrick, 118
    Peter, 86
Ring, Michael, 97
Rippey, Elijah, 35, 82
    Patrick, 113
Rippley, John, 134
Risdal, William, 114
Rising, O., 1
Risten, William, 132
Ritchie, Alexander, 126
Riter, Daniel, 51
Ritewaner, Bernard, 89
Ritter, Daniel, 51
    Tobias, 102
Ritterman, Jacob, 134
Rittlemyers, George, 94
Rively, P., 92
Roach, Patrick, 83, 85
    Sadler, 74
Roack, William, 75
Roase, Jonathan, 130
Robbins, Isaac, 27
    Jacob, 39
    Jeremiah, 40
Roberson, Roberts, 89
Robert, Jonathan, 106
Roberts, Caleb, 107
    John, 12
    Josiah, 41
    Moses
    Paul, 32
    Reuben, 50
    Stephen, 26
    Thomas, 32
    Warren, 114
Robertson, George, 75
    Isaac, 29
    James, 126, 131
    Richard, 113
Robeson, James, 83
Robins, William, 32

Robinson, Andrew, 88, 89,
        113
    Caleb, 56, 59
    Daniel, 35, 86, 129
    Edmund, 32
    Edward, 88, 89
    James, 35, 60, 83,
        118, 123, 129
    John, 19, 37, 62, 102
    Mack, 101
    Noah, 56, 62
    Richard, 51
    Robert, 132
    Stephen, 107
    William, 32, 131
Robson, Cornelius, 29
Roch, John, 102
Rockley, George, 22
Rodey, Patrick, 82
Rodgers, Andrew, 72
    James, 27
Roe, James, 49
    John, 27
    Simon, 124
    William, 124
Roese, James, 49
Roger, William, 8
Rogers, Abram, 21
    Allen, 81
    David, 26
    Henry, 140
    James, 23, 37
    Jno, 98
    Samuel, 37
    William, 3, 34, 35,
        75, 105
Roll, Matthias, 12
Rollings, Aaron, 61
Rollins, Aaron, 61
    Thomas, 59
Romander, John, 86
Romer, William, 114
Rood, Ezra, 43
Roome, Benjamin, 126
Roosa, Jacob, 133
Root, Ezra, 43
Rose, Albert, 116
    Andrew, 126
    Benjamin
    Ephraim, 33
    Jacob, 90, 110, 133
    James, 109
    John, 13, 18, 29, 113
    Jonathan, 130
    Joseph, 27
    Levy, 15
    Peter, 108
    William, 19, 28
Roseborough, John, 29
Rosecrans, Richard, 37
Rosekrans, James, 128, 130
Rosengrants, Richard, 37
Ross, George, 2
    John, 3, 16, 116, 133

169

Ross, cont.
    Peter, 108
    William, 28, 124
Rossett, Robert, 82
Roucastle, John, 28
Rouch, Conrad, 91
Roucrasts, Richard, 37
Rough, Conrad, 91
    John, 93
Roundsiner, Richard, 102
Rounsavella, John, 28
Rourke, Andrew, 75
Rouse, Pierre R.
Rovet, Anton, 142
Rowe, John, 52, 61
    Joseph, 27
    William, 68
Rowell, James, 59, 63
    Israel
    Samuel, 66
    William, 56, 61
Rowen, Jno, 66
Rowik, William, 75
Rowlins, Daniel, 67
Royal, David, 26
    John, 26
    Thomas, 13
Royall, Michael, 136
Royce, Jacob, 50
    Joel, 48, 50
    Peter, 86
    Thomas
Rulgus, Henry, 84
Rumfieldt, Henry, 94
Runcastle, Jno, 23
Rundel, Jeremiah, 137
Rundlett, William, 67
Runnells, Enos, 42
    Israel, 63
    Joseph, 108
    Moses, 58
    Samuel, 67
    Stephen, 63
    Timothy, 122
Runnellson, William, 94
Runyan, Conrad, 27
Ruppert, Jacob, 94
Rush, John, 11
Rushmore, William, 96
Russell, Amos, 40
    Casper, 14
    Edward, 26
    Jacob, 60
    James, 130
    Jonathan, 123
    Joseph, 116
    Swain, 25
    Thomas, 132
    William, 29, 67, 81, 130, 132, 133
Rutgers, Henry, 142
Rutt, Martin, 35
Ryan, John, 35, 81, 100

Ryan, cont.
    Patrick, 24, 114
    Robert, 116
    Thomas, 11
Ryant, Joseph, 68
Ryburn, James, 136
Ryggars, Peter, 19
Ryle, Peter, 86
Rylay, John, 113
Rylie, Sylvester, 134
Rynard, John, 124

Sackett, Samuel, 120, 122
Saffin, Thomas, 41
Sailheimer, Nicholas, 99
Sailor, Alex, 90
Sain, Jno, 91
Salkman, Frederick, 141
Saint, Clare, George, 20
Saint Lawrence, George
Salmond, William, 85
Sambert, Adraim, 143
Sampson, Isaac, 132
    John, 53
Samuel, Jeremiah, 101
Sanborn, John, 57
    Joseph, 54, 66
    Matthew, 68
    Paul, 60
    Seamey, 63
Sandell, Leo, 18
Sander, Abijale, 11
Sanders, John, 19, 25
Sanderson, David, 49
    Thomas, 48
Sandford, John, 126
Sandley, Christian, 88, 89
Sanford, Daniel, 123
    John, 126
Santferd, John, 31, 34
Sargents, Samuel, 69
Sarjerson, William, 108
Sartwell, Simon, 45, 47, 48
Saterlee, Elisha, 104
Saulsbry, John, 12
Saunders, Abraham, 78
Savage, William, 83
Sawyer, Jonathan, 54
Sax, Jacob, 116
    Josef, 116
Saxton, Jesse, 22
Say, John, 21
    Thomas, 99
Scaits, James, 123
Scammell, Alex, 64
Scanning, David, 40
Scantland, Jeremiah, 124
Sceele, James, 48
Schaffer, Charles, 98
Schaffner, George, 140, 141
    Thomas, 83
Schameau, Peter, 141
Scharf, John, 140

Schelig, Ludawig, 142
Schelle, Ludewig, 142
Schemers, George, 141
Schindler, John, 142
Schmidt, Dedrich, 144
    Heinrich, 144
Schools, John, 2, 4
    Paul, 4
Schoonmaker, Henry, 133, 134
Schoot, John, 4
    Paul, 102
Schrader, John J., 116
Schrampf, Niclaus, 144
Schraner, Lodewick
Schriber, Peter, 119
Schriner, Christian, 116
Schroder, John
Schrupp, Henry, 94
Scott, David, 71
    Henry, 126
    James, 106
    John, 37, 81
    Thomas, 50
    William J., 45, 47, 49, 60, 82
Scouten, Henry, 129
Scrals, Thomas, 119
Scythin, Jno, 19
Seabeck, Anthony, 73
Seabrook, Nathan, 73
Seagar, George, 80
Seagull, Jacob, 69
Seamey, John, 63
Seaming, David, 40
Searles, Constant, 104
Sears, Isaac, 13
    Samuel, 15
    Thomas, 119
Seary, Lawrence, 29
Season, John, 29
Seasor, John, 29
Seavey, John, 63
Seby, Isaac, 97
Secheveral, George, 37
Secomb, Thomas, 43
Secore, John, 130
Secus, Francis, 130
    John, 130
Seeds, George, 123
Seeley, John, 16
    Samuel, 9, 10
Seelingham, Benjamin
    Henry, 68
    Jacob, 68
Seely, John, 20
Seevy, Joseph, 113
Seillcker, Frederick, 141
Seilheimer, Niche, 99
Seils, James, 48
Selin, Anthony, 4, 102
Sellars, Michael, 110
Sennett, Richard, 26

Senter, Abraham, 63
    Asa, 45, 47
Seperal, Frederick, 90
Seprile, William, 80
Sepruli, Nicholas, 81
Dequern, Frederick, 140
Serals, Thomas, 19
Sergent, Benjamin, 68
    David, 15
    Ebenezer, 61
    Valentine, 60
    Volent, 60
Sertain, James, 109
Sesshons, John, 70
Sessions, John, 70
Sessor, Daniel
    John, 70
Settlemyer, Christian, 93
Severance, Thomas, 50
Sevey, Isaac, 97
Seqall, Lewis, 97
Sewalt, Lewis, 97
Sexton, Timothy, 28
Shaddock, Levi, 13
Shade, Nathan, 53
Shaffer, Adam, 93
    George, 132
    John, 44, 94
Shaffner, Francis, 83
Shaftser, Adam
    George, 75
    John
Shandonet, Francis, 46
Shane, Caspar, 98
Shankling, Andrew, 41
Shannon, James, 76
    Samuel, 81
Shapher, Theophilus, 26
Shappo, Anton
Sharer, Robert, 86
Sharkey, Thomas, 132
Sharp, John, 141
Shaver, Jacob, 22
    Joseph, 22
Shaw, David, 104
    Jno, 84, 85
    Samuel, 81
    Thomas, 67
Shay, Markom, 132
Sheaport, Jacob, 91
Shear, Abraham, 134
    Samuel
Shearer, Philip, 91
Shearlock, John, 19
Shearina, Richard, 26
Sheels, James, 116
Sheels, Daniel, 102
Sheldon, Elisha, 7
    Jacob
    Joseph, 34
Shell, Christopher, 116
    George, 113
Shelock, John, 19, 113

Shelton, John, 43
Sheppard, George, 69
    Nathaniel, 20
    Robert, 101
    Samuel, 23, 26
    Stephen, 41
Sheridan, Peter, 35
    Richard, 113
Sheriff, Cornelius, 2
Sherlock, John, 19, 115
Sherman, Jesse, 108, 110, 111
    John, 108
    Richard, 67
Sherter, William, 81
Sherwood, Abraham, 110
    Andrew, 15
    Henry, 110
    James, 15
    Jonas, 24, 25
    Nathan, 107
Shevellier, John, 125
Sheyfey, Daniel, 85
Shicker, Caspar, 74
Shieds, James, 116
Shift, George, 113
Shipe, Caspar, 74
    William, 75
Shipman, Eliphalet, 70
    William
Shippen, William, 96
Shiras, Richard, 12
Shirk, Jacob, 94
Shirley, Daniel, 52
    Thomas, 132
Shiskey, Thomas, 132
Shitz, Matthian, 29
    Nathaniel
    Peter, 113
    Samuel, 113
Shitz, Jacob, 93
Shively, John, 94
Shoars, Jonathan, 25
Shockey, Christian, 85
Shoemaker, Frederick, 88, 89, 90
    Michael, 88, 89
    Peter, 35, 80
    William, 20
Shoppe, Anton, 44
Shorter, William, 81
Shotz, John, 88, 89
Shoup, Henry, 91
Showers, Adam, 13
Shrawder, Philip, 90
Shrive, Isaac, 16
    Israel, 3
    John, 16
Shrunna, Lodewick
Shryack, Jno, 94
Shryer, Matthias, 93
Shubert, Armitage, 97
    Fred, 97
    Niclaus, 143

Shucraft, John, 108
Shudy, Martin, 92
Shffley, William, 14
Shugat, Martin, 94
Shuler, Henry, 92
Shullian, Thomas, 139
Shulter, John, 110
Shute, Daniel, 100
    John, 19, 95, 97
Shweitser, Frederick, 90
Sibbic, Thomas, 120
Sickels, Samuel, 20
Sickle, Abraham, 114
    Jacob, 28
Sigler, Henry, 17
Sigougne, Lois de 140, 142
Silk, Michael, 48
Sill, Elsha, 104
    Shadwick, 104
Sillnan, John, 116
Sills, Elisha, 104
Silver, Samuel, 66, 71
Silvia, James, 139
Simmers, Peter
Simmonds, William, 83
Simmons, Bennett, 41
    Ezekiel, 129
    John, 54, 123
    Joshua, 126
    Levi, 54
    Silas, 54
Simojohn, Martin
Simon, Ezeriah, 104
    John, 108
    Martin, 110
Simmonds, William, 83
Simons, Samuel, 129
Simpkins, Gideon, 113
    Jeremiah, 133
Simpson, John, 14
    Michael, 100
    Robert, 69
    Thomas, 65
    William, 50, 52, 53
Sims, Stephen, 100
Sinclair, Joshua, 51
    Samuel, 51
Sinkler, Noah, 66
    Richard, 66
Sinnott, Pattrick, 120, 123
Sipprell, Nicholas, 81
Sisco, Samuel, 54
Sithin, Jno, 19
Sitzer, Barent, 126
Size, Abraham, 134
Skiff, Stephen, 104
Skeggs, Richard, 102
Skiffington, John, 115
Skilman, Thomas, 9
Skinner, Jonathan, 134
Slack, Joseph, 61
Slaughter, John, 18
Slautry, Thomas, 81

Sleeper, Benjamin, 66
Slicker, Caspar, 74, 77
Slife, John, 94
Slonter, Evert, 132
Sloven, James, 134
Slutt, Abraham, 129
    Maivel, 129
    William, 129
Sluyter, Jacob, 116
Sly, Samuel, 37
    William, 129
Small, John, 58
Smaller, John, 89
Smalley, Thomas, 132
Smalls, Frederick,
Smart, Moses, 70
    Richard, 70
Smick, Raynard, 99
Smitard, John, 88, 89
Smith, Abner, 134
    Alexander, 51, 117
    Asa, 104
    Azariah, 104
    Benjamin, 51, 52, 69, 121
    Caleb, 106
    Christian, 93
    Christopher, 106
    Daniel, 37
    David, 123
    David, Sr., 132
    David, Jr., 132
    Duncan, 114
    Ebner, 126
    Edward, 53, 83
    Elijah, 59
    Elisha, 59
    Ezeriah, 104
    Frances, 39
    Frederick, 141
    Gad, 39
    George, 91
    Hershom, 125
    Henry, 94
    Isaac, 51, 64, 65, 70
    Isaac, Jr., 104
    Israel, 120, 124
    Jacob, 94, 101
    James, 22, 90, 102, 104
    Jeremiah, 66, 71
    Jesse, 132
    John, 17, 63, 67, 86, 90,
        92, 94, 102, 108,
        111, 116, 118, 124
    Joseph, 35, 70, 80, 115,
        132
    Josiah, 124, 126
    Larrence, 12
    Matthew, 32, 94
    Michael, 63, 94
    Nathaniel, 69, 72
    Oliver, 62
    Patt, 97
    Peter, 27, 166
    Reuben, 134

Smith, cont.
    Reynard, 99
    Richard, 110
    Robert, 94
    Samuel, 32, 132
    Solomon, 113
    Theodore, 43
    Thomas, 134
    Weight, 37
    William, 31, 33, 37, 74,
        81, 107
    William, Jr., 104
Smithly, John, 90
    Philip, 90
Snakeker, Moses, 126
Snead, William, 96
Snell, Jacob, 96, 99
Snider, John, 24
Snow, John, 10
    Joshua, 66
Snowden, Jonathan, 3, 9
    John, 123
Snyder, Christian, 27
    Frederick, 86
    Henry, 36
    John, 94
    Peter, 129
Socks, Andrew, 75
Sollman, William, 40
Sollas, Thomas, 75
Sollen, Frederick, 94
Solomon, John, 100
    William, 85
Somers, Hugh, 117
Sooper, Joseph, 13
Soper, Thomas, 29
Sorguy, John, 80
Southerland, James, 36
Space, John, 22
Spade, Jno, 99
Spafford, Tyler, 51
Spank, Marries, 74
Sparer, Robert
Sparks, David, 42
Spaulding, John, 72, 73, 104
    Simon, 103, 104
Spear, Samuel, 71
Spears, John, 118
Specht, Adam, 71
Speed, George, 134
    Henry, 134
    Thomas, 67
Speldon, E., 3
Spencer, Joseph, 76
    Moses, 58
    Oliver, 3
Spenck, John, 92
Spicer, Jacob, 125
    John, 29
Spoor, John, 115, 116
Sprage, Seth, 129
Spring, John, 63
Springer, Henry, 70
    Levi, 17

Springstead, Abraham, 10
    George, 132
Springsteen, Harmanus, 1
Springsten, George, 132
Springstone, George, 132
    John
Sproat, William, 2, 3, 7
    73
Sproule, Moses, 23, 24,
Sprown, Thomas, 67
Squire, Joseph, 36
Squirrel, Jacob, 124
Staats, Gerritt, 114
Staber, Nichilas
Stack, Archibald
Stackhouse, Amos, 14
Stacy, John, 44
Stademan, Anton, 142
Stafford, Jno, 98
Stagg, Abner, 71
    Adam, 136
    Cornelius, 139
    Jasper, 119
    Jno, 31
    John, 2, 36
Stain, Edward, 81
Stalker, Seth, 129
Stall, Adam, 41
Stamford, Henry, 75
Stanbury, Elijah, 134
Stanford, Henry, 75
Stanley, Samuel, 20
    Thomas, 42, 132
Stansbury, Elijah, 134
Stanton, Charles, 50, 60
    John, 93
Staples, Stephen, 40
Stark, Archibald, 70
    Caleb, 45, 46
    James, Jr., 104
    John, 45, 46, 104
    Nathaniel, 104
States, Peter, 137
Statler, Henry, 90
Stearns, Daniel, 48
Stebbins, Samuel, 40
Stediford, Garret, 72
Steel, James, 129
    John, 107
    Solomon, 43
    Thomas, 17
    William, 80
Steele, John, 2
Steeples, Thomas, 17
Steigle, Valentine, 86
Stenson, Samuel, 80
Stephens, Charles, 18
    Ephram, 48
    Henry, 110
    Isaac, 28
    Nicholas, 32
    Peter, 35
    William, 100
Stephenson, William, 82

Sterling, Levi, 114, 115
Stett, Isaac, 75
   John, 123, 124
Stevens, Bartholomew, 53
   Ephraim, 51
   Francis, 104
   Henry, 51
   Ira, 104
   Richard, 133
   Roger, 54
Stevenson, Cornelius, 17
Steves, Caleb, 108
   Philip, 108
Steward, Hugh, 37
Stewart, Alexander, 20
   Charles, 74
   George, 136
   James, 73, 82, 132
   Jno, 98
   John, 34
   _____, 2
Stickhan, Gotlieb, 142
Stickle, Valentine, 86
Stickney, Levi, 69
   Thomas, 49, 52
Stiles, Aaron, 33
   Henry, 39
   Job, 10
Still, Isaac, 75
   Stephen, 104
Stillinger, Levi
   Thomas, 16
Stillwell, James, 110
   Thomas, 109
   William, 14
Stites, Job, 10
Stiver, William, 27
Stober, Niclous, 91
Stocker, Samuel, 54
Stocketts, Robert, 61
Stone, Andrew, 68
   Caspar, 75
   Hugh, 76
   John, 85
Stonebraker, Adam, 90
Stoner, John, 85
   Michael, 88, 89
   Nathaniel
Storm, Abram, 10
   John, 131
Storts, Jno, 99
Story, Samuel, 95
Stouffer, George, 94
Stout, Elisha, 32
   Joseph, 11
   Wessel, 23
Strate, Henry, 129
   William, 129
Strattin, Arrias, 19
Stratton, David, 125
   Jona, 44
Staughan, John, 101
Straw, John, 68

Strawbridge, John, 10
Street, Benjamin, 78
   Samuel, 109
Stricker, John, 95, 96
Strider, Philip, 88
Strieter, Joseph, 94
Strimple, John, 21
Stringham, James, 126
Stroam, Henry, 126
Strobridge, John, 10
Strong, John, 122
   William, 19
Stroud, Phillip, 44
Strouffer, George
Strough, George, 90
Stroughen, James, 37
   Jno
Struble, Nicholas, 84, 85
Stryker, W. S., 1, 8
Stuart, James, 128
   William, 12
Stubbes, Robert, 81
Stull, Adam
Stump, John, 132
Sturges, Isaac, 114
   Jonathan, 19
Suddett, William, 101
Suertity, Echard, 143
Sullivan, Daniel, 26, 60, 81
   Dennis, 114, 115
   John, 1, 4, 36, 82
   Joshua, 32
   Owen, 76
   Patrick, 2, 19
   Peter, 34
   Timothy, 25
Summers, Peter, 72
Sunliter, Jno, 92
Susong, Andrew, 81
Sutherland, Daniel, 116
   James, 118
Suttliff, John, 134
Sutton, Ephraim, 33
   William, 22
Swaine, Hezekiah, 68
Swan, Hezekiah, 68
   John, 71
   Joseph, 20
   Peter, 37
Swanheiser, Christian, 102
Swartout, Bernardine, 106
   Cornelius, 118
Swartz, Gotfried, 92
Sweat, Samuel, 46
Sweten, Stephen, 67
Sweating, Richard, 25
Sweatt, Abraham T., 66
Sweden, Caspar, 29
Swedge, Henry, 91
Sweeney, Daniel, 35
   Isaac, 79, 86
   John, 80
Sweet, John, 54
   Moses, 61

Sweeten, Richard, 25
Sweetsar, Stephen, 67
Swift, James, 27
   John, 104
Swiss, Jacob, 134
Switcher, Stepheh, 67
Swords, Hugh, 86
Syms, William, 97
Synchiser, John, 102
Syron, John, 37

Taeger, John, 141
Taggart, James, 46, 71
   John, 61
   Joseph, 61
   William, 54, 59
Tainey, George, 18
Taits, Martin, 75
Talbott, William, 97
Talladay, Solomon, 132
Talleday, John, 129
   Solomon, 132
Taller, James, 130
Tallmadge, Samuel, 100, 121, 123
Tapp, William, 114
Tarbill, Nathan, 28
Tarna, John, 97
Tater, John, 21
Tatten, William, 96
Tay, John, 126
Taylor, Benjamin, 52
   Broadstreet, 59
   Edward, 68, 111
   Jacob, 48
   John, 19, 58
   Medad, 49
   Nathan, 56
   Nathaniel, 61
   Oliver, 68
   Peter, 11
   William, 18, 35, 88, 89
Teanning, David, 40
Teats, Martin, 75
Teets, Michael, 37
   William, 37
Tegan, Hugh, 99
Tempel, Stephen, 40
Temple, Stephen, 40
Templeton, James
Tendcal, Samuel, 29
Tenegan, George, 131
Teneyer, George, 131
TenEyck, Isaac
   John, 111
   Joseph, 130
Tennent, Thomas, 44
TerBoss, Isaac, 130
   John, 130
   Simon, 122
Terbush, Simon, 122
Terrell, Jeremiah, 82
   Lawrence, 81

Terwilliger, Jacobus, 133
Terry, John, 19
    William, 104
Tharp, Benjamin, 13, 32, 35
    Peter, 27
    Thomas, 138
Thatcher, Benjamin, 90
Thayer, John, 131
They, William, 86
Thicks, John, 36
Thomas, Edmund, 23, 27
    Enoch, 66
    George, 46, 130
    Henry, 109
    Jacob, 69
    John, 13, 18, 35
    Luke, 33
    Matthew, 21
    Morgan, 28
    Richard, 121
    Valentine, 28
    William, 14
Thompson, Aaron, 29
    Adam, 50
    Alexander, 100
    Benjamin, 123
    Elias, 133
    George, 96
    Henry, 54
    James, 53, 81
    John, 19, 59, 111, 113, 121
    Joshua, 45, 47, 48, 52
    Loring, 48
    Price, 13
    Robert
    Samuel, 45, 47
    Seth, 49
    Stanley, 108
    William, 32, 139
Thomson, James, 17
    William, 139
Thorn, Obadiah, 134
Thornbury, Francis, 78
Thorne, Daniel, 137, 138
Thornton, Herms, 98
    James, 130
Thorp, Abel, 32
    Eliphalet, 39, 43
    Sal, 12
    Thomas, 137, 138
Thorton, Herms, 98
    James, 130
Thrackmorton, Halmes, 32
Thulmin, Peter, 31, 34
    Robert, 31
Thurston, Benjamin
    James, 83
    Michael, 96
    Oliver, 62
    Robert, 69
Tibbits, Isaac, 41
Tice, Elijah, 32
Tidd, John, 101

Tiebout, Henry, 118
Tiemand, Peter, 125
Tilston, Benjamin, 40, 42
Till, Henry, 102
Tilley, Samuel, 42
    Thomas, 41
Tilton, John, 13
    Peter, 132
Timlin, John, 88, 89
Timmas, Henry, 142
Timmey, Henry, 25
Timmons, Abner, 107
Timms, Absalom, 17
Timy, Henry, 25
Tinis, Abraham, 17
Tinkham, James, 34
Tiny, Boston, 40
    Cornwell, 40
Titcomb, Benjamin, 55, 56
Tite, James, 93
Titus, James, 130
    Jonathan, 120, 124
    Shadrick, 17
Tiverdy, Thomas, 98
Toad, Enock, 41
Tobbs, Richard, 9
Tobles, Richard, 9
Tobs, Richard, 9
Todd, James, 81
    John, 15
    Solomon, 53
Tofet, Peter, 134
Tolland, Elias, 101
Tolman, John, 44
    Samuel, 44
Tom, Nathaniel, 31
Tompkins, Abraham, 113
    Jonas, 36
    Nathaniel, 123
Ton, Gullam, 143
Toole, Edward, 97
    Patrick, 21
Topham, Daniel, 2
Toplin, Jno, 98
Torguy, John, 80
Torr, Vincent, 58
Torrance, Thomas, 41
Torrey, Daniel, 66, 71
Torry, Daniel, 71
Towle, William, 62
Town, Joseph, 11
Townley, Joshua, 9
Townsend, Samuel, 82, 132
Tozer, Peter, 68
Traverse, Abraham, 132
Travis, James, 109
    Scott, 130
    Uriah, 108
Trickey, Samuel, 61
Trifgen, Jona, 10
Trimler, Henry, 80
Trimmin, Jonathan, 110
Trookey, John, 80
Trout, Michael, 107

Trowbridge, Luther, 44
Truax, John, 23
Trucks, John, 93
True, Henry, 52
Tubbs, Samuel, 104
Tubec, John, 125
Tubert, Francois, 143
Tubu, John, 125
Tuby, John, 125
    Julien, 125
Tucker, Jonathan, 60
    Joseph, 38, 39, 42,
    Joshua, 132
    William, 42
Tuckett, Aariah, 12
    Thomas, 104
Tudor, George, 72, 74
Tuffs, Jeder, 101
Tumands, Peter, 125
Tummey, Henry, 25
Tumond, David, 124
Tupley, John, 82
Tupper, Nathan, 131
Turner, Ezra, 54
    James, 71
    Thomas, 93
    William, 42, 76
Turtle, Azariah, 120
Tuthill, Azariah, 120, 1
    Joel, 106
    William
Tuttle, Daniel, 10
    John, 12
    Nathan, 51
    William, 27
Tway, John, 27
    Timothy, 29
Tweedy, Thomas, 99
Twombly, William, 56, 57
    62
Tye, William, 86
Tyerman, William, 86
Tyler, Ephraim, 104

Ulett, Samuel, 102
Ulrig, Henry, 142
Unbehand, John, 35, 81
Underwood, Isaac, 104
    Joseph, 40
Upright, George, 116
    Nathan, 116
Uthest, John, 114
Utley, Asa, 122
Utter, Gilbert, 131
    Isaac, Sr., 131
    Isaac, Jr., 131

Vacher, John F., 120
Vaille, Jean, 43
Valentine, Jacob, 25
    Joseph, 113
    Peter, 117
Vallarey, John, 134
Vallence, William, 36

Vame, William, 43
VanAllen, Peter, 121
VanAlta, John, 115
VanAmbro, Abraham, 112
VanAngleus, John, 3, 9
VanAtten, Peter P., 121
VanAtter, Jacobus, 110
VanBlaricum, James, 119
VanBonbaugle, C., 119
    John, 119
VanBrimer, Abraham, 73, 76
VanBuschaten, Peter, 120, 124
Vance, John, 50
    Joseph, 102
    Thomas, 36
Vances, Cornelius, 107
VanCleaf, Peter, 32
VanCortlandt, Nicholas, 1
VanCourtland, Philip, 4, 106
Van D'Bogert, John, 122
Vandemark, Gilbert, 132
    Oliver, 132
    Zachariah, 110
VanDenMark, Cornelius, 128
Vanderburgh, Henry U., 129
VanderHayden, Adam
    Gershom
Vanderlite, Abraham, 12
VanderVorst, James, 114
VanDiver, Jacob, 86
VanDorn, Eseck, 32
VanDike, John, 20
Vanduser, Abraham, 119
VanduHale, Abraham, 12
Vane, John, 50
    Thomas, 36
VanEmsburg, Abraham, 113
Vaness, Cornelius, 107
VanEvery, Martin, 35
VanGelder, Isaac, 121
    Jacobus, 133
    Matthew, 131
VanHoevenburgh, Rudolphus, 20, 25
VanHooser, Ryncer, 122
VanHoover, Rymer, 122
    William, 28
VanHorn, Simon, 13
VanKlack, James, 113
VanKleck, James, 113
VanKleefs, Lawrence, 116
VanMarter, John, 25
VanNoren, Gorst, 134
Vanny, Vincent, 130
VanOrder, Charles, 118
VanOrmond, James, 25
VanOstrand, Jno, 97
VanOte, Joseph, 134
VanRensselaer, Jeremiah
VanSire, John, 113
VanSise, Gilbert, 122
VanTasel, Cornelius, 109
Vantine, Frances, 128

Vantine, cont.
    Isaac, 129
    Robert, 129
VanVarrick, James, 26
VanVorhies, Peter, 9, 13
VanWaganen, Tunis, 106, 109
VanWye, Hndk, 22
Variere, Guilliam, 143
Varshe, John F., 120
Vaughan, Cornelius, 98
    William, 25
Vaultz, Conrad, 122
Veasey, Eliphalet, 62
Veccor, Ambrose, 37
Vece, John, 110
Venett, John, 14
Verdrius, Christian, 142
Vergan, John, 108
Vermilian, Peter, 131
Verrian, John, 108
    Joseph, 129
Very, George, 118
Vessels, John, 114
Vetter, Frederick, 144
Viccor, Ambrose, 37
Victor, Adam
    Jacob, 93
Vincent, Adam, 19
    William, 93
Voges, John, 42
Voghum, Benjamin, 21
Voinnards, Joseph, 141
Voorhees, Hendrck, 32
Voorhies, Tunis, 13
Voorhis, Albert, 36
Vouck, William, 117
Vorse, Albert, 36
Vose, Amonale, 139
    Amoah, 139
Vredenburgh, William, 18, 117
    James, 121

Wabby, Roger, 113
Wachtet, John, 88, 89
Waddell, Robert, 131
Wade, Edward, 62
    Henry, 26
    John, 88, 89
    Nehemiah, 144
Wadleigh, Elijah, 66, 71
Wagerman, Emanl, 115
Waggermer, Jacob, 93
Waggoner, Caspar, 91
    Christian, 90
Wait, Jason, 45, 47, 51
    John, 64
Waitsell, Jacob, 78, 80, 81
Walcott, William, 30
Waldron, Ebenezer, 60
    Nathaniel, 66
Walker, Andrew, 79, 83
    Benjamin, 120, 123
    Edward, 104, 121

Walker, cont.
    Elijah, 104
    Francis, 12
    George, 16, 20
    Israel, 110
    Joseph, 41
    Matthew, 121
    Matthias, 121
    Meseck, 10
    Obadiah, 104
    Samuel, 132
    William, 9, 50, 53
Walkers, Francis, 12
Walking, Zaccheus, 41
Wallace, Caesar, 58
    John, 48, 51, 116
    William, 15
Waller, Robert, 33
Wallasa, William, 15
Walling, James, 33
Wallinger, Jacob, 17
Wullis, William, 42
Walls, Francis, 62
Wally, Roger, 113
Walsh, Michal, 29
Walter, Conradt, 114
Walters, John, 28
Wandle, Jacob, 32
    John, 133
Waner, Eliliu
    John, 122
Wanton, Abiel, 50
    Rufus, 51
    Samuel, 53
Ward, Ebenezer, 10
    Isaac, 27
    John, 17, 59, 73, 94
    Melcher, 59
    Michael, 59
    Robert, 120, 121
    Samuel, 63
    Stephen, 51
Warden, Caleb, 104
    Nathan, 116
    Thomas, 20
Warner, Benjamin, 38, 41
    Edmund, 129
    Ephraim
    Martin, 75
Warren, Benjamin, 41
    Christian, 39
    Thomas, 57
Warring, Benjamin, 115
Warwick, Hugh, 42
Watason, Hugh, 137
Waters, Thomas, 67
Waterson, Hugh, 137
Watkins, Thomas, 20
Watson, Daniel, 60
    David, 63
    Glosten, 61
    Isaac, 58
    Jon, 100

Watson, cont.
    Joseph, 113
    Levi, 130
    Thomas, 37
    William, 15, 20, 119
Watt, Francis, 62
Watts, Bowen, 19
    Robert, 21
Way, John, 114
Waygant, Tobias, 107
Wayman, Abel, 18
Weare, Nathan, 68
Weatherby, Benjamin, 33
Weatherley, William, 99
Weaver, Albert, 100
    Christopher, 117
    George, 96
    Henry, 116
    Johanneal, 130
    John, 126
    Michael, 90
Weaverlin, Peter, 12
Webb, Andrew, 83
    Nathaniel, 105, 106
Webber, Samuel, 42
Webster, Elihu, 10
    John, 45
    Jonathan, 54
    Stephen, 68
    Thomas, 58
Weed, David, 113
    Samuel, 129
Weeks, Abraham, 106
    Jacob, 114
Weidam, John, 90
Weidman, John, 90
Weir, James, 82
    Samuel, 48
Weisenfels, Frederick, 4
Weissenfels, Charles F., 106
    Frederick, 4
    George, 110
    John, 107
Weitz, Michel, 29
Weitzell, Jacob, 78, 80, 81
Welch, David
    Garrit, 80
    James, 19
    Nathan, 29
    Richard, 119
    Thomas, 20
Welden, Jeremiah, 113
    Robert, 112
Welding, Robert, 112, 115
Welger, Daniel, 81, 84
Wella, James, 29
Wells, James, Jr., 104
    John, 115
    Samuel, 50
    Thomas, 60
Welsh, Benjamin, 58
    Garret, 80
    John, 58

Welsh, cont.
    Joseph, 126
    Richard, 119
    Thomas, 61
    William, 17
Wemire, Frederick, 133
Wendell, Jacob, 40
Wentworth, Ebenezer, 44
    Enoch, 44
    Phinehas, 58
Wentz, Jacob, 92
Wesaman, Henry, 142
Wessels, Joseph, 114
Wessenger, Ludwig, 88
West, Asa, 125
    Jacob, 134
    John, 132
    Nehemiah, 66
Westfall, Levi, 122
Wethenhauk, James, 35
Wetherstine, John, 116
Wetzell, Philip, 98
Weyant, Tobias, 107
Whalin, John, 42
    Patrick 42
Wharrey, Robert, 79
Wheelan, Edward, 85
Wheeler, Benjamin, 101
    John, 41, 42, 126
    Reuben, 51
    Richard, 107
    Samuel, 43, 130
    Stephen, 130
    Thomas, 93
    William, 110
Wheelock, Jonathan, 48
Whelan, Patrick, 42
Whentworth, Fred, 41
Wherry, Robert, 15
Whidon, Samuel, 50
Whiley, John, 115
Whillock, Epraim, 14
Whipple, Nathan, 108
Whilaker, John, 28
White, Andrew, 106, 107
    David
    Ephraim, 122
    John, 37, 124
    Jonathan, 138
    Joseph, 113
    Peter, 20
    Thomas, 10, 20
    William, 25, 41, 110
Whitehal, Jacob, 12
Whitehead, James, 15
    John, 129
    Samuel, 22
    William, 125, 131
Whitham, William, 113
Whiting, Daniel, 3
Whitlock, Ephraim, 9
    Thomas, 48
Whitlow, Benjamin, 99

Whitman, Lemuel, 103
Shitmore, James, 137, 138
Whitney, Jacob, 110, 126
Whittemore, Amox, 137
    James, 138
    Pelatiah, 56, 61
Whittier, Benjamin, 66
Whittow, Benjamin, 99
    John, 70
    Simeon, 41
Wice, James, 75
Wickham, Stephen, 125
Wideman, Jno, 93
Wier, Jeremiah, 122
Wiggins, Winthrop, 63
Wiggins, Thomas, 96
Wiglon, Samuel, 27
Wilborn, Esau, 116
Wilbur, Esau, 116
    Ichabod, 130
    Jacob, 130
Wilcox, James, 10
    John, 107
Wiley, William, 83
Wilger, Daniel, 81
Wilhele, John, 106
Wilhelm, George, 90
Wilhite, Jesse, 101
    John, 101
Wilker, Daniel, 81
Wilkerlay, William, 99
Wilkerson, Robert, 114
Wilkes, Daniel, 81
Wilkins, Asa, 69
    James, 69
    Robert, 65
Wilkinson, Amos, 97
    Nathan, 3
    Nathaniel, 23
Wilks, Jno, 96
    Melatiah, 130
Willard, Jonathan, 45, 47
    Wilder, 49, 50
Willcox, James, 10
Willet, Alfrecht, 142
    Francis, 113
Willett, Marinus, 113
Willgar, Samuel, 81
William, Frederick, 92
Williams, Adam, 42
    Arthur, 113
    Benjamin, 54
    David, 80
    Ebenezer, 48
    Elias, 96
    Garret
    Henry, 37
    Isaac, 35, 129
    James, 73
    John, 13, 21, 72, 118, 126
    Joseph, 94
    Nathaniel, 104

Williams, cont.
    Peleg, 46
    Reese, 34
    Richard, 114, 134
    Samuel, 60, 61
    Solomon, 116
    Thomas, 12, 103, 141, 143
    William, 17, 83
Williber, John, 101
Willis, Aaron, 15
    John, 133
    Thomas, 41, 60
    William, 134
Williss, Isaac, 21
    John, 116, 130
Williamson, Garret, 11
    Jacob, 13
    James, 122, 123
Wills, Peter, 130
    Thomas, 60
Willson, James, 10
    Moses, 10
    Robert, 83
    Thomas, 86
    Walter, 124
Wilmott, John, 74
Wilsey, Isaac
    William, 113
Wilson, Abraham, 132
    Alexander, 41
    Andrew, 12
    Benjamin, 42
    George, 51
    James, 25, 53, 101
    John, 14, 117, 129, 132
    Joshua, 62
    Robert, 53, 117
    Samuel, 59
    Thomas, 14, 51, 117
    William, 73, 80
Winand, Jno, 90
Winchell, Samuel, 126
Wingate, Daniel, 63
    Enoch, 63
Wink, Jacob, 93
Winkler, Fred, 99
    Henry, 91
Winters, James, 81
Wisdom, Henry, 58
Wise, Abner, 50
    James, 75
Wissenback, Hendrick, 117
Wisso, Lewis, 51
Witlock, Thomas, 49
Witmore, Amos, 14
Witt, Charles, 102
Wolf, Henry, 19
Wolfe, Frederick, 83
Wolff, Anton, 142
Wood, Abijah, 123
    Abraham, 81
    Edward, 70
    Francis, 25

Wood, cont.
    George, 10
    Gideon, 70
    Isaac, 10
    James, 129
    John, 124
    Thomas, 70
    William, 10, 56, 57
Woodamore, Cornelius, 108
Woodbury, Israel, 59
    Luke, 56, 57
    William, 59
Woodcock, Jonathan, 70
    Richard, 104
Woodell, Timothy, 59
Woodman, Cornelius, 108
    Daniel, 63
    John, 2
    Nathan, 42
    Nathan, Jr., 43
Woodruff, Daniel, 33
    Ebenezer, 19
    Epraim, 120, 123
    John, 29
    Samuel, 137
Woods, Daniel, 52
    Hugh, 76
    Thomas, 86
Woodside, Abraham, 81
    Robert, 18
Wooster, John, 41
Woodstock, Richard, 104
Woodward, John, 134
    Robert, 71
Woodworth, Asa, 42
Wool, Isaac, 139
    Josiah, 139
    Paul, 52
Woolcut, William, 130
Wooley, Isaac, 11
    Jonathan, 69, 70
    Ledidiah, 32
Woolsey, Isaac, 12
Wooton, Morris, 23, 24
Worcester, James, 67
Worden, Cabel, 104
    Davis, 124
    John, 104
    Nathan, 126
    Samuel, 27
Wright, Abraham, 119
    Barrock, 109
    David, 11, 49
    Edward, 117
    Jacob, 106, 109
    James, 141
    John, 80, 121
    Jonathan, 49
    Joseph, 11, 51
    Peter, 39
    Phinehas, 49
    Samuel, 11, 119
    Thomas, 101
    William, 20

Wrine, William, 118
Wyatt, Stephen, 41
Wybert, Frederick, 116
Wyer, James, 35
Wylie, John, 115
Wyman, Daniel, 58
Wyochover, Jacob, 115
Yackley, Michael, 90
Yaden, William, 36
Yaple, Henry, 93
Yarington, William, 123
Yatas, James, 115
    Jno, 13
    William, 14
Yattis, Jno, 13
Yeaple, Henry, 92
Yeardon, William, 36
Yengle, Johan T., 115
Yeomans, Elezer, 126
    Isaac, 116
    William, 36
Yockley, Michael, 90
Yores, John, 109
Yorety, Frederick, 18, 19
York, Joseph, 51
Yost, John, 100
Young, Aaron, 27
    Charles, 98
    Daniel, 153
    David, 37
    James, 63
    John, 97
    Joseph, 40, 63
    Marcus, 93
    Philip, 33
    Robert, 97
    Thomas, 20
Youngman, John, 69
    Thomas, 69
Yourns, John, 109

Zeaster, Michael, 113
Zimmerman, John, 142
    Jonathan, 88, 89
    Jonce, 142

www.ingramcontent.com/pod-product-compliance
Lightning Source LLC
Chambersburg PA
CBHW080247170426
43192CB00014BA/2592